Customer Copy

Box No **330-F12-PCK-10190**

Order No 26660773
Placed On 05-Sep-2012
Invoice Date 10-Sep-2012

Sold To

hannah Doherty

Phone (732)796-8385
E-Mail: hdoherty3@liberty.edu

Ship To

hannah Doherty

Shipping Method : Store Pickup

Pickup Location:At Store
Pickup by Name:hannah doherty

Ship from

Liberty University Bookstore

1971 University Blvd.,Bldg. #65
Lynchburg, VA - 24502, US
E-Mail:sm330@bncollege.com
Website
http://liberty.bncollege.com
Phone: **(434)582-2316**

1 Your Order

Item #	Description	Price	QTY	Total
1	INTRO TO EDUCATION >CUSTOM<, New	$55.55	1	$55.55

Sub-total		$55.55
+ Shipping		$0.00
+ Tax		$0.00
Total Amount	1 Item(s)	$55.55

2 Processed Payments

Payment Type	Account No.	Date	Amount
SFA	XXXX9258	10-Sep-2012	$55.55
		Total Payments Processed	$55.55
		Order Total	$55.55
		Outstanding balance	$0.00

3 SFA Summary

HANNAH DOHERTY

Account No. XXXX9258

Amount Authorized	Description	Balance
$55.55	12 BKPS NEW INTL STUDENT BOOK	$220.55

Questions about your order? For fastest service, refer to your Box Number (see top of page) when contacting the bookstore.
Details about our Refund and Exchange policies are on the bookstore's website. We look forward to serving you again soon.

SHOP ONLINE with your bookstore website. We are the headquarters for textbooks, college gear, school supplies and gifts. Be sure to sign up for emails to find out about special offers.

Senior Vice President, Editorial and Marketing: Patrick F. Boles
Senior Sponsoring Editor: Natalie Danner
Development Editor: Abbey Briggs
Assistant Editor: Jill Johnson
Operations Manager: Eric M. Kenney
Production Manager: Jennifer Berry
Art Director: Renée Sartell
Cover Designer: Kristen Kiley

Cover Art: "Textbooks and apple" used by permission of iStock; "Teacher and students" used by permission of iStock; "Classroom, globe on desk, US flag hanging from blackboard" Copyright © 1999–2008 Getty Images, Inc. All rights reserved. "Mulitcolored crayons"— Courtesy of iStockphoto. "Colorful crayons"— Courtesy of iStockphoto. "Toddler boy playing with alphabet puzzle"— Courtesy of Mimi Haddon/Getty Images. "School Hallway" courtesy of Matt symons/iStockphoto Lp. "Locker" courtesy of Jose Gil/ iStockphoto Lp.

Printed in the United States of America.
V092
Please visit our website at *www.pearsoncustom.com.*

Attention bookstores: For permission to return any unsold stock, contact us at *pe-uscustomreturns@pearson.com.*

Pearson Learning Solutions, 501 Boylston Street, Suite 900, Boston, MA 02116
A Pearson Education Company
www.pearsoned.com

ISBN 10: 1-256-22070-1
ISBN 13: 978-1-256-22070-1

PEARSON CUSTOM
Education

Liberty University
School of Education
EDUC 125
Introduction to Education

Pearson Learning Solutions

New York   Boston   San Francisco
London   Toronto   Sydney   Tokyo   Singapore   Madrid
Mexico City   Munich   Paris   Cape Town   Hong Kong   Montreal

Contents

Teaching in Focus

Meet the Focus Teachers and Students

"You just had to be there!" we often exclaim when words aren't enough. Learning about teachers, students, and schools is one of those situations when photos or video clips can help convey what a thousand words cannot. Is it as good as being there? No, but it helps.

Throughout this text you will learn about 4 schools, 10 teachers, and 12 students. These people and places are real. You will get to know 10 teachers through interviews, room tours, and lesson clips in MyEducationLab and in *Teaching in Focus* features. You will watch 12 students grow through real-life scenarios in both the text and in video segments that include student-teacher conversations and parent interviews. You'll see their smiling faces in the photos throughout chapters.

Explore these classrooms. Reflect on the teaching, the learning, the student diversity you see. Use these teachers, students, and schools to help you develop your own teaching identity. These 10 teachers and 12 students put faces on our discussions of development, diversity, teaching, and learning. Take your time as you read about, watch, and listen to them. Let their stories sink in. Think about the ones who speak to you most deeply. Let them help guide you toward your teaching identity!

FOCUS SCHOOL

Sara Davis Powell

Summit Primary School
Summit Station, Ohio
Kindergarten–second grade
Principal: Laura Hill

Summit Primary is a thriving school serving kindergarten through second grade students just outside Columbus, Ohio. Once a rural farm community, Summit Station where the school is located is becoming a suburban area that is increasingly diverse. In the last decade the student population of Summit Primary has changed from basically white and all English speaking to a rich mixture of races and ethnicities speaking at least 17 different languages. It's an exciting time of growth for the community, the school, and the teachers who spend their days with students in the early childhood phase of development.

Get to know the school and its principal, Laura Hill, and follow the teachers and students you are about to meet in the Teaching in Focus section on the MyEducationLab that accompanies this text.

Focus Teachers

Sara Davis Powell

Brandi Wade
Kindergarten teacher
Summit Primary School, Ohio
Teaching experience:
Grades 5–6 (2 years),
Preschool and K (14 years)

Brandi says she has found her place in life. From her family to her friends to her teaching career, everything fits for this exuberant kindergarten teacher. One look around her classroom and one brief conversation are enough to know that 5- and 6-year-olds who spend time in Brandi's care are fortunate children.

Brandi believes in active involvement of children. She finds ways to teach the Ohio kindergarten curriculum standards through lots of movement, music, hands-on experiences, and play. Each year she spends whatever time is necessary to help her 15 to 25 kindergarten students per class form positive habits so the necessary routines of the classroom take care of themselves. She knows that classroom management and learning go hand in hand.

"My heart is where the children are" is a phrase Brandi says and lives. She believes that children must feel comfortable and loved in their environment before they can learn and thrive. She laughs and cries with her students, allows herself to be vulnerable to their needs, and provides a warm, developmentally appropriate setting in which children learn and grow.

Brandi and her husband have two sons, a Jack Russell terrier, and two turtles. Brandi enjoys swimming, camping, reading mysteries, and going to movies.

Sara Davis Powell

Renee Ayers
Second grade teacher
Summit Primary School, Ohio
Teaching experience:
Reading teacher (2 years)
First grade (3 years)
Second grade (4 years)

Renee exudes enthusiasm for life. From the soccer field to the energy she puts into teaching second grade, Renee's personality shines through. She says summers as a camp counselor influenced her teaching philosophy of infusing active learning and fun into instruction.

Renee is a reflective teacher who spends time in her classroom diagnosing student needs. She says her biggest challenge is to design learning experiences for each child that take into account what the child already knows and is able to do. She believes strongly in individualizing assignments even when her instruction is geared toward the whole class. The children in Renee's class are learning to be reflective too. She saves samples of work from the beginning of the school year and periodically shows the samples to the students so they can compare and recognize their own progress. This is a simple process that's good for children.

At the end of the school year a very shy little boy said, "Mrs. Ayers, can you go to third grade with us?" The children pull at her heartstrings. All the effort is worth it.

Renee and her husband have a baby daughter, the delight of their lives. In addition to her adult women's soccer league, Renee enjoys skiing, snowboarding, mountain biking, and taking evening walks with her family.

Focus Students

Dylan Todd
Kindergarten
Summit Primary School, Ohio

Kindergarten
Provided by the
Todd family

*Dylan with Mom and
Dad* Provided by the Todd
family

Dylan is the only child of Brandon and Lisa Todd. Their pride is obvious as they talk about what a delightful little boy he is. When Dylan smiles, everyone smiles. When he giggles, his pure expression of joy is contagious.

Dylan is in his second year as a kindergarten student. During his first year, Dylan made progress and perhaps could have gone on to first grade. However, in consultation with the school staff, Mom and Dad decided it would benefit Dylan to experience another year of kindergarten, giving him time to mature a bit more socially.

We meet Dylan in the winter of his second year of kindergarten. His teacher, Brandi Wade, says that he has made wonderful progress in learning to read. In terms of the reasoning ability needed for progress in math, Brandi says Dylan is continuously growing and learning.

Sherlonda Francis
Second grade
Summit Primary School, Ohio

Kindergarten Provided by the Francis family *2nd grade* Provided by the Francis family *Sherlonda with Mom and Dad*
Sara Davis Powell

Sherlonda's personality shines. The challenge is to help her develop academically and find success in school so high school graduation will be in her future. Renee Ayers, her teacher, is afraid that if Sherlonda doesn't experience academic success soon, her penchant for socializing may actually get in the way of her success.

Sherlonda is doing fine in second grade. However, in first grade she had some difficulty paying attention and staying on task. Although this isn't unusual for early childhood students, it was chronic enough to concern the Summit Primary staff. Renee talked extensively with Sherlonda's first grade teacher, and they worked together to plan Sherlonda's second grade experience so she would experience success.

Sherlonda's mom is the sponsor of her church dance group, and her dad is very active in Sherlonda's life, saying his daughter loves to learn new things and figure out how things work. Both parents say they have always read to Sherlonda, and now she is reading to them.

FOCUS SCHOOL

Sara Davis Powell

Rees Elementary School
Spanish Fork, Utah
Kindergarten–fifth grade
Principal: Mike Larsen

Rees Elementary is a school for kindergarten through fifth grade students in Spanish Fork, Utah, just south of Salt Lake City. Located in a suburban area at the base of the Wasatch Mountains, Rees incorporates an emphasis on the arts supported by an experienced and enthusiastic faculty. While each grade level provides traditional classrooms, Rees also has a dynamic team of three teachers who spend their days in multiage classrooms of third, fourth, and fifth grade students, all learning together.

 *On the MyEducationLab that accompanies this text, you can hear about Rees Elementary from principal Mike Larsen. You will also hear from each of this school's focus teachers and students.*

Focus Teachers

Sara Davis Powell

Tim Mendenhall
Third, fourth, and fifth grade teacher
Rees Elementary School, Utah
Teaching experience:
Fifth–eighth grade science (4 years);
Multiage third, fourth, and fifth grade (11 years)

Tim Mendenhall's ready laugh sets the tone for his classroom where third, fourth, and fifth grade students enjoy being actively involved in their own learning. Tim's comfortable manner allows his students to get to know him and one another in his multiage classroom.

Tim's approach to science is to provide interesting objects and books to grab his students' attention. Nothing compares to the excitement generated by the classroom's pet tarantula, Rosie. As Tim teaches his kids how to hold her, Rosie playfully crawls up and down his arm and onto the hand of a willing student (with a little coaxing from Tim!). Take a look at page 102 in Chapter 4!

The reading area in Tim's classroom is surrounded by bookshelves. Inside the area are couches and pillows. Tim says the arrangement is his *kiva,* a Native American meeting space that traditionally was hollowed out with room for seating all around and reserved for important and/or spiritual gatherings. In Tim's reading kiva, his students find a comfortable place to enjoy his collection of varied and interesting books.

Before deciding to teach, Tim was a forestry major. His wife and three sons share his love of the outdoors. Tim finds ways to balance a wonderful family life with his responsibilities as a classroom teacher. Teaching school may not be the most lucrative profession, but it's what Tim loves to do.

Sara Davis Powell

Chris Roberts
Third, fourth, and fifth grade teacher
Rees Elementary School, Utah
Teaching experience:
Special education (14 years)
Multiage third, fourth, and fifth grade (13 years)

Chris Roberts's adventurous spirit and active lifestyle permeate both his personal and his professional life. Chris has climbed Mount Kilimanjaro, rafted his way through the rapids of the Grand Canyon, and explored the shores of remote islands.

Chris brings his treasures to the classroom and shares his adventures with his students. Listening to real-life stories of scuba-diving encounters with giant sea rays and six-foot eels makes learning about ocean life and geography pure joy! Imagine spending three straight years in Mr. Roberts's class!

Chris is a fan of all kinds of art. He has posters of some of his favorite paintings on the walls of his classroom along with inspirational poems, essays, and even cartoons. Chris infuses lessons in math, science, social studies, and language arts with a sense of curiosity and elements of critical thinking. One of his goals is for his students to see beyond the classroom walls, beyond Spanish Fork, beyond Utah and the United States, to learn there's a whole world to experience.

Chris's family all share his love of adventure. Chris and his wife raised their children without television. He says there's nothing inherently wrong with television, but it distracts people from doing more worthwhile things like reading and experiencing life rather than just watching other people experience it.

Sara Davis Powell

Brenda Beyal
Third, fourth, and fifth grade teacher
Rees Elementary School, Utah
Teaching experience:
Third grade (8 years);
Multiage third, fourth, and fifth grade (13 years)

The teaching profession is very personal to Brenda Beyal, and she approaches it with a sense of calling. The classroom environment she creates is warm and inviting.

Brenda's favorite subject to teach is language arts. She views literature as a child's window on the world, and reading as a way of experiencing both events and points of view. When her class of third, fourth, and fifth graders read a book together, they explore meanings, not just words. They enjoy finding out about the author and rereading the story for deeper meaning. They write in their journals about story themes and act out sequences.

The fact that Brenda is Native American brings extra richness to her classroom. The wisdom of generations of her ancestors influences her. She has meaningful Native American objects and posters in her classroom and feels it's important for her to share parts of her heritage with her students. As they grow and encounter other Native Americans, Brenda wants her students to recall, "I know a Native American. I like the kind of person Ms. Beyal is. I'd like to get to know this person I have just met."

Brenda's family time with her husband, son, and daughter is very meaningful to her. She also enjoys drawing, sculpting, and collecting Native American artifacts.

Focus Students

Kindergarten
Provided by the
Wiley family

1st grade
Provided by the
Wiley family

3rd grade
Provided by the
Wiley family

Amanda and Mom
Sara Davis Powell

Amanda Wiley
Third grade,
Rees Elementary School, Utah

Amanda's mom, president of the Rees Elementary PTA, describes Amanda as "just plain fun." All it takes is five minutes of classroom observation to know the description fits. Amanda loves school now, but reading did not come easily for her, and first grade proved to be very challenging. Toward the end of second grade, things began to click for Amanda. Now in third grade, she is an avid reader.

Introduction

Amanda is crazy about math. Mom says Amanda doesn't behave like a stereotypical girl. She would rather be involved in rough-and-tumble play than to do what most girls want to do. Amanda is the middle of three sisters and doesn't seem to have time for relationships with other girls.

The summer before going to third grade, when Amanda would be in Tim Mendenhall's homeroom, she talked her family into letting her be the caretaker of Rosie, the class pet. As it turns out, the class pet is not a cuddly guinea pig or a cute little rabbit, but a large hairy tarantula.

Hector Mancia
Fourth grade,
Rees Elementary School, Utah

Kindergarten
Provided by the
Mancia family

2nd grade
Provided by the
Mancia family

4th grade
Provided by the
Mancia family

Hector and Mom
Sara Davis Powell

Hector's smile would warm the heart of any teacher. As a fourth grader, he is a fluent English speaker, vibrant, curious, and determined to succeed. Hector's family came to Utah from Mexico. One of his biggest challenges is to help his family learn English. Mrs. Mancia understands and speaks some English, but his dad and older brother do not.

Hector enjoys school. He fits right in with other third, fourth, and fifth graders in Chris Roberts's multiage class at Rees Elementary. Hector tells us that he really enjoys reading, sports, recess, and lunch—pretty typical of fourth graders. His mom tells us he enjoys basketball, school, and cleaning his room. This last may seem surprising, but Hector likes to please those around him.

Hector enjoys Mr. Roberts's lessons and says his teacher's travels add a lot to the classroom. Chris Roberts's teaching style draws him in and keeps him excited about school.

Josie Ford
Fifth grade,
Rees Elementary School, Utah

Kindergarten
Provided by the
Ford family

3rd grade
Provided by the
Ford family

5th grade
Provided by the
Ford family

Josie and Mom
Sara Davis Powell

At age 10, Josie loves school, reads fluently, enjoys math, and is quite proficient on the computer. She thrives in a multiage setting with children in grades 3, 4, and 5. She enjoys spending her days with her classmates, sharing the social aspects of children her own age and younger, as well as the academic challenge of learning fifth grade standards while assisting third and fourth grade students learn their standards. When Josie was a third grader she was assisted by the older children in her multiage classroom. Josie enjoys helping in the same way she was helped.

Josie has a well-rounded life and lots of advantages, evident both in her school performance and her home life. Mom tells us they have an active, outdoor-oriented family. She and her sister and parents often go on adventures in the Utah desert and mountains.

FOCUS SCHOOL

Sara Davis Powell

Cario Middle School
Mt. Pleasant, South Carolina
Sixth–eighth grade
Principal: Carol Bartlett

Cario Middle School serves sixth, seventh, and eighth grade students and is located in Mt. Pleasant, South Carolina, a medium-size city just across the Wando River from historic Charleston. Cario provides young adolescents with the foundational components of a true middle school, including teams of teachers who teach specific groups of students, close teacher-student relationships, high expectations, and a support network that boosts both academic and personal growth.

Meet Cairo's principal Carol Bartlett in the Teaching in Focus section on the MyEducationLab that accompanies this text. Here you will also be able to have a look at each focus teacher's classroom and meet each of the students and their parents.

Focus Teachers

Sara Davis Powell

Traci Peters
Seventh grade math teacher
Cario Middle School, South Carolina
Teaching experience:
Seventh grade math/science (6 years);
Seventh grade math (2 years)

Traci's classroom is filled with math—the shelves, the walls, the tables—math is everywhere. The seventh graders in her classes know they'll be actively involved in tasks that help them understand concepts. From geoboards to examine perimeter and area, to paper triangles they tear apart to prove the angles add up to 180 degrees, problem solving becomes something they do, rather than something they just read about. One of Traci's primary goals is to show students that learning math can be lots of fun.

Traci offers her students before-school tutoring to help with concepts that may be difficult. The sessions also help students who have been absent to get caught up. The tutoring not only gives an academic boost, but it also gives Traci and her students time to get to know one another better.

Traci believes it's important for teachers to reveal some of their personal selves to students. She freely talks about her son and proudly shows students pictures of him as she encourages students to talk about their families and what they like to do in school and out of school.

Traci is married and has a 2-year-old son. She says she loves the fact that she is his first teacher. Walking on the beach, traveling to see family and friends, and spending everyday time with her husband and son make life a real joy for Traci.

Sara Davis Powell

Deirdre Huger-McGrew
Sixth–eighth grade language arts, social studies teacher
Cario Middle School, South Carolina
Teaching experience:
First, fourth, fifth grade (7 years)
Sixth–eighth grade language arts, social studies (4 years)

Deirdre Huger-McGrew has taught a variety of grade levels and subjects. She says each one is interesting and challenging, but none so much as her current assignment on a two-person team charged with implementing a new program at Cario Middle School called CARE: Cario Academic Recovery and Enrichment. The program is designed to assist low-achieving sixth, seventh, and eighth graders in working toward grade-level competency.

Deirdre and her teaching partner, Billy, have been given a unique opportunity to begin a program and design it in ways that are responsive to their students. Principal Carol Bartlett has given them a good deal of professional autonomy. Deirdre says she is thriving in this situation even though her students are among the most challenging at Cario.

Deirdre's ability to talk with students about their interests, hopes, fears, and dreams makes her the ideal teacher for CARE students. She's the "mom" figure for the students.

Deirdre not only has students at Cario to care for, but her own home is brimming over with children. She and her husband have six children, all under 19 years old. Deirdre's attitude is "the more, the merrier." She says she's a teacher 24 hours a day! In her little free time, she enjoys writing and pursuing art activities.

Focus Students

Kindergarten
Provided by the McBeath family

3rd grade
Provided by the McBeath family

5th grade
Provided by the McBeath family

David and Mom
Sara Davis Powell

David McBeath
Sixth grade
Cario Middle School, South Carolina

At 6 feet and 195 pounds, David doesn't appear to be 12 years old. However, looking at his childlike face and hearing his soft voice, you realize he is a young adolescent whose emotional and social development are yet to catch up with his physical growth. David wants teachers to be friendly and organized. What he doesn't like are teachers who are boring or who cover material too quickly.

David enjoys music. He plays the bass guitar with a church rock band several times a week. David's mom tells us he hummed before he spoke. Music is his favorite pastime and a way of expressing himself. This kind of interest and talent are particularly important for students with learning disabilities. David has struggled academically since kindergarten.

David's mom makes the most of his auditory skills by encouraging him to listen to books on CD and follow the words as he does so. David will need all the help he can get to succeed in public school for the next six years because of his academic difficulties.

Patrick Sutton
Seventh grade
Cario Middle School, South Carolina

Kindergarten
Provided by the
Sutton family

2nd grade
Provided by the
Sutton family

5th grade
Provided by the
Sutton family

7th grade
Sara Davis Powell

Patrick is a very self-assured 13-year-old seventh grader who likes school. He enjoys being with friends the most and doing homework the least (no surprise here!). He says he likes teachers who challenge him and dislikes teachers who are mean and yell at kids. Patrick says he would like to join the NFL. But if that's not in his future, he would like to be an architect.

Patrick's mom tells us he is a delight at home. She says he is independent, easy to be around, loves his family, and enjoys attention. The main challenge Patrick has faced is that the family has moved often. Patrick has had to make new friends and start over several times in his eight years of schooling. Mom thinks that has made him stronger and a better student. Her hope for him is that he will retain his love of learning and be true to himself.

Trista Kutcher
Ninth grade
Wando High School, South Carolina

Preschool
Provided by the
Kutcher family

Kindergarten
Provided by the
Kutcher family

3rd grade
Provided by the
Kutcher family

9th grade
Provided by the
Kutcher family

Trista is as friendly as any high school freshman could be. Other Wando students pass her and smile when they say hello. Trista is a cheerleader and an athlete—and she has Down syndrome.

Trista's coach and fellow cheerleaders tell us they anticipated problems because of Trista's disability. They soon discovered that their fears were not justified. Trista has proven to have both the skill and the attitude to be an asset to the squad.

Trista, her parents, ReBecca and Joe, and her two sisters form a loving, supportive family. ReBecca and Joe are both teachers. When at Cario Middle School, ReBecca was there to make sure Trista had every advantage possible in a public school setting. At Wando High School, Joe is her homeroom teacher. Their interest and involvement have played a major role in Trista's success.

FOCUS SCHOOL

Sara Davis Powell

Roosevelt High School
Fresno, California;
Ninth–twelfth grade
Principal: Maria Romero

Roosevelt High School in Fresno, California, is a large urban school for ninth through twelfth graders. The student population of Roosevelt is predominantly Hispanic and Asian. Many of the Roosevelt students are children of migrant farm workers, and a significant number have only recently moved to the United States. The dedicated and creative faculty of Roosevelt High provides rich learning opportunities for all students, regardless of race, ethnicity, primary language, or socioeconomic status.

Get to know the school and its principal, Maria Romero, and follow the teachers and students you are about to meet in the Teaching in Focus section on the MyEducationLab that accompanies this text.

Focus Teachers

Sara Davis Powell

Craig Cleveland
History, government, economics
Roosevelt High School, California
Teaching experience:
History, government, economics (18 years)

Every day, during lunch as well as in the five-minute passing periods between classes, students gather in Mr. Cleveland's classroom to play a tune on his piano or strum a chord or two on his guitar. Several other students sit on desks and listen or participate. This doesn't happen by accident. It happens because Craig Cleveland welcomes students to express themselves, to be comfortable finding their own voice in his classroom and in his presence.

Craig's philosophical stance concerning teaching and learning involves his belief that students learn best when they are interested and involved through authentic reading, writing, speaking, and listening activities. The lessons he plans in his history, government, and economics classes include reading materials that push students to think and to interact with the text and one another. Students form opinions and write about them. Students speak to both question and persuade, to communicate in order to learn. The first rule of thumb in Craig's planning is "Give the students something worth thinking about."

Craig is an avid observer of human nature and the learning process both at school and in his home. He considers the home a fascinating lab for learning as he and his wife delight in watching their five daughters read, draw, create skits, and solve problems. Craig enjoys playing tennis and writing songs.

Jessica O'Rourke

Derek Boucher
History, reading
Roosevelt High School, California
Teaching experience:
History (12 years)
Reading intervention (4 years)

Derek Boucher is an intense teacher whose conscientious involvement in the teaching profession sets a standard for all of us. His background in social sciences and his initial years in teaching led him to the realization that until students can read with fluency and comprehension, they will not be the kind of lifelong learners he would hope for them to be.

Although high school may seem much too late to learn to read, the reality is that many 15- to 18-year-olds can read only well enough to barely pass classes, and some not even to that extent. English-language learners often have even more difficulty.

Derek involves the students in all his classes in current events that impact their lives. He helps them put events and ideologies in context. They explore issues such as media influence and bias. He pushes them to think through issues, form opinions, and then find ways to express their opinions. He teaches them to be wise consumers of information.

Derek and his wife enjoy family time with their two sons and daughter. Derek is an avid reader of professional literature. He also contributes to it by writing opinion editorials in the local newspaper, the *Fresno Bee,* and articles in professional journals.

Sara Davis Powell

Angelica Reynosa
Modern World History
Roosevelt High School, California
Teaching experience:
World history (3 years)

Angelica Reynosa's tenth grade bilingual modern world history class is filled with enthusiasm. There are 34 students in the class, all of whom have been in the United States for less than two years. Angelica is a young Latina whose fluency in both Spanish and English makes her an ideal teacher at Roosevelt High School.

The students' enthusiasm for the class is enhanced by the fact that Angelica teaches in both Spanish and English. But language is not the only reason students are engaged. Angelica says her goal is to make every day enjoyable, memorable, and meaningful for all her students. She admits that it can be difficult to continually search for interactive, hands-on activities for teaching history, but the effort is worth it.

With a master's degree in school counseling, Angelica sees herself teaching several more years and then becoming a guidance counselor. She has aspirations to pursue a doctoral degree and plans to be part of the education profession for a long time.

Something that is particularly enjoyable for Angelica is the fact that she married a high school history teacher who teaches at a nearby school. Angelica says their conversations are filled with empathy because they each understand the other's dilemmas and can listen attentively and make helpful suggestions when challenges arise.

Focus Students

Kindergarten
Provided by the
Reyes family

3rd grade
Provided by the
Reyes family

6th grade
Provided by the
Reyes family

10th grade
Provided by the
Reyes family

Mayra Reyes
Tenth grade
Roosevelt High School, California

Mayra was born in the United States and is fluent in both Spanish and English. Friends are at the center of her life. Mayra would much rather be at school than at home. She enjoys going out with friends and playing sports. She says she didn't like to read before enrolling in Derek Boucher's class. Now that she has read her first real book, she says she reads better and faster and enjoys it.

On the day that Mayra's mother had agreed to come to school to talk, she didn't show up because of a domestic dispute involving Mom's boyfriend. Mayra's dad has been out of her life for years, and she doesn't understand how he can stay away. She confided that one of her fondest wishes is to be reunited with her father. Her home life often lacks the support that would help her be successful.

Mayra receives support at school through a program for Hispanic students focused on the arts called Folkloria. When asked about her future, she says she would like to be either a teacher or a nurse.

Guillermo Toscano
Eleventh grade
Roosevelt High School, California

Kindergarten
Provided by the Toscano family

3rd grade
Provided by the Toscano family

6th grade
Provided by the Toscano family

10th grade
Provided by the Toscano family

Guillermo and Mom
Sara Davis Powell

Guillermo represents the first generation in his family to go to high school. In conversation, his maturity and thoughtful demeanor are engaging. Guillermo tells us his dad came to the United States to give his family a better life.

Guillermo says he learns best when he experiences the concepts and content to be learned through class activities. He enjoys lots of teacher-student interaction.

Mom says Guillermo is always pleasant and kind. In fact, she affectionately calls him her "gentle bear." She says he enjoys school but is sometimes a little lazy. She lets us know with a giggle that even this trait endears Guillermo to her. He loves sports, both playing them and watching them. Mom hopes Guillermo will go to college and get into a business of his choice. She quickly adds that she hopes he can do all this right there in Fresno so he will be close to her. What a loving environment.

Hugo Martinez
Eleventh grade
Roosevelt High School, California

11th grade
Provided by the Martinez family

Hugo with Mom and Dad
Sara Davis Powell

Hugo is a 17-year-old junior with a very outgoing personality. Are you wondering why there's only one school picture of him? When Hugo, his mom and dad, and three brothers crossed the Mexican border into California 18 months ago, they only brought the clothes they were wearing.

Angelica Reynosa, Hugo's bilingual teacher, interprets the question about what he would like to do in the future. He responds in English, "I have a dream in my life." Then in Spanish he says he wants to graduate from high school, go to college, and be a doctor or a teacher. Hugo's mom and dad, with Angelica interpreting, express their pride in Hugo and say he is responsible, does his chores and homework, and is well rounded. Their hope is that Hugo's teachers be positive and continue to motivate him.

Perhaps the biggest road block for Hugo is his lack of U.S. citizenship. This precludes him from receiving grants and government loans. Without financial assistance, Hugo will likely not go from high school to college.

Khammany Douangsavanh
Twelfth grade
Roosevelt High School, California

Kindergarten
Provided by the
Douangsavanh family

2nd grade
Provided by the
Douangsavanh family

5th grade
Provided by the
Douangsavanh family

Khammany and Mom
Sara Davis Powell

Khammany speaks fluent English at school but only Laotian at home. She participates consistently and demonstrates an appreciation for the value of education. As a learner, Khammany says interest in a subject is the key to motivating her to succeed. Khammany says she likes history in Craig Cleveland's class because there's so much in the past to think about and so much in the future to predict.

Khammany's mom, who speaks no English and relies on Khammany to interpret, is very emotional when she says she wants her daughter to receive a good education to help her succeed. This is especially important since the death of Khammany's dad about a year ago. Mom views her daughter as the hope of their family. She's bright and determined, and her mother is obviously proud of her.

Khammany will be the first in her family to graduate from high school and would be the first to enter college. However, she will likely feel compelled to help support her mom and extended family, making four years of college fairly elusive.

Teachers and the Teaching Profession

In *Meet the Focus Teachers and Students* you were introduced to 10 focus teachers with whom you will interact throughout this text. Getting to know our focus teachers helps you explore how accomplished lifelong learners approach the classroom and the profession of teaching. Among the many questions to consider about teachers and teaching, here are some we address:

✦ Who teaches in the United States and why?

✦ How do we prepare to teach?

✦ Is teaching a profession?

✦ What is teacher professionalism?

✦ What are the characteristics of effective teachers?

No African tribe is considered to have warriors more fearsome or more intelligent than the Masai. It is perhaps surprising, then, to discover that the traditional greeting between Masai warriors is *Kasserian ingera,* which means "And how are the children?"

This traditional tribal greeting acknowledges the high value the Masai place on their children's well-being. Even warriors with no children of their own give the traditional answer, "All the children are well," meaning that peace and safety prevail, that the priority of protecting the young, the powerless, is in place, that Masai society has not forgotten its proper function and responsibility, its reason for being. "All the children are well" means that life is good.

If we greeted each other with this same daily question, "And how are the children?" how might it affect our awareness of children's welfare in the United States? If we asked this question of each other a dozen times a day, would it begin to make a difference in the reality of how children are thought of and cared for in the United States?

If everyone among us, teacher and nonteacher, parent and nonparent, comes to feel a shared sense of responsibility for the daily care and protection of all the children in our community, in our town, in our state, in our country, we might truly be able to answer without hesitation, "The children are well. Yes, all the children are well."

Sara Davis Powell

Shutterstock

From Chapter 1 of *Your Introduction to Education: Explorations in Teaching*, 2/e. Sara Davis Powell.

Where DO I Stand?

This inventory helps you explore your personal reasons for considering teaching as a career. Read each item and decide how meaningful it is to you. If an item resonates very strongly within you, then choose "4: I strongly agree." Reserve a choice of "4" for those items you genuinely care most about. If you agree with a statement, but are not overly enthusiastic about it, then choose "3: I agree." If you really don't care one way or the other about a statement, choose "2: I don't have an opinion." If you simply disagree with a statement, choose "1: I disagree." If you feel adamantly opposed to a statement, choose "0: I strongly disagree." There are no right or wrong answers, just differing experiences and viewpoints. Following the inventory are directions for how to organize your responses and what they may indicate in terms of where you stand.

> 4   I strongly agree
> 3   I agree
> 2   I don't have an opinion
> 1   I disagree
> 0   I strongly disagree

_____ **1.** Some of my fondest memories involve experiences working with children/teens.

_____ **2.** The health insurance and retirement benefits of teaching mean a lot to me.

_____ **3.** In K–12 school I enjoyed and excelled in a particular subject.

_____ **4.** As a teacher, I look forward to growing professionally.

_____ **5.** At least one member of my family is an educator.

_____ **6.** I am considering teaching because I believe education has necessary societal value.

_____ **7.** Teaching is most worthwhile because of the opportunity to influence students.

_____ **8.** Although I may be interested in other professions, the stability of a career in the public school system draws me to teaching.

_____ **9.** Both the daily work hours and the yearly schedule of a teacher appeal to me.

_____ **10.** Doing the same thing in the same way repeatedly does not appeal to me.

_____ **11.** My desire to teach is based on my love of a particular subject.

_____ **12.** There was a teacher in my K–12 experiences who had a profound impact on my life.

_____ **13.** My family is pleased with my decision to teach.

_____ **14.** A teacher's primary task is to help students become productive citizens.

_____ **15.** Being with children/adolescents is something I enjoy and look forward to.

_____ **16.** I am anxious to read whatever I can about the teaching profession.

_____ **17.** A major reason for choosing the teaching profession is the appeal of having holidays and spring break time off.

_____ **18.** Being a teacher means always having a job.

_____ **19.** Education is necessary for the continued success of our country.

_____ **20.** I have very fond memories of my relationship with one or more teachers in K–12 school.

21. Having a long summer vacation means a lot to me.

22. I have been drawn to a particular subject area for years.

23. Professional self-growth motivates me.

24. I am interested in teaching because I want to work with children and/or adolescents.

25. I plan to teach because someone in my family is encouraging my choice.

26. I want to teach because of the promise of job security.

27. Being a camp counselor appeals to me.

28. I want to teach to positively benefit society.

29. Content knowledge is the primary goal of education.

30. Someone in my family enjoys teaching and relays positive stories about the profession.

31. I would like to be able to personally thank a former teacher for influencing me to be a teacher.

32. I like the idea of having days off when my own children will also have time off.

33. I have a passion for a content area.

34. Even in difficult economic times, the fact that teachers will always be needed appeals to me.

35. My family values education and emphasizes the worth of teachers.

36. My career goal is to emulate a teacher I have known.

37. Without quality public education our society suffers.

38. I am still in touch with at least one of my K–12 teachers.

39. Being home by about 4 P.M. is important to me.

40. Teaching appeals to me most because I love to learn new things.

In the tables, record the number, 0 to 4, that you responded for each indicated item. Then find the sum for each table's responses.

ITEM #	MY #	ITEM #	MY #	ITEM #	MY #	ITEM #	MY #	ITEM #	MY #	ITEM #	MY #	ITEM #	MY #	ITEM #	MY #
1		6		3		12		9		5		2		4	
7		14		11		20		17		13		8		10	
15		19		22		31		21		25		18		16	
24		28		29		36		32		30		26		23	
27		37		33		38		39		35		34		40	
Sum A		Sum B		Sum C		Sum D		Sum E		Sum F		Sum G		Sum H	

Now it's time to graph your responses. Mark and then shade your sums on the **Choosing to Teach** *bar graph. The results show how much you value, relatively speaking, eight reasons for becoming a teacher that we discuss in this chapter. Your instructor may ask you to share your graph with others as part of the exploration of teachers and the teaching profession.*

By the end of this book you will have explored many aspects of the teaching profession in very personal ways. As teachers, the better we know ourselves, the closer we come to understanding our students and finding ways to address their needs to help them grow. At the end of this chapter we revisit elements of Where Do I Stand? *by responding to follow-up questions in* Where Do I Stand Now?

Throughout this book you are asked to respond to ideas and questions. **Points of Reflection** *features provide mental exercises that involve you in an extended conversation about teaching.* **Reflection** *requires us to honestly think about what we believe and do, why we believe it and how we do it, and the consequences of our beliefs and actions.*

Are you surprised by your graph? Is this the first time you actually analyzed your reasons for choosing to teach or for at least considering being a teacher?

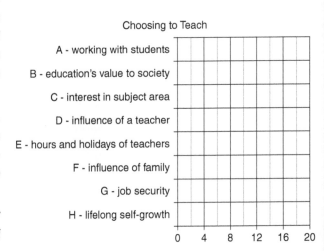

Choosing to Teach

A - working with students
B - education's value to society
C - interest in subject area
D - influence of a teacher
E - hours and holidays of teachers
F - influence of family
G - job security
H - lifelong self-growth

0   4   8   12   16   20

Teaching in Focus

Traci Peters teaches seventh grade math at Cario Middle School in South Carolina. By all accounts she's an excellent teacher—just ask her principal, her colleagues, and, most importantly, her students. Outside school Traci enjoys a very happy home life with husband Dwayne and young son Robert. The seventh graders in Traci's classes know all about these two very important people in her life, and that's the way Traci wants it. Although math is the subject she has chosen to teach, she is conscious of the fact that her responsibilities go well beyond fractions and equations. She views each student as an individual with relationships and often complex growing-up issues. Traci reveals herself to them, and they, in turn, feel comfortable enough to share with her.

In a prominent place in the classroom Traci has a "Mrs. Peters" bulletin board on which she displays, among other things, family photos (from her childhood to the present), her favorite poems and book titles, her own seventh grade report card, and her 5 x 7 middle school picture. Traci says her students spend lots of time examining the board's contents, laughing and asking questions.

Traci sees herself as a role model of a healthy, positive adult who makes good choices and tries to make a difference in other people's lives. When asked if she would just as freely share with students the not-so-positive aspects of her life, she replies yes. When she's not feeling well, she lets her students know. If her son Robert is sick and she needs to stay home to care for him, she tells her students.

Traci attends her students' basketball games, concerts, spelling bees, Odyssey of the Mind competitions—the typical year-long parade of events. She views this as a tangible way to show her students she is interested in them, their growth, and their lives.

Watch Traci's room tour, as well as her interview, in the Teaching in Focus section for Chapter 1 in MyEducationLab for this course.

Who Teaches in the United States and Why?

Teaching is the largest profession in the United States, with almost 4 million teachers in both public and private schools (National Center for Education Statistics [NCES], 2009). Examine Figure 1.1 to see who teaches in the United States.

Figure 1.1 U.S. teachers

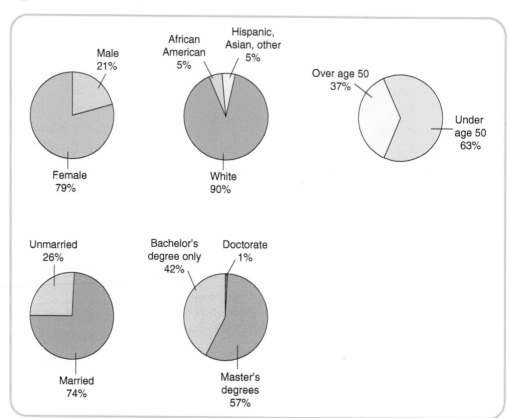

Source: National Education Association. (2003). Status of the American public school teacher 2000–2001. Retrieved May 15, 2005, from www.nea.org/edstats/images/status.pdf.

Teachers and the Teaching Profession

TEACHERS IN THE UNITED STATES

In Figure 1.1 you'll see that teachers are better educated than ever—more than 50% hold master's degrees. About 75% of U.S. teachers are married, 15% are single, and 11% are widowed, divorced, or separated. About a third of teachers have school-age children themselves (National Education Association [NEA], 2003). However, if you ask, they'll all likely tell you they "have" 20 or more children every year!

Also note that most teachers are white and female. There is considerable need for more diversity and gender balance in the teaching force. Do we want to discourage white women from becoming teachers? Absolutely not. Is there a need for more male teachers and teachers from minority population groups? Absolutely yes.

Most people join the teaching profession purposefully. In a large-scale survey of teachers with fewer than 5 years in the classroom, only about 12% said they "fell into teaching by chance." Some enter directly upon graduation from college, and some become teachers after pursuing one or more other careers. This same survey found that most teachers possess a strong inclination toward their career choice: 86% of the surveyed teachers believe that teaching requires a "sense of calling," and 96% say that teaching is work they love to do. The inference is that entering the teaching profession requires a commitment beyond that required by many other careers and, once in the profession, relatively new teachers overwhelmingly view teaching in positive ways (Public Agenda, 2003). But why did they choose to become teachers?

DECIDING TO TEACH

Helping you first make the decision to teach and then find your teaching identity is at the heart of this book. Exploring why other people choose to teach may help you clarify your own thoughts and desires. In 2001 the National Education Association (NEA) surveyed almost a thousand teachers, asking why they chose the teaching profession. The teachers were given a list of 21 possible reasons and asked to choose their top 3. Our discussion of the reasons for choosing to teach is organized around the eight reasons most often chosen by the teachers in the survey. As you read, think about your own reasons for considering teaching as your career.

DESIRE TO WORK WITH YOUNG PEOPLE.

Because 6 to 7 hours of a teacher's day are spent in direct contact with students, enjoying their company is a must. Getting to know the students we teach allows us to become familiar with their emotional and social needs as well as their cognitive needs. You may hear teachers talk about teaching the **whole child**. This simply means attending to all their developmental stages and needs, along with teaching them grade-level and subject-area content. When we view the whole child, we realize the depth of our responsibilities as classroom teachers.

VALUE OF EDUCATION TO SOCIETY.

Education is widely viewed as the great equalizer. This means that differences in opportunity and privilege diminish as children reach their potential through quality education. In other words, the achievement gap narrows with the increased educational success of the students who historically underachieve. An **achievement gap** is a disparity among students, as some excel while others languish with respect to learning and academic success. Through teaching you will make a difference in the lives of individuals and thereby benefit society as a whole.

Traci Peters values young adolescents as individuals and develops strong positive relationships with them. Sara Davis Powell

Teachers and the Teaching Profession

INTEREST IN SUBJECT MATTER. According to the National Education Association (2003), high school teachers choose "interest in subject matter" more often than elementary teachers. An intense interest in a subject area is important if you are going to teach that subject all day. Middle school is a happy compromise for people who have both a strong desire to work with students and a passion for a specific subject. Most middle school teachers teach one or possibly two subjects all day to students whose development is challenging and intriguing.

INFLUENCE OF TEACHERS. Can you name the last five vice presidents of the United States? How about the current Miss America? Who represents your home district in the state legislature? Who was your fifth grade teacher? Who taught your favorite class when you were a freshman in high school? The last two questions are the easiest, aren't they? That's because teachers influence us. They are uniquely positioned to shape students' thoughts and interests during the formative years of childhood and adolescence.

LONG SUMMER VACATION. A joke that's been around for a long time goes like this: "What are the three best things about teaching?" Answer: "June, July, August." Here's another. "What's the best time to be a teacher?" Answer: "Friday at 4." Within our ranks we smile at these harmless jokes.

Those who have not taught, or don't understand the pressure of having 15 or 25 or even 100 students dependent on them for at least part of each day, may view the schedule of a teacher as excessively punctuated with days off. However, time away from school is well deserved, even if it is used to catch up on teaching-related tasks. The change of pace is refreshing, allowing opportunities for revitalization.

Aside from summer vacation and days off, other aspects of scheduling make teaching a desirable choice for many. During the school year most teachers do not have students after about 3:30 in the afternoon. To people who work 8 to 5 jobs, 3:30 seems like a luxury. However, most teachers spend additional time either at school or at home planning for the next day and completing necessary administrative tasks. The teaching schedule allows for this kind of flexibility. A teacher's schedule is also ideal for families with school-age children. Having a daily routine similar to that of other family members has definite benefits.

INFLUENCE OF FAMILY. Most of us who consider being teachers grew up in families that valued education and respected teachers. If there are teachers in your family who are energetic and enthusiastic about their careers, they may influence you to follow in their footsteps.

JOB SECURITY. We will always need teachers. Those who are competent are generally assured positions even in difficult economic times. Other benefits related to job security include the availability of group health insurance and a reasonable retirement plan. It's unlikely that a career in teaching is chosen because of salary, although some districts and states are making progress in raising teachers' pay to be competitive with other fields that require a bachelor's degree. Table 1.1 shows average teacher salaries by state.

In almost all states and school districts, teachers are paid for both longevity in the profession and levels of education completed. A beginning teacher with a master's degree will receive a higher salary than a beginning teacher with a bachelor's degree. Two teachers with bachelor's degrees will be paid differently if one has 3 years of teaching experience and the other has 15 years in the classroom. In most cases, the fact that the teacher with 3 years can point to contributing to outstanding verifiable improvement and student achievement whereas the more experienced teacher has little to show with regard to influencing measurable student learning makes no difference in compensation. Is this fair? No. Have we found ways to measure student growth and pay teachers accordingly? Some ideas exist. But for decades school systems have tried to pay teachers based on performance, or

Teachers and the Teaching Profession

TABLE 1.1 Average teacher salaries, 2006–2007

Rank	State	Salary	Rank	State	Salary
1	California	$63,640	26	Wisconsin	$46,707
2	Connecticut	$61,039	27	North Carolina	$46,137
3	New Jersey	$59,730	28	Colorado	$45,832
4	New York	$59,557	29	Texas	$45,392
5	Rhode Island	$58,420	30	Idaho	$45,094
6	Illinois	$58,275	31	Arizona	$44,700
7	Massachusetts	$58,178	32	Arkansas	$44,493
8	Maryland	$56,927	33	South Carolina	$44,355
9	Michigan	$55,541	34	Tennessee	$43,815
10	Pennsylvania	$54,977	35	Kentucky	$43,787
11	Alaska	$54,678	36	Alabama	$43,389
12	Delaware	$54,537	37	Kansas	$43,318
13	Ohio	$53,536	38	Iowa	$42,922
14	Hawaii	$51,916	39	Louisiana	$42,816
15	Oregon	$51,080	40	New Mexico	$42,780
16	Wyoming	$50,771	41	Oklahoma	$42,379
17	Georgia	$49,836	42	Maine	$42,103
18	Minnesota	$49,719	43	Nebraska	$42,044
19	Nevada	$49,426	44	Montana	$41,146
20	Virginia	$49,130	45	West Virginia	$40,534
21	Washington	$47,880	46	Missouri	$40,384
22	Indiana	$47,832	47	Mississippi	$40,182
23	Vermont	$47,645	48	North Dakota	$38,586
24	Florida	$47,219	49	Utah	$37,775
25	New Hampshire	$46,797	50	South Dakota	$35,378
	U.S. average	**$51,009**			

Source: American Federation of Teachers (2008).

merit, but without the kind of success that perpetuates merit pay to the satisfaction of those affected, the teachers themselves.

When considering salary, investigate the cost of living where you want to live. For example, in 2005, thousands of experienced teachers in the suburbs outside New York City made more than $100,000 a year (Fessenden & Barbanel, 2005). However, an examination of the cost of living in such places as Westchester County, New York, shows that $100,000 there is equivalent to a much lower salary in most of small-town America.

OPPORTUNITY FOR A LIFETIME OF SELF-GROWTH. This is exactly what teaching offers. Few careers are as exciting or as rewarding on a daily basis, including the satisfaction of positively impacting the future of children. Teachers experience growth, both personally and professionally, in many ways: through relationships, reading, attending conferences, and the wide variety of professional development opportunities available. Teaching is not a stagnant career; rather, it continually presents new experiences, all of which offer opportunities for self-growth.

Sonia Nieto (2009), a respected educator and writer, offers additional, and perhaps more intriguing, reasons for becoming and remaining a teacher in Figure 1.2. Nieto's reasons are somewhat more complex than the eight we just explored and require thoughtful consideration. All of the reasons for choosing to teach are positive of course. Yet only discussing all the benefits and rewards of teaching presents a picture that's out of balance. No career is without challenges; no career is without frustration.

Points of Reflection 1.1

We've looked at eight reasons for choosing teaching as a career. Which are your top three reasons for considering the teaching profession and why?

Figure 1.2 Additional reasons for choosing to teach

Desire to engage in intellectual work
Belief in the democratic potential of public education
Anger at the current conditions of education
Sense of mission
Empathy for students
Enjoyment of improvisation
Comfort with uncertainty
Passion for social justice

Source: From S. Nieto (2009). From surviving to thriving. *Educational Leadership, 66*(5), 8–13.

Brandi Wade, one of our focus teachers at Summit Primary School in Ohio, tells us that perhaps we don't choose teaching, but rather teaching *chooses us.* Read about her philosophy in **Teaching in Focus**.

TEACHER SATISFACTION

Regardless of why teachers choose their profession, few will remain if their choice is not satisfying. As in any life's work, there are good days and bad, successes and failures, questions with answers often difficult to find. Talking with real teachers who spend their days with real students yields stories and opinions as varied as the individuals themselves.

For over 25 years MetLife, Inc. has surveyed teachers, encouraging them to express their opinions about many aspects of teaching. Teacher responses concerning their satisfaction with the teaching profession in Figure 1.3 are revealing and encouraging. The graphic depicts a comparison between teacher views in 1984 and teacher views in 2008. In both years teachers said they love to teach at the same rate, 82%. That's where the similarities end. As you can see, in responses to every other statement, teachers were significantly more positive about their profession in 2008 than in 1984, with three quarters of the teachers in 2008 saying they would advise others to enter the profession.

Teaching in Focus

Brandi Wade, kindergarten, Summit Primary, Ohio. *In her own words. . . .*

It may not so much be that you choose teaching, but that teaching chooses you. It will be in your heart and on your mind constantly. Although it's never easy for more than 5 minutes at a time, teaching is the most important profession you can pursue. I am truly blessed to be a kindergarten teacher. I get to teach a different lesson, meet a different challenge, and see life from different perspectives every day in my classroom.

Laugh with the children, laugh at yourself, and never hold a grudge. Don't be afraid to say "I'm sorry" to a child when you have done something unprofessional or hurtful. If children do hurtful things, just hug them a little more tightly and make them feel safe. Children learn best when they feel safe and loved no matter what.

Sara Davis Powell

I don't teach to be remembered, although it's nice to think that you'll never be completely forgotten. I teach so that I can remember. I remember their personalities and how they grow. I remember the times we struggled with learning and succeeded, as well as those times when we fell short of our goals. I remember the laughter and the tears we shared.

Some people say, "Leave school at school." The best teachers I know often lose sleep thinking about and worrying about their students. It's worth every toss and turn!

Figure 1.3 25-year perspective on teacher satisfaction

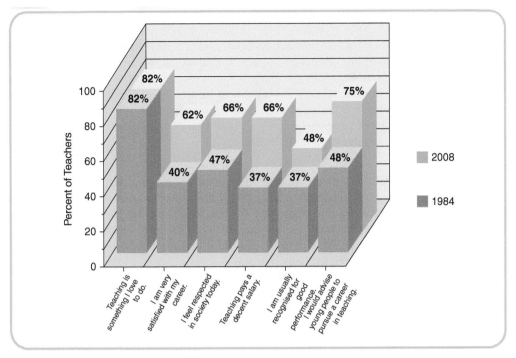

Source: MetLife. (2008). The MetLife survey of the American teacher. Available at: www.metlife.com/assets/cao/contributions/foundation/american-teacher/ MetLife_Teacher_Survey_2009.pdf.

How Do We Prepare to Teach?

You may have heard it said of someone, "He's just a natural-born teacher." There's some truth in this statement. Teaching comes more naturally to some than to others. With varying degrees of natural talent and inclination for teaching, we all have much to do to prepare to effectively make the teaching and learning connection. Our nature-given attributes must be enhanced by the knowledge and skills gained through studying content, learning about theory and methods of teaching, being mentored, reading, observing, practicing, and reflecting.

Each state has its own preparation requirements for those who teach in public school classrooms. Most states require a prospective teacher to pass a test before they grant certification or licensure. The most widely used tests are part of the **Praxis Series** published by the Educational Testing Service (ETS). The state issues a teaching certificate or license when a teacher candidate is determined to be sufficiently qualified. Let's examine two broad paths to initial teacher preparation: traditional and alternative.

TRADITIONAL PATHS TO TEACHER PREPARATION

The traditional paths to initial teacher preparation come through a university department of education. National and state organizations carefully scrutinize university programs and evaluate how teacher candidates are prepared. About two thirds of states require university teacher education programs to be accredited (authorized to prepare teachers) through the **National Council for Accreditation of Teacher Education (NCATE)**.

All three of the following initial teacher preparation paths—bachelor's degree, fifth-year program, master's degree—include one or two semesters of **student teaching,** also called **clinical internship**. During this extended fieldwork, teacher candidates teach lessons and, for a designated time frame, take over all classroom duties. A classroom teacher serves as the **cooperating teacher** (host and mentor) while a university instructor supervises the experience.

BACHELOR'S DEGREE. A 4-year undergraduate teacher preparation program consists of a combination of general education courses, education major courses, and field experiences. Most early childhood and elementary teacher preparation programs result in a degree with a major in education. Many programs in middle-level education result in a degree with a major in education and two subject area concentrations (15 to 24 hours). To teach in high school, most programs require a major in a content area and a minor, or the equivalent of a minor, in education coursework.

FIFTH-YEAR PROGRAM. Some universities offer a fifth-year teacher preparation program. Teacher candidates complete a major other than education and stay for a fifth year for more education coursework plus student teaching. For instance, a teacher candidate interested in science may major in biology and then stay a fifth year to become a certified, or licensed, teacher. Some of these programs include a master of arts in teaching degree rather than an extended bachelor's degree.

MASTER OF ARTS IN TEACHING. People who have a bachelor's degree in an area other than teacher education may pursue teacher preparation through a master of arts in teaching (MAT) degree. Most early childhood and elementary MAT programs consist of all teacher education courses and fieldwork, whereas middle-level MAT programs typically require 18 to 24 hours of subject area coursework in addition to education courses. High school MAT programs generally require a degree in a content area or the accumulation of enough content hours to be considered a concentration.

ALTERNATIVE PATHS TO TEACHER PREPARATION

There is a growing movement toward alternative paths to teacher preparation. In the 1980s alternative certification began as a way to address projected shortages of teachers. Since the first efforts, we have seen various models for recruiting, training, and certifying people who already have at least a bachelor's degree and want to become teachers.

Since 1983 the number of teachers entering the classroom through alternative means has rapidly increased. Now all 50 states offer one or more of over a hundred different programs offering alternative certification/licensure, with some estimates stating that as many as a third of new teachers are using alternative routes to the classroom. Adults who decide that teaching is for them after having other careers are likely to enter the profession through alternative paths (Feistritzer, 2009).

Many alternative programs grow out of specific needs and are developed and coordinated through partnerships among state departments of education, school districts, and university teacher education programs. Their structures vary widely, and they tend to be controversial. Some people doubt that teacher preparation is as effective outside the realm of university-based programs.

Perhaps the most widely known alternative path to the classroom is through the nonprofit organization **Teach for America** (TFA). Teach for America's goal is to increase the number of teachers willing to tackle the challenges of classrooms in low-income areas. TFA recruits individuals who are college seniors or recent graduates who agree to teach in high-needs rural or urban schools for at least 2 years in exchange for a salary plus reduction or elimination of college debt. In 2009 there were over 7,000 TFA teachers (Teach for America, 2010).

Diversity is an issue when hiring teachers, regardless of how they are prepared. Read about Mike Larsen's plans to hire a more diverse teaching force at Rees Elementary in *Diversity Dialogue*.

Mike Larsen, principal of Rees Elementary School, Utah

In this text you will read about teachers, students, principals, and schools as they struggle with issues involving diversity. All of the scenarios are based on our focus people and places introduced in *Meet the Focus Teachers and Students*. These *Diversity Dialogues* put what we are discussing in context so you can see how teachers, students, and principals address issues in schools and communities.

Sara Davis Powell

Mike Larsen of Rees Elementary School south of Salt lake City, Utah, is in his first year as principal of this K–5 school. Rees boasts a rich racial and ethnic diversity. The students are white, black, Hispanic, Native American, and Asian, all the broad racial distinctions recognized by the federal government. Their **ethnicities,** or where their families come from, represent an even greater spectrum of diversity.

Rees is a very good school as determined by multiple measures. The students achieve at levels above the state average, there are few real discipline issues, the facilities are more than adequate, and the teaching staff is both effective and stable. Mr. Larsen is quite pleased to have been appointed principal of such a school. If he simply maintained the status quo Rees would hum along just fine. But one thing bothers him. Although he considers every one of the Rees teachers to be good teachers, Mr. Larsen is concerned that the profile of the teaching staff closely mirrors the national average. Of the 45 teachers, 36 (80%) are female and 42 (92%) are white.

In March of his first year at Rees, Mr. Larsen finds out that three of his teachers are not returning to Rees in August. Two teachers plan to retire and one is marrying a Marine and moving to San Diego. All three are white. Mr. Larsen immediately recognizes an opportunity to introduce more diversity into the Rees teaching staff.

Respond to these items by writing one well-developed paragraph for each.

1. Mr. Larsen is aware that at Rees the tradition is for an entire grade level of teachers to spend time with candidates for teaching positions. The openings will be in second grade, fourth grade, and on one of the third/fourth/fifth grade multiage teams. Mr. Larsen plans to meet with each group of teachers to express his desire to hire teachers who are more diverse. What kinds of things might he say to the groups?

2. Mr. Larsen plans to do some recruiting at local colleges. Why might he find a more diverse pool of teacher candidates in alternative programs?

GETTING TO KNOW SCHOOLS, TEACHERS, AND STUDENTS

Regardless of the route you take to become a teacher, the more experiences you have in schools with teachers and students, the better prepared you will be to have a classroom of your own. The more experiences you have, the more certain your decision will be concerning whether teaching is for you. Experience in classrooms will also lead to more informed decision making about your teaching identity.

Most preparation programs require field experiences throughout. You may begin with observations in one course and then work with individual students and small groups in another, with whole group lessons before and during student teaching/clinical practice. These experiences may hold many surprises for you. Having a 5-year-old nephew you enjoy seeing several times a year is very different from working all day with 20 5-year-olds in a kindergarten classroom. Your memories of senior advanced placement literature that inspired you to want to teach high school English may be a romantic picture of students paying rapt attention as the sonnets of Elizabeth Barrett Browning are discussed. However, this may be a far cry from an actual freshman English class. If you fit the profile of most teachers and are a white woman from suburbia, chances are classrooms in urban America will expand your view of what it's like to be a teacher. You can read about differences in settings and students in this and other books and be somewhat informed. Seeing for yourself brings reality into view.

The Teaching in Focus videos aligned with this text allow you inside four real schools to get to know 10 real teachers and 12 real students. The videos may be accessed through MyEducationLab for this course.

Preparing to teach requires reflection on the many roles involved in the profession. Sara Davis Powell

There are other ways to gain insights into the classroom. Finding opportunities to have conversations with teachers is an excellent way to learn more about the realities of the classroom. Volunteering at schools, places of worship, and community organizations will present opportunities both to get to know kids and to observe adults interacting with them. Being a summer camp counselor, tutoring in an after-school program, and coaching in community recreation leagues all provide valuable experiences.

Is Teaching a Profession?

This text repeatedly refers to teaching as the *teaching profession*. Whether a particular job or career qualifies as a **profession** depends, in large measure, on who is making the determination. We hear references to the plumbing profession, the culinary profession, the cosmetology profession, but there are established guidelines for determining if a career or job is universally considered a profession. These characteristics of a profession will likely not affect common usage of the word, but examining teaching with regard to them helps spotlight aspects of what we do that may need to be strengthened.

CHARACTERISTICS OF A PROFESSION

For decades authors have delineated characteristics of a "full" profession. For equally as long, educators and others have debated whether teaching is indeed a profession. This debate is healthy because as we consider the characteristics of a profession and measure teaching by them, we see what teaching is and is not, what teachers have evolved into, and what teachers may still need to become. A summary of a full profession's characteristics, from both a historical perspective and a modern one, is presented in Figure 1.4. Let's look briefly at these 10 characteristics and think about whether each applies to teaching.

Considering that in the United States children ages 5 through 16 are required to receive a formal education, and that most do this through public schools, a dedicated teaching workforce can collectively deliver this *essential service* (1). Members of this teaching workforce agree that teaching requires *unique knowledge and skills* (2), whether acquired through traditional or alternative paths. On-the-job *training, ongoing study* (2), and development are encouraged, but not necessarily required, although most teachers must renew their teaching

Figure 1.4 Characteristics of a full profession

1. Provides an essential service no other group can provide.
2. Requires unique knowledge and skills acquired through extensive initial and ongoing study/training.
3. Involves intellectual work in the performance of duties.
4. Individual practitioners are committed to service and continual competence.
5. Identified performance standards guide practice.
6. Self-governance in admitting, policing, and excluding members.
7. Allows for a considerable amount of autonomy and decision-making authority.
8. Members accept individual responsibility for actions and decisions.
9. Enjoys prestige, public trust.
10. Granted higher-than-average financial rewards.

Sources: Howsam et al. (1976); Ingersoll (1997); Rowan (1994); Webb, Metha, and Jordan (2007).

certification/license every 5 years or so by completing graduate coursework or participating in other forms of professional development.

Teaching definitely *involves intellectual work* (3). Teachers pass along intellectual concepts and skills, which is the very heart of what teachers do. To enter and remain in a teaching career requires a *commitment to service* (4) and, hopefully, *continual competence* (4) as guided and measured by *performance standards* (5). The word "hopefully" is included because teachers rarely *police their own ranks* (6) to the point of excluding someone who does not live up to accepted teacher standards. If policing occurs, it is generally accomplished by administrators.

When the classroom door closes, teachers have a great deal of *autonomy* (7), sometimes approaching isolation. However, public school teachers must accept any student placed in their classrooms and must teach a set curriculum over which they have little or no control. Even with certain constraints, we are *decision makers* (7), and we must *accept individual responsibility* (8) for the decisions we make.

A great level of *trust* (9) is placed in teachers. After all, for 7 to 10 hours a day families allow teachers to have almost exclusive control over their children. In most communities, teachers enjoy a degree of positional *prestige* (9), but they are rarely *granted higher-than-average financial rewards* (10).

As you can see, not all 10 characteristics of a full profession apply to teaching. We still have few mechanisms for policing our own ranks (6), and the financial rewards of teaching are not higher than average (10). Teachers should continue to work together to perpetuate each of the eight characteristics we exemplify while exploring ways to incorporate the other two. Many associations and organizations are helping teaching to be a profession by allowing teachers through collaborative efforts to set common goals, speak with a collective voice, and build research-based foundations to support what we do and how we do it.

PROFESSIONAL ASSOCIATIONS

National and regional professional associations provide leadership and support for teachers. Some serve the general teacher population; others are specific to a grade span or subject area. Most associations solicit members, hold annual conferences, publish materials, provide information, and advocate for those who teach and those who learn. Participating in professional organizations is a positive step toward growing as a professional.

The **National Education Association (NEA)** and the **American Federation of Teachers (AFT)** are the largest professional education associations in the United States, with a total of more than 5 million members, including teachers, administrators, professors, counselors, and other educators. Both organizations are unions and represent their members in **collective bargaining,** or negotiating with employers and states to gain additional benefits for their members. Large nonunion professional organizations such as ASCD Learn. Teach. Lead., Kappa Delta Pi (KDP), and the Council for Exceptional Children (CEC) serve a wide spectrum of educators. Most national organizations have regional and state affiliate associations. These more local groups provide easily accessible face-to-face opportunities for interaction among members.

An organization that specifically deals with the needs of, and standards for, beginning teachers is the **Interstate New Teacher Assessment and Support Consortium** (INTASC, 1992). The standards endorsed by INTASC address what beginning teachers should know and be able to do. They provide the framework for beginning teacher performance.

Each subject area has a professional organization that provides guidelines for what to teach, sponsors annual conferences, publishes relevant books and journals, represents subject areas in educational and political arenas, and both encourages and disseminates research on teaching and learning. Table 1.2 lists some of the professional associations available to teachers to assist with their professionalism. Visiting their Web sites will give you valuable insight into just how important these, and other professional organizations, are and can be.

TABLE 1.2 Professional Organizations

Teacher Unions

AFT	American Federation of Teachers	www.aft.org
NEA	National Education Association	www.nea.org

Subject-Area Organizations

AAHPERD	American Alliance for Health, Physical Education, Recreation and Dance	www.aahperd.org
ACTFL	American Council on the Teaching of Foreign Languages	www.actfl.org
IRA	International Reading Association	www.reading.org
MTNA	Music Teachers National Association	www.mtna.org
NAEA	National Art Education Association	www.naea-reston.org
NATIE	National Association for Trade and Industrial Education	www.skillsusa.org/NATIE/
NBEA	National Business Education Association	www.nbea.org
NCSS	National Council for the Social Studies	www.ncss.org
NCTE	National Council of Teachers of English	www.ncte.org
NCTM	National Council of Teachers of Mathematics	www.nctm.org
NSTA	National Science Teachers Association	www.nsta.org/
RIF	Reading Is Fundamental	www.rif.org

Level-Specific Organizations

ACEI	Association for Childhood Education International	www.acei.org
NAEYC	National Association for the Education of Young Children	www.naeyc.org
NMSA	National Middle School Association	www.nmsa.org

Need-Specific Organizations

INTASC	Interstate New Teacher Assessment and Support Consortium	www.intasc.org
CEC	Council for Exceptional Children	www.cec.sped.org
NAGC	National Association for Gifted Children	www.nagc.org
SCA	Speech Communication Association	www.isca-speech.org
TESOL	Teachers of English to Speakers of Other Languages	www.tesol.org

General Associations

ASCD	ASCD Learn. Teach. Lead.	www.ascd.org
KDP	Kappa Delta Pi	www.kdp.org
PDK	Phi Delta Kappa	www.pdkintl.org

Teachers and the Teaching Profession

What Is Teacher Professionalism?

Professionalism is a way of being. It involves attitudes and actions that convey respect, uphold high standards, and demonstrate commitment to those served. Fulfilling responsibilities and making the most of growth opportunities are core aspects of teacher professionalism. Patricia Phelps, former academic editor of the *Kappa Delta Pi Record* (a publication of KDP), presents a philosophical framework within which characteristics of teacher professionalism may be placed. Phelps (2003) states that teachers achieve greater levels of professionalism when they are willing to do what it takes, to do what must be done. In other words, professionalism involves hard work. This hard work requires commitment in three broad areas.

COMMITMENT TO MAKE STUDENTS OUR FIRST PRIORITY

Student welfare and learning must be paramount. Ask yourself, as a Masai might, "And how are the children? Are they all well?" Putting students first requires that we become advocates for their welfare.

ADVOCATING FOR STUDENTS. To be an **advocate for students** is to support and defend them, always putting their needs first. How do we become advocates for our students? Here are some components of advocacy to consider.

- Understand that advocacy takes multiple forms with individuals, groups, or causes, in both large endeavors and small actions.
- In all conversations, with educators and noneducators alike, keep the focus on what's best for students.
- Take an informed stance on issues that affect children. Actively promote that stance to have widespread impact.
- Support families in every way possible.

Advocacy guides our efforts and decisions directly toward our goal—improving students' learning, which, ultimately, improves students' lives.

MAKING WISE DECISIONS. As teachers we continually make decisions. Some of the decisions are made on autopilot, especially those that have to do with routines in the classroom. The quality of other decisions often rests on common sense and maturity, characteristics that are enhanced by preparation and experience. It's important to remember that our decisions have consequences and require thoughtful consideration to make sure we are advocating for our students and maintaining a classroom climate that is conducive to learning.

DETERMINING CLASSROOM CLIMATE. Our classrooms can be respectful environments that promote learning, or not. The sobering words of Haim Ginott (1993), a respected teacher and psychologist, should occupy a prominent position in both your classroom and your consciousness.

> I've come to a frightening conclusion. I am the decisive element in the classroom. It's my personal approach that creates the climate. It's my daily mood that makes the weather. As a teacher, I possess a tremendous power to make a child's life miserable or joyous. I can be a tool of torture or an instrument of inspiration. I can humiliate or humor, hurt or heal. In all situations, it is my response that decides whether a crisis will be escalated or de-escalated, a child humanized or de-humanized.

Points of Reflection 1.2

Does the commitment to put students first sound like something you are willing to do? Explain the reason(s) for your answer.

Advocating for students is important at all grade levels. Renee, a second grade teacher, and her twin sister, Tara, a high school physics teacher, both advocate for their students in developmentally appropriate ways.
Sara Davis Powell

COMMITMENT TO QUALITY

Quality should characterize our knowledge of content and our relationships and interactions with students, colleagues, administrators and families. Phelps (2003) tells us that "modeling quality is the most significant way to motivate others to put forth the same effort" (p. 10). Modeling quality requires that we have positive and productive values leading to teaching that facilitates learning.

FACILITATING LEARNING. Making the teaching and learning connection is the primary role of a teacher. Learning is why students are in school, and teaching is how we guide and facilitate learning. Our effectiveness as teachers should be measured by how much and how thoroughly students learn.

We can categorize the responsibilities involved in facilitating learning in a number of valid ways. Perhaps none is more important than evaluating each of our actions in terms of its contribution to academic rigor and developmental appropriateness. **Academic rigor** refers both to teaching meaningful content and to having high expectations for student learning. **Developmental appropriateness** means that our teaching addresses students' physical, cognitive, social, emotional, and character development. Academic rigor without developmental appropriateness will result in frustration for teachers and foster discouragement and defeatism in students. Developmental appropriateness without academic rigor will accomplish little in terms of student learning. Neither concept is mutually exclusive. In fact, they shouldn't be exclusive at all but rather should interact in supportive ways and balance one another as they guide our decision making.

Points of Reflection 1.3

Are these dispositions part of your personal beliefs? What other dispositions do you think contribute to being a teacher who promotes academic rigor and development appropriateness?

DEVELOPING DISPOSITIONS. **Dispositions** are composed of our attitudes, values, and beliefs. They powerfully influence our teaching approaches and actions. Dispositions that are favorable to effective teaching include, among many others:

- I believe all students can learn.
- I value student diversity.
- I respect individual students and their families.
- I am enthusiastic about the subjects I teach.
- I value other teachers as colleagues and partners in teaching and learning.
- I believe families are important in making the teaching and learning connection.

COMMITMENT TO CONTINUAL GROWTH

Teacher effectiveness is enhanced when a lifelong learning orientation is in place. A commitment to continual growth provides a powerful model for students.

BECOMING A REFLECTIVE PRACTITIONER. We grow when we reflect on our teaching practices. As discussed earlier in this chapter, reflection with regard to teaching is thinking about what we do, how we do it, and the consequences of our actions or inactions, all with the goal of being better teachers. To be **reflective practitioners** means that we deliberately think about our practice, that is, what we do as teachers. We do this with the purpose of analysis and improvement. Sounds pretty automatic and unavoidable, doesn't it? But it's not. A teacher can repeatedly go through the motions of planning, teaching, and assessing throughout a career yet seldom engage in reflection that results in improved practice.

John Dewey (1933), one of the great American educators, described reflection using words such as *active, persistent,* and *careful.* So how do we become reflective practitioners who actively, persistently, and carefully think about how we teach? Here are some concepts to consider:

- Reflective practice requires conscious effort.
- Self-knowledge is vital and can be aided by thoughtfully completing the *Points of Reflection* throughout this text.

- Reading about and researching aspects of teaching will ground our practice and provide subject matter on which to reflect.
- Talking with other educators will both inform and strengthen what we do and how we do it.
- Being deliberate—doing what we do for a reason—will result in better decisions based on reflection.

21ST-CENTURY KNOWLEDGE AND SKILLS. Teachers committed to continual growth are determined to increase their knowledge and skills to keep up with current research and thought concerning teaching practices. During the first decade of the 21st century some major forces both inside of, and external to, the education community recognized and espoused the need for knowledge and skills that reflect the realities of the 21st-century world. Perhaps the most influential source of information about teacher and learner characteristics for the new century is the **Partnership for 21st Century Skills (P21)**.

In 2009 there were 14 states officially and voluntarily aligned with the Partnership for 21st Century Skills: Arizona, Illinois, Iowa, Kansas, Louisiana, Maine, Massachusetts, Nevada, New Jersey, North Carolina, Ohio, South Dakota, Wisconsin, and West Virginia. On the P21 Web site we find the organization's self-description. "The Partnership for 21st Century Skills has emerged as the leading advocacy organization focused on infusing 21st century skills into education. Bringing together the business community, education leaders, and policy-makers, we have defined a powerful vision for 21st century education to ensure every child's success as citizens and workers in the 21st century" (Partnership for 21st Century Skills, 2009).

The Partnership for 21st Century Skills outlines characteristics of teachers that help them teach students in ways that lead to success, including

- Critical thinker
- Problem solver
- Innovator
- Effective communicator
- Effective collaborator
- Self-directed learner
- Information and media literate
- Globally aware
- Civically engaged
- Health conscious
- Financially and economically literate

These are characteristics for teachers to spend their careers developing and improving. A commitment to continual growth requires it.

Points of Reflection 1.4

Do you have a desire to continually grow professionally and personally? If so, how do you know? If you are hesitant to answer this question, what areas of your own motivation do you think you need to consider?

DELAWARE VISION 2015

Teacher professionalism is required for any large-scale education initiative to succeed. Vision 2015 is Delaware's plan to transform its public education system, focusing on student achievement, fairness, and accountability. To accomplish this transformation, teachers who exemplify Phelps's three areas of professional commitment—putting students first, quality, continual growth—are absolutely necessary.

Delaware's stated goal is to create the best schools for every student, no exceptions and no excuses. In other words, Vision 2015 calls for professional educators to respect the uniqueness of each student and provide the schools necessary for all students to succeed. Delaware proposes to make the changes necessary closest to the students—in the schools and in the classrooms—and sets high expectations for every child and every educator. The initiative revolves around six major areas of reform: setting high sights, investing in early childhood education, developing and supporting great teachers, empowering principals to be great school leaders, encouraging innovation and requiring accountability, and establishing a simple and fair funding system (Delaware Department of Education, 2006).

This chapter's *Letter to the Editor* covers a lot of ground, with topics related to Delaware's Vision 2015. The writer suggests that the lofty goals of Vision 2015 will not be accomplished without eliminating ineffective teachers.

Letter to the Editor

This letter appeared in the Wilmington, Delaware, newspaper, the *Wilmington News Journal.*

NOVEMBER 12, 2009 SAME TEACHERS, ADMINISTRATORS WILL NOT GET REFORM JOB DONE

I applaud Marvin "Skip" Schoenhals and his team at Vision 2015 for trying to turn around our public school system here in Delaware and for giving us a report on the current status of education in Delaware.

Unfortunately, his report of some progress contained no quantitative assessments. The only numbers were those related to possible additional federal funding— throwing more money at the problem. Again, unfortunately, the Vision 2015 team is trying to produce a winning team with the same old players (teachers and administrators). Some of these players may well respond favorably to their new coaches.

However, many will probably not, and, at best, will do so grudgingly as new strategies and plays are being developed and attempted to be implemented—these teachers simply carry too much old baggage. In turn-around situations, even the best of coaches will need substantially new players. Players with more talent should be recruited; old players should be given five years to demonstrate new talent or find themselves alternate occupations—they won't make the cut.

Existing players should be given five years to obtain degrees in the subject matter they are teaching—subject matter degrees, not degrees in education or pseudo-subject matter degrees such as physics for non-scientists. All new teachers should be required to have such substantive degrees.

James R. Thomen

Montchanin

Now it's your turn. Write a letter to the editor from the perspective of a future teacher expressing your views concerning the letter writer's concerns. You may comment on any, or all, of the writer's expressed opinions.

The following information and questions may help you frame your thinking but should not limit nor determine what you write.

1. The writer expresses apparent disgust at what he calls "throwing more money at the problem." As a future teacher, how would you answer this common criticism?

2. Does the sports metaphor work in this case? Are there problems with the analogy you want to point out?

3. Is characterizing experienced teachers as "carrying too much baggage" a generalization that's fair? Do you think it likely applies to some teachers?

4. What do you think about the 5-year time frame to demonstrate new talent?

5. Should all teachers, regardless of the grade level they teach, be required to have subject-area degrees as opposed to maybe a degree in elementary education or early childhood education? What about middle and high school teachers?

6. How does what you know about what's considered a full profession relate to the writer's view of getting rid of teachers who are judged to be ineffective?

Write your letter in understandable terminology, remembering that readers of newspaper letters to the editor are citizens who may have limited knowledge of school practices and policies.

Figure 1.5 is a scoring guide that may be used to assess your letter to the editor. It is the same guide that the Educational Testing Service uses to assess the writing portion of the Praxis II *Principles of Learning and Teaching* exam many states require for either initial teacher licensure/certification or at the completion of the first year of teaching. You will refer to Figure 1.5 in subsequent chapters as you write additional letters to the editor.

Figure 1.5 General scoring guide for *Letter to the Editor* features

A response that receives a score of 3:

- Demonstrates a thorough understanding of the aspects of the case that are relevant to the question
- Responds appropriately to all parts of the question
- If an explanation is required, provides a strong explanation that is well supported by relevant evidence
- Demonstrates a strong knowledge of pedagogical concepts, theories, facts, procedures, or methodologies relevant to the question

A response that receives a score of 2:

- Demonstrates a basic understanding of the aspects of the case that are relevant to the question
- Responds appropriately to one portion of the question
- If an explanation is required, provides a weak explanation that is supported by relevant evidence
- Demonstrates some knowledge of pedagogical concepts, theories, facts, procedures, or methodologies relevant to the question

A response that receives a score of 1:

- Demonstrates misunderstanding of the aspects of the case that are relevant to the question
- Fails to respond appropriately to the question
- Is not supported by relevant evidence
- Demonstrates little knowledge of pedagogical concepts, theories, facts, procedures, or methodologies relevant to the question

No credit is given for blank or off-topic responses.

Deirdre Huger-McGrew expresses her views about continual professional growth in the *Teaching in Focus*.

This text will continue to refer to a career in teaching as the *teaching profession* and to teachers as *professionals.* Commitment to students, quality, and growth—everything a professional teacher does can be placed within this framework. Remember these three commitments as we examine what it means to be an effective teacher.

Teaching in Focus

Sara Davis Powell

Deirdre Huger-McGrew, language arts/social studies, Cario Middle School, South Carolina. *In her own words. . . .*

Throughout my 12 years as a teacher, I've taken many courses beyond my initial teacher training. I have been involved in teaching-related projects, most by choice and others as directed by my principal to achieve school and district goals. I have taken my professional development personally because I feel it is a part of my responsibility to nurture my growth as a teacher. It is my identity. It is who I am as a teacher. Seeking to enhance my skills makes a difference in my classroom. I take delight in embracing changing views and trying strategies that have the potential to improve my teaching.

What makes athletes, doctors, or lawyers the best in their fields? I believe it is their desire and ability to seek ways to improve what they do as professionals. This gives them an edge. Teachers should want the same. I want to continually accomplish growth-enhancing professional goals.

What Are the Characteristics of Effective Teachers?

"From the moment students enter a school, the most important factor in their success is not the color of the skin or the income of their parents, it's the person standing at the front of the classroom." This powerful statement was made in a speech to the Hispanic Chamber of Commerce in 2009 by President Barack Obama. Sobering, isn't it? The president of the United States is stating what recent research corroborates. Teachers make the most difference when it comes to student learning. Our effectiveness, or lack of it, matters.

The search for a neatly packaged description of an effective teacher dates back for centuries, even millennia. The best we can come up with are lists of characteristics based on observation and available data, along with narrative anecdotal descriptions. There's a lot to be learned from considering a number of perspectives.

Standards for teachers are expectations for what they should know and be able to do. All teacher education standards address teacher effectiveness. School-level organizations such as the National Middle School Association (NMSA) and the Association for Childhood Education International (ACEI) prescribe standards for new teachers. The 10 standards of the Interstate New Teacher Assessment and Support Consortium (INTASC) describe what effective teachers should know and be able to do regardless of the level they teach (Figure 1.6).

The **No Child Left Behind Act of 2001 (NCLB),** the 2001 to 2010 reauthorization of the Elementary and Secondary Education Act, was the most sweeping school legislation in decades. One of the major aspects of NCLB was the requirement that teachers be **highly qualified,** meaning that they have a standard of content knowledge and specialized

Figure 1.6 INTASC standards

1. The teacher understands the central concepts, tools of inquiry, and structures of the discipline(s) he or she teaches and can create learning experiences that make these aspects of subject matter meaningful for students.
2. The teacher understands how children learn and develop and can provide learning opportunities that support their intellectual, social, and personal development.
3. The teacher understands how students differ in their approaches to learning and creates instructional opportunities that are adapted to diverse learners.
4. The teacher understands and uses a variety of instructional strategies to encourage students' development of critical thinking, problem solving, and performance skills.
5. The teacher uses an understanding of individual and group motivation and behavior to create a learning environment that encourages positive social interaction, active engagement in learning, and self-motivation.
6. The teacher uses knowledge of effective verbal, nonverbal, and media communication techniques to foster active inquiry, collaboration, and supportive interaction in the classroom.
7. The teacher plans instruction based upon knowledge of subject matter, students, the community, and curriculum goals.
8. The teacher understands and uses formal and informal assessment strategies to evaluate and ensure the continuous intellectual and social development of the learner.
9. The teacher is a reflective practitioner who continually evaluates the effects of his/her choices and actions on others (students, parents, and other professionals in the learning community) and who actively seeks out opportunities to grow professionally.
10. The teacher fosters relationships with school colleagues, parents, and agencies in the larger community to support students' learning and well-being.

Source: The Interstate New Teacher Assessment and Support Consortium (INTASC) standards were developed by the Council of Chief State School Officers and member states. Copies may be downloaded from the Council's Web site at www.ccsso.org. Council of Chief State School Officers. (1992). *Model standards for beginning teacher licensing, assessment, and development: A resource for state dialogue.* Washington, DC: Author.

preparation for their chosen level. The federal government set guidelines for the quality of teachers in public schools, but each state determines its own policy for what teachers must do to be considered highly qualified. Experienced teachers have options in terms of how to meet the highly qualified stipulations.

WHAT PARENTS SAY ABOUT TEACHER EFFECTIVENESS

In the 41st annual *Phi Delta Kappan/Gallup Poll of the Public's Attitudes Toward the Public Schools*, parents were asked to rank nine teacher traits. From most important to least, the parents polled chose the following:

1. Dedication to, and enthusiasm for, the teaching profession
2. Caring about students
3. Intelligence
4. Ability to communicate, to understand, to relate
5. High moral character
6. Friendliness, good personality, sense of humor
7. Ability to discipline, to be firm and fair
8. Patience
9. Ability to inspire, motivate students (Bushaw & McNee, 2009)

A surprising and welcome statistic to come from the 2009 poll is that 7 of 10 parents report that they would like their children to become public school teachers. This whopping 70% is the highest percentage to respond favorably concerning their own children becoming teachers in over 30 years.

WHAT TEACH FOR AMERICA HAS DISCOVERED ABOUT EFFECTIVE TEACHERS

While attempting to determine why some teachers are significantly more effective than others in facilitating student learning, Teach for America has systematically observed and analyzed the results achieved by TFA teachers. They found some intriguing characteristics linked to teachers who facilitate student learning beyond what might be predicted for the mostly poor, mostly minority, student population taught by TFA teachers. Effective teachers tend to . . .

1. set high, long-term goals for their students
2. perpetually look for ways to improve their effectiveness
3. constantly reevaluate what they are doing
4. recruit students and their families into the teaching and learning process
5. maintain focus, making sure everything they do contributes to student learning
6. plan exhaustively and purposefully
7. refuse to surrender to poverty, bureaucracy, and budgetary shortfalls
8. establish efficient classroom routines
9. possess a relentless mind-set of perseverance
10. reflect on their performance and adapt accordingly
11. show signs of contentment with their lives
12. have a history of personal goal achievement
13. know the content they teach (Ripley, 2010)

Although not necessarily a trait appropriate for this list, Teach for America tells us that a predictor of a TFA teacher's classroom success is grade point average (GPA) in the last 2 years

Effective teachers purposefully and collaboratively plan for instruction.
Sara Davis Powell

of college, rather than overall GPA. In other words, a GPA that starts out mediocre and then improves appears to be associated with greater teacher effectiveness than a 4.0 all 4 years. Another interesting point is that the more college extracurricular accomplishments, the better the teacher. These are areas you can work on *right now* that will help shape the teacher you will become. Encouraging, isn't it?

WHAT STUDENTS SAY ABOUT TEACHER EFFECTIVENESS

Emphasis has shifted recently from the teacher to the pupil as the focal point for defining teacher effectiveness. Very simply stated, the "ultimate proof of teacher effectiveness is student results" (Stronge, 2002, p. 65). But what results? What seems like a simple statement has complicated nuances because accurately assessing student learning is itself complex. Do we judge the effectiveness of a teacher solely by the standardized test scores of students? That would be easy if standardized test scores told the whole story.

In a survey of about 400 urban, low-income middle and high school students conducted by Corbett and Wilson (2002), all of them identified their teachers as the main factor in determining how much they learned. They listed a variety of characteristics of the diverse teachers most effective in helping them learn, all of which fit into the following six categories. Effective teachers . . .

1. push students to learn
2. maintain order
3. are willing to help
4. explain until everyone understands
5. vary classroom activities
6. try to understand students (pp. 19–20)

EFFECTIVE TEACHERS MAKE A DIFFERENCE

"Substantial research evidence suggests that well-prepared, capable teachers have the largest impact on student learning" (Darling-Hammond, 2003, p. 7). This is not to say that other factors we discuss throughout this book do not significantly influence student learning. However, Linda Darling-Hammond, a noted expert on teacher quality, and others contend that an effective teacher can overcome many of the circumstances in students' lives and positively impact student learning. When the outside influences on student learning result in an achievement gap, Kati Haycock (2003), director of the Education Trust, tells us, "If we insist on quality teachers for every student, we can dramatically improve the achievement of poor and minority students and substantially narrow the achievement gap" (p. 11). Reiterating the need for effective teachers, James Stronge (2002), another respected educator, writes, "Teachers have a powerful, long-lasting influence on their students. They directly affect how students learn, what they learn, how much they learn, and the ways they interact with one another, and the world around them" (p. vii).

Teachers can be effective using very different approaches. You can probably name two teachers in your own experience who were effective but who had different traits. Stronge (2002) tells us "teaching effectiveness draws on a multitude of skills and attributes in different combinations and in different contexts to produce the results that define effectiveness" (p. 64).

Points of Reflection 1.5

Think about the teachers you have had. What made some effective and others relatively ineffective?

An important factor to understand when it comes to the characteristics of effective teachers and teaching is that much of what makes teachers effective comes through experience in the classroom. This is not to say that new teachers can't be effective. Of course they can! But think about this. Teaching is a profession that expects a brand-new teacher to do the same job as an experienced veteran (Johnson & Kardos, 2005). Don't count on someone saying, "Hey, it's okay if only half your kids learn about half of what you attempt to teach. After all, you're new." David Berliner (2000), a noted leader in teacher education, estimates that it takes about 5 years to "get smart about teaching" (p. 360). Some of the characteristics of effectiveness take time to develop: It takes time to be able to make decisions with automaticity and to draw on experience to supplement formal training.

Throughout this text you are urged to ask repeatedly, as the Masai do, "And how are the children? Are they all well?" However, when you are a novice teacher, your primary question may often be "How am I doing?" In *Educating Esme: Diary of a Teacher's First Year,* Esme Codell (1999) reveals that her mentor told her that with experience the question "How am I doing?" increasingly becomes "How are the children doing?"

Effective teachers, regardless of whom or what they teach, share many common characteristics. Teacher professionalism is a thread that binds them all. But although there are many similarities, the day-to-day responsibilities may vary in many ways. Teachers of students with special needs; teachers who specialize in art, music, or physical education; teachers who teach all or most subjects to one group of students; and teachers who teach the same content area each day to several groups of students—all have specific preparation requirements and position responsibilities.

CONCLUDING THOUGHTS

Learning to be a teacher . . . teaching so others learn . . . learning to be a better teacher—this life-affirming cycle can be yours. Think of the cycle as a wheel that gathers momentum and takes you on a profound journey. You have begun to grow toward the profession. As a teacher you'll grow within the profession. Read what becoming a teacher meant to one young man, Jamie Sawatsky, a seventh grade history teacher in Chantilly, Virginia.

> I noticed the change in myself the first time I walked into my classroom. I was no longer Jamie. That was the name of the young man who had delivered pizzas or worked at the office. My newfound teaching life had metamorphosed me into "Mr. Sawatsky." My previous work experiences had taught me a variety of skills, but accepting the title of teacher has cast me into a world where I am charged with the awesome responsibility of sculpting young minds and preparing students for positive participation in their community. When asked why they entered the profession, many teachers respond, "I wanted a chance to make a positive change in the world." In my case, perhaps selfishly, I wanted to be in a profession that would make a positive change in me. With my first year of teaching about to conclude, I can say that I am happy to be a teacher and happy to be "Mr. Sawatsky." (Tell, 2001, p. 18)

After reading the *Chapter in Review,* interact with Traci Peters in this chapter's *Developing Professional Competence.*

Chapter in Review

Who teaches in the United States and why?

- Teaching is the largest profession in the United States.
- Most teachers are white women, leading to a need for more men and people of color in teaching.
- Almost 90% of teachers believe teaching requires a "true sense of calling."

- The most common reasons for choosing to teach include the desire to work with young people, the value of education to society, interest in a subject, the influence of a teacher or of family, the teaching schedule, job security, and the opportunity for a lifetime of self-growth.
- Teacher satisfaction with the profession has grown over the last 25 years.

Teachers and the Teaching Profession

How do we prepare to teach?

- States issue a certificate or license to teach in public schools based on their own criteria.
- The traditional path to becoming a teacher is through a university-based teacher preparation program.
- Alternative paths to teacher preparation provide timely, but somewhat controversial, routes to teacher certification.
- There are many ways to get to know teachers, students, and schools, including field experiences through teacher preparation programs, volunteer opportunities, watching movies about teachers, and participating online through this and other texts.

Is teaching a profession?

- A profession is an occupation that includes extensive training before entering, a code of ethics, and service as the primary product.
- Teaching meets most of the criteria generally agreed upon for a full profession.
- Numerous professional organizations support teachers and teaching.

- Teachers can and should make contributions to the knowledge base of the teaching profession.

What is teacher professionalism?

- Teacher professionalism involves a commitment to make students the first priority.
- Teacher professionalism involves a commitment to quality in both our work and our relationships.
- Teacher professionalism involves a commitment to continual growth.

What are the characteristics of effective teachers?

- Effective teachers may have very different styles of teaching.
- The most important factor in determining teacher effectiveness is the extent of student learning.
- There are established standards for teacher effectiveness through organizations like the Interstate New Teacher Assessment and Support Consortium and the National Board of Professional Teaching Standards.
- Both individuals and organizations have opinions about what makes a teacher effective. There is much to learn from the differing viewpoints.

Developing Professional Competence

Visit the Developing Professional Competence section on Chapter 1 of the MyEducationLab for this text to answer the following questions and begin your preparation for licensure exams.

You met Traci Peters in *Meet the Focus Teachers and Students* and again in the beginning of this chapter in the *Teaching in Focus* section. She is the math teacher on her four-person interdisciplinary team at Cario Middle School. In March one of her teammates, Melanie Richardson, announced that her husband was being sent to Iraq and that without his help with their five children, she was going to have to move to another state where her parents live. Melanie teaches English-language arts and has been on Traci's team, the Dolphins, for 3 years. This is a big blow to Traci and her two other teammates. Melanie will leave Cario in mid-April. The Dolphin team teachers are very easy to work with and have enjoyed a collegial relationship with Melanie.

Carol Bartlett, principal of Cario, understands the importance of finding the right person to fill the position, but she is told that a teacher from another school will be placed in Melanie's classroom for the remainder of the school year. Ms. Bartlett knows the teacher the district personnel office plans to place on the Dolphin team. Linda Merchant's reputation is that of a veteran teacher who does not collaborate, sits behind her desk during class, and consistently finds ways to undermine administrators. Ms. Bartlett suspects her position was purposefully eliminated at the other school and the district just needs to find a place for her. Ms. Bartlett is certain the Dolphin teachers will not be pleased with the district's choice.

1. Which of the following attributes of a full profession does this scenario directly violate?
   a. A full profession enjoys prestige and public trust.
   b. A full profession admits, polices, and excludes members.
   c. A full profession provides an essential service no other group can provide.
   d. A full profession involves intellectual work in the performance of duties.

2. Which of the following statements applies least to this situation?
   a. The three teachers on the Dolphin team will likely have to put out extra effort to keep their students from being affected by what they anticipate will be substandard teacher performance.
   b. The three teachers are likely most concerned about INTASC Standard 10: "The teacher fosters relationships with school colleagues, parents, and agencies in the larger community to support students' learning and well-being."
   c. The three teachers will continue to instill academic rigor while making their classrooms developmentally appropriate.
   d. Ms. Merchant has a master's degree in education, so the rumors about her are very likely exaggerated.

3. As they have always done, the Dolphin teachers take individual responsibility for the success of their team of students. Which of the following would not be evidence of this?
   a. They use opportunities to say positive things about their students in the community.
   b. They don't get involved in decisions that affect their students because they believe that designated experts know best.
   c. They invite families to come to school to discuss areas of concern for their children.

d. They consistently talk about and act on what they believe to be best for their students.

Now it's time for you to respond to two short essay items involving the scenario. In your responses, be sure to address all the dilemmas and questions posed in each item. Each response should be between one half and one double-spaced page.

4. Traci and her teammates understand that Ms. Merchant will be a temporary member of their team, or at least that's their hope. They have been assured by the school district that they will be able to interview candidates for the English-language arts position and that a new teacher can be in place by August. This helps them get through the remainder of the school year. As they look to the future, what are three qualities you would recommend they look for as they, along with Ms. Bartlett, choose a new teacher for their team?

5. U.S. Secretary of Education Arne Duncan (2009) believes that teacher evaluation is broken. The seventh grade team at Cario is about to experience some of the consequences of a system that not only fails to discriminate between effective and ineffective teachers but also allows ineffective teachers to remain in the classroom. How would meaningful formative assessment help fix the system? What would you recommend be done with the results of annual summative evaluation?

Where DO I Stand NOW?

In the beginning of this chapter you completed an inventory that helped you explore your reasons for choosing teaching as your career. Now that you have read the chapter, completed exercises related to the content, engaged in class discussions, and so on, answer the following questions in your course notebook.

1. If you rated **desire to work with young people** as one of your top reasons for choosing to teach, is it still among your top reasons? If so, why? If not, why not? If **desire to work with young people** was not among your top reasons, has it become more important to you after giving your reasons more consideration? If so, why? If not, why not?

2. If you rated **value of education to society** as one of your top reasons for choosing to teach, is it still among your top reasons? If so, why? If not, why not? If **value of education to society** was not among your top reasons, has it become more important to you after giving your reasons more consideration? If so, why? If not, why not?

3. If you rated **interest in subject matter** as one of your top reasons for choosing to teach, is it still among your top reasons? If so, why? If not, why not? If **interest in subject matter** was not among your top reasons, has it become more important to you after giving your reasons more consideration? If so, why? If not, why not?

Teachers and the Teaching Profession

4. If you rated **influence of teachers** as one of your top reasons for choosing to teach, is it still among your top reasons? If so, why? If not, why not? If **influence of teachers** was not among your top reasons, has it become more important to you after giving your reasons more consideration? If so, why? If not, why not?

5. If you rated the **schedule/vacations of teachers** as one of your top reasons for choosing to teach, is it still among your top reasons? If so, why? If not, why not? If the **schedule/vacations of teachers** was not among your top reasons, has it become more important to you after giving your reasons more consideration? If so, why? If not, why not?

6. If you rated **influence of family** as one of your top reasons for choosing to teach, is it still among your top reasons? If so, why? If not, why not? If **influence of family** was not among your top reasons, has it become more important to you after giving your reasons more consideration? If so, why? If not, why not?

7. If you rated **job security** as one of your top reasons for choosing to teach, is it still among your top reasons? If so, why? If not, why not? If **job security** was not among your top reasons, has it become more important to you after giving your reasons more consideration? If so, why? If not, why not?

8. If you rated **opportunity for a lifetime of self-growth** as one of your top reasons for choosing to teach, is it still among your top reasons? If so, why? If not, why not? If **opportunity for a lifetime of self-growth** was not among your top reasons, has it become more important to you after giving your reasons more consideration? If so, why? If not, why not?

MyEducationLab

The MyEducationLab for this course can help you solidify your comprehension of Chapter 1 concepts.

- Explore the classrooms of the teachers and students you've met in this chapter in the Teaching in Focus section.

- Prepare for licensure exams as you deepen your understanding of chapter concepts in the Developing Professional Competence section.

- Gauge and further develop your understanding of chapter concepts by taking the quizzes and examining the enrichment materials on the Chapter 1 Study Plan.

- Visit Topic 1, The Teaching Profession, to watch ABC videos, explore Assignments and Activities, and practice essential teaching skills with the Building Teaching Skills and Dispositions unit.

References

American Federation of Teachers. (2008). Survey and analysis of teacher salary trends (2006–2007). Retrieved February 1, 2010, from http://archive.aft.org/salary/

Berliner, D. C. (2000). A personal response to those who bash teacher education. *Journal of Teacher Education, 51*(5), 358–371.

Bushaw, W. J., & McNee, J. A. (2009). The 41st annual Phi Delta Kappa/Gallup poll of the public's attitudes toward the public schools. *Phi Delta Kappan, 91*(1), 8–23.

Codell, E. R. (1999). *Educating Esme: Diary of a teacher's first year.* Chapel Hill, NC: Algonquin Books of Chapel Hill.

Corbett, D., & Wilson, B. (2002). What urban students say about good teaching. *Educational Leadership, 60*(1), 18–22.

Council of Chief State School Officers. (1992). *Model standards for beginning teacher licensing, assessment, and development: A resource for state dialogue.* Washington, DC: Author.

Darling-Hammond, L. (2003). Keeping good teachers: Why it matters, what leaders can do. *Educational Leadership, 60*(8), 7–13.

Delaware Department of Education. (2006). Vision 2015. Retrieved July 28, 2010, from

http://www.vision2015delaware.org/resources/Vision2015report1-26.pdf

Dewey, J. (1933). *How we think: A restatement of the relation of reflective thinking to the educative process.* Boston: D.C. Heath.

Duncan, A. (2009/2010, Winter). Evaluating the teaching profession. *American Educator, 33*(4), 1–5. Retrieved January 31, 2010, from http://www.aft.org/pdfs/americaneducator/ae_winter09.pdf

Feistritzer, C. E. (2009). Alternative teacher certification: A state-by-state analysis 2009. Retrieved January 24, 2010, from www.teach-now.org/overview.cfm

Fessenden, F., & Barbanel, J. (2005). The rise of the six-figure teacher. *The New York Times.* Retrieved May 20, 2005, from http://www.nytimes.com/2005/05/15/nyregion/15/iteach.html

Ginott, H. G. (1993). *Teacher and child.* New York: Collier Books/Macmillan.

Haycock, K. (2003). Toward a fair distribution of teacher talent. *Educational Leadership, 60*(4), 11–15.

Howsam, R. B., Corrigan, D. C., Denemark, G. W., & Nash, R. J. (1976). *Educating a profession.* Washington, DC: American Association of Colleges of Teacher Education.

Ingersoll, R. (1997). *The status of teaching as a profession: 1990–1991.* Washington, DC: U.S. Department of Education.

Johnson, S. M., & Kardos, S. M. (2005). Bridging the generation gap. *Educational Leadership, 62*(8), 8–14.

Metropolitan Life Insurance Company. (2008). METLife survey of the American teacher. Retrieved August 24, 2010, from www.metlife.com/assets/cao/contributions/foundation/american-teacher/MetLife_Teacher_Survey_2009.pdf

National Center for Education Statistics. (2009). Fast facts. Retrieved August 4, 2010, from http://nces.ed.gov/fastfacts/display.asp?id=28

National Council on Teacher Quality. (2009). Evaluation and tenure policies do not consider what should count the most about teacher performance: classroom effectiveness in 2009. State teacher policy yearbook. Retrieved January 31, 2010, from www.nctq.org

National Education Association. (2001). *Attracting and keeping quality teachers.* Washington, DC: Author. Retrieved May 15, 2005, from http://nea.org/teachershortage.index

National Education Association. (2003). *Status of the American public school teacher 2000-2001.*

Washington, DC: Author. Retrieved May 15, 2005, from http://www.nea.org/edstats/images/status.pdf

Nieto, S. (2009). From surviving to thriving. *Educational Leadership, 66*(5), 8-13.

Partnership for 21st Century Skills. (2009). About us. Retrieved November 17, 2009, from http://www.21stcenturyskills.org/index.php?option=com_content&task=view&id=42&Itemid=69

Phelps, P. H. (2003). Teacher professionalism. *Kappa Delta Pi Record, 40*(1), 10-11.

Public Agenda. (2003). Attitudes about teaching. New York: Author.

Public Education Network. (2003). *The voice of the new teacher.* Washington, DC: Author.

Ripley, A. (2010, January/February). What makes a great teacher? *The Atlantic.* Retrieved January 29, 2010, from http://www.theatlantic.com/doc/201001/good-teaching

Rowan, B. (1994). Comparing teachers' work with work in other occupations: Notes on the professional status of teaching. *Educational Researcher, 23*(6), 4-17, 21.

Stronge, J. H. (2002). *Qualities of effective teachers.* Alexandria, VA: Association for Supervision and Curriculum Development.

Teach for America. (2010). *Growth plan.* Retrieved January 24, 2010, from http://www.teachforamerica.org/about/our_growth_plan.htm

Tell, C. (2001). Who's in our classrooms: Teachers speak for themselves. *Educational Leadership, 58*(8), 18-23.

Webb, L., Metha, A., & Jordan, K. F. (2007). *Foundations of American education* (5th ed.). Upper Saddle River, NJ: Merrill/Prentice Hall.

Teachers and the Teaching Profession

Schools

Sara Davis Powell

In this chapter we explore schools in the United States by addressing these focus questions:

✦ What are the purposes of public schools in the United States?

✦ What is the culture of a school?

✦ How do school venues differ?

✦ What is school like at different levels?

✦ What are the three principal settings of U.S. schools?

✦ What is an effective school?

Schools are centers of our communities, foundations of our citizenry, targets of political and ethical debate, mirrors and shapers of our society, and keepers of the hopes and dreams of parents and children. Without exception the greeting "And how are the children?" should be on the lips and in the hearts of every adult in every U.S. school.

Before we discuss schools in the United States, explore your own preferences regarding your future career in this chapter's *Where Do I Stand?*

Shutterstock

From Chapter 2 of *Your Introduction to Education: Explorations in Teaching*, 2/e. Sara Davis Powell.

Where DO I Stand ?

Responding to these items provides generalizations of where your interests lie in terms of who you want to teach, in what kind of school, and the setting you may prefer. After reading an item, indicate your level of agreement by choosing a number and placing it in the blank before the statement. Following the inventory are directions for how to organize your responses and what they may indicate in terms of where you stand.

4   I strongly agree
3   I agree
2   I don't have an opinion
1   I disagree
0   I strongly disagree

_____ **1.** Teaching routines to young children appeals to me.

_____ **2.** I enjoy living out in the country, away from cities.

_____ **3.** I believe that public schools best serve our country's students.

_____ **4.** Teaching children to comprehend topics through reading is an exciting process to me.

_____ **5.** Having a shopping mall nearby is important to me.

_____ **6.** Teaching middle school appeals to me.

_____ **7.** I would be most comfortable teaching in a private school.

_____ **8.** I am drawn to kids who have fewer advantages than others.

_____ **9.** I want to teach students whose parents have specifically chosen their school.

_____ **10.** Teaching basic math concepts in understandable ways would be fun.

_____ **11.** Social and civic opportunities in the suburbs attract me.

_____ **12.** I want to spend my days with students who are quickly becoming young adults.

_____ **13.** I want to teach one or two specific subjects.

_____ **14.** I have a positive view of public schools.

_____ **15.** Children in grades 3 to 5 are the ones with whom I would most like to work.

_____ **16.** Being somewhat isolated geographically is all right with me.

_____ **17.** Teaching different levels, or branches, of one subject, appeals to me.

_____ **18.** I look forward to the challenges presented by inner-city students.

_____ **19.** Neighborhoods with single-family homes and schools close by compose what I envision as my teaching situation.

_____ **20.** Private schools provide valuable options to students.

_____ **21.** Being part of a team of teachers who share a specific group of students sounds inviting.

_____ **22.** Teaching in a rural setting appeals to me.

_____ **23.** I want to teach in a school that all children have the opportunity to attend.

_____ **24.** I enjoy being with 5-year-olds.

_____ **25.** I want to spend my days with students with whom I can hold an adult-like conversation.

_____ **26.** I function best when I have ready access to stores and services.

_____ **27.** Teaching in a school that aligns with a particular religious faith will be best for me.

_____ **28.** Children who are ready to explore multiple topics and comprehend much of what they read would be a population I would like to relate to.

_____ **29.** Small communities appeal to me.

_____ **30.** The ups and downs of preteens will provide a challenge I am anxious to tackle.

_____ **31.** Students who live in low-income circumstances draw me to the teaching profession.

_____ **32.** The challenges of being a teenager in today's world interest me as a future teacher.

_____ **33.** Teaching children to read is an exciting prospect.

_____ **34.** I want to teach kids who traditionally have had a harder time benefiting from school.

_____ **35.** Within the public schools students have ample opportunity to thrive.

_____ **36.** I would enjoy teaching two subjects and having a homeroom group in grades 4 and 5.

Find the sums as indicated.

ITEM	MY #	ITEM	MY #	ITEM	MY #	ITEM	MY #	ITEM	MY #	ITEM	MY #	ITEM	MY #	ITEM	MY #	ITEM	MY #
1		4		6		12		2		5		8		3		7	
10		15		13		17		16		11		18		14		9	
24		28		21		25		22		19		31		23		20	
33		36		30		32		29		26		34		35		27	
Sum A		Sum B		Sum C		Sum D		Sum E		Sum F		Sum G		Sum H		Sum I	

Now shade this grid with Sums A, B, C, and D to get an idea of how you feel about teaching at a specific grade level.

A = early childhood   C = middle

B = elementary   D = high

16				
15				
14				
13				
12				
11				
10				
9				
8				
7				
6				
5				
4				
3				
2				
1				
	A	B	C	D

Now shade this grid with Sums E, F, and G to get an idea of how you feel about teaching in particular settings.

E = rural

F = suburban

G = urban

16			
15			
14			
13			
12			
11			
10			
9			
8			
7			
6			
5			
4			
3			
2			
1			
	E	F	G

Now shade this grid with Sums H and I to get an idea of your preference for public school or private school.

H = private school

I = public school

16		
15		
14		
13		
12		
11		
10		
9		
8		
7		
6		
5		
4		
3		
2		
1		
	H	I

Does the inventory reflect part of your perceived teaching identity? If not, how do you see yourself differently from these results?

Teaching in Focus

Brandi Wade teaches kindergarten at Summit Primary School in Summit Station, Ohio. She has witnessed many changes at her school as families have moved into the once rural area just outside Columbus. Housing developments have sprung up all around the school, and change has been ongoing for several years. The small town of Summit Station is now surrounded by a thriving suburban-like area, and there are no signs that growth is slowing down. The Licking Heights School District continues to build bigger schools to accommodate the influx of families.

Summit Primary is the only K–2 school in the district. This is a purposeful configuration. Principal Laura Hill says she likes the format because she has every kindergarten, every first grade, and every second grade teacher in the district right in her building. This lends a great deal of consistency to how children are taught and what and when they learn as Summit Primary retains its specialty of early childhood education. The grade-level teachers work together as teams to provide instruction that is developmentally appropriate for young children.

Along with the growth has come diversity. Once a school of predominantly white children with a relatively small African American population, all English speaking, Summit Primary now serves children with a variety of heritages who speak one of 17 different languages. This diversity of languages presents a major challenge for the Summit teachers. In Brandi's two kindergarten classes, five native languages are represented along with twin boys from Somalia. A special teacher works with these learners who speak limited or no English to help them acquire the English they need to make learning kindergarten skills an easier and more natural process. Brandi's dedication to all children in her kindergarten classes, regardless of their background, is evident in her interactions and conversations about "her kids."

Watch an interview with Brandi in the Teaching in Focus section for Chapter 2 in MyEducationLab for this course.

What Are the Purposes of Public Schools in the United States?

Mandatory attendance makes some form of schooling a common factor in our society. As such, we have all experienced schools. But as with all human endeavors, our perspectives differ. Perspective, however, isn't the only reason we view schools differently; the schools themselves are different. We begin our discussion of the similarities and differences among schools by considering distinctions between education and schooling. We then consider the purposes of **public schools** in the United States, those funded *by* the public, and accountable *to* the public, through local, state, and federal governments.

DISTINCTIONS BETWEEN EDUCATION AND SCHOOLING

Remember in geometry class when the teacher told you that a straight line on the chalkboard wasn't a line but rather a line segment? You may have rolled your eyes and mumbled, "What difference does it make?" Well, for the content of the geometry class (and the inevitable test), it certainly mattered. But did your English teacher ever ask you to draw a *line segment* under a prepositional phrase in a sentence? Probably not. Outside the context of geometry class, most of us find it unnecessary to make a distinction between a line and a line segment.

So it is with the words *education* and *schooling*. As teachers, we need to understand the differences. Once we do, we may use the words interchangeably in some contexts, always aware that distinctions do exist.

EDUCATION. Although it may not seem obvious, there is a distinct difference between education and schooling. Education is the lifelong process of learning. Every day of our lives, in every possible setting, we learn. When we see, hear, feel, or sense, we are learning. This is education—our lifelong formal and informal process of learning.

SCHOOLING. Schooling is one specific, formalized element of education. Schools are institutions specifically designed to educate in formal ways. They involve organization and

Schools

structure, both of which should be determined primarily by the needs of those who learn, as well as those who teach.

A discussion of American schools is often called a discussion of American education. That's fine. It's understood that we are talking about what goes on in school settings. The hope is that education occurring in school is productive and accurate in nature, but regardless, learning of some kind is taking place just like it does continually in every walk of life. As teachers we are called educators. As long as we recognize and acknowledge that the whole world educates children, we may continue to interchange the words *education* and *schooling*, and *educator* and *teacher*.

COMPLEMENTARY PURPOSES OF PUBLIC SCHOOLS

There's no need to settle on, or settle for, narrowly defined purposes for public schooling. Although there are many, we will consider eight. These purposes may be best understood and put into perspective using the concept of balance. Each pair of purposes discussed is more complementary than oppositional. They balance each other.

TRANSMITTING SOCIETY AND RECONSTRUCTING SOCIETY.

Both of these purposes deal with societal knowledge and values. On the more conservative side, *transmitting society* involves public schools both reflecting and supporting our American society. This is a process called socialization. **Socialization** occurs through a variety of influences including home, family, place of worship, print and electronic media, peers, and, of course, school. Students are influenced through the subjects we offer and the content of those subjects, as well as through our instruction, both actions and words. Transmitting society means promoting the concepts that preserve our democratic way of life and discouraging concepts that oppose it. Transmitting society is unifying, emphasizing what we have in common rather than our differences.

Teachers walk a fine line when it comes to achieving the purpose of transmitting society while continuing to respect the students and their families who bring a differing societal view with them to the classroom. What many of us take for granted may be new and unusual to a growing number of our students. A democratic way of life involves acceptance of differences; in American schools, acceptance should escalate to the embracing of differences. This in itself is transmitting a society that preserves democracy.

The complement of transmitting society is *reconstructing society,* challenging knowledge and values with an eye toward improvement. The concept of social reconstruction involves teaching students to recognize what needs to change, identifying the means of change, and encouraging students to work proactively for a common goal. Rather than only passing down knowledge and values to preserve society's status quo, students are urged to examine aspects of our society, keep what is worthwhile, and seek to change or discard what isn't.

As you can see, transmitting society and reconstructing society do not have to be opposing purposes. When they are balanced, it is possible to pass on the best of society while questioning and changing aspects of society for the better.

PARTICIPATION IN SOCIETY AND ACADEMIC LEARNING.

Preparing students to *participate in society* involves socialization plus the teaching of survival skills that will help them get along with others; obtain and keep employment; be politically, morally, and socially proactive; and be productive members of a community with a sense of responsibility. Public schools, along with other institutions and groups, certainly help prepare students for participation in society.

At the same time as we prepare students to participate in society we facilitate *academic learning.* Every subject area includes a body of knowledge that is, by and large, "society free," or independent from what's going on at the time within society. For instance, mathematical formulas, classic literature, history, and geography all have academic aspects that change little with time. Plato maintained that this kind of academic knowledge is the foundation for seeking truth that is not dependent on, or influenced by, current society, and that seeking of truth is a necessary purpose of education. He encouraged students to look

Schools

at possibilities through the lens of formal academic learning and to question the world around them.

In *A Place Called School*, Goodlad (1984) looked at many documents that have addressed the question "What is the purpose of schooling?" He concluded there are four broad goals:

1. Academic: Imparting knowledge and intellectual skills
2. Vocational: Preparing for the world of work
3. Social and civic: Participating in a democratic society
4. Personal: Developing self-expression and talent

Goal 1 obviously fits into the academic learning purpose, whereas the other three prepare students to participate in society.

INDIVIDUAL NEEDS AND COLLECTIVE NEEDS. These two purposes most certainly go hand in hand. A citizenry of formally educated individuals serves the collective good. American public schools provide opportunities for children to reach their learning potential. Some schools make this opportunity more feasible, more readily attainable, than others. Throughout this book we explore differences in schools that either bring out the best in individual children or that, in either overt or sometimes subtle ways, stand in the way of individual student learning potential.

Meeting the *individual needs* of students is sometimes referred to as the development of *human capital.* These words seem mechanistic and cold until we consider them separately. The word *human* describes us. The word *capital* in this sense is a noun meaning the knowledge and skills derived from education, training, and experience. The development of human capital is directly related to the well-being of individuals. It takes groups of people—the collective—to preserve our democratic way of life.

To serve *collective needs*, then, is to view the purpose of American schools as ensuring strong, free communities by teaching knowledge and values, such as honesty, hard work, civility, respect, compassion, and patriotism. The goals for the collective include economic prosperity, maintenance of our national security, and the development of a sense of both humanity and democratic ideals.

In American public schools we teach individual students who, together, form the collective of our country. The stronger the collective, the more opportunities there are for the individual. These two purposes of public education are complementary and interdependent.

SUSTAINING FOR TODAY AND PREPARING FOR TOMORROW. Schools *sustain for today* by providing a set of experiences for students. Yes, many of them will be successful in school. Some will go on to college and most will have productive careers. But some will not. Not because American public schools want it to be so, but because the reality is that not all students will make the step from school to adulthood to be citizens who contribute in positive ways. Some will drop out of school and lack the knowledge, skills, and/or credibility to fulfill their potential in adult life. Some will experience debilitating life circumstances or even death before they complete high school. What we need to remember in terms of schools serving to sustain for today is that children, regardless of what their futures hold, deserve a warm, caring, nurturing environment where they have opportunities to learn and grow. Ideally, home and family provide this environment. Whether that's the case or not, American public schools should provide this environment day after day, year after year as we ask one another, "And how are the children?"

Elliot Eisner (2004), one of our most influential educators, wrote, "Preparation for tomorrow is best served by meaningful education today" (p. 10). American public education that sustains for today, *prepares for tomorrow.* It's a building process, a self-perpetuating cycle.

Preserving our democratic way of life is accomplished through the fulfillment of these eight purposes and other related goals. Craig Cleveland writes about the learning that occurs both inside and outside of school, the education that you, as teacher candidates, are experiencing. He tells us that both education and schooling, as defined earlier, lead to

Points of Reflection 2.1

With which three of the eight complementary purposes of public schools do you identify most? Explain your choices.

Schools

Teaching in Focus

Craig Cleveland, history teacher, Roosevelt High School, California. *In his own words. . . .*

Much of what you need to know about effective teaching and learning is found within yourself already. The environment and circumstances in which you learned powerful and life-changing lessons may have been in school or elsewhere in life. The relevant and meaningful lessons your students learn will need to be both inside and outside the school if education is going to have the power to transform them into thoughtful mature people.

Essential to creating a learning environment in the classroom is a researched and clearly articulated philosophy about how learning happens. When such a philosophy is in place, teachers are able to make sound and reliable instructional decisions and refinements.

Continuing my education in a graduate program, reading professional literature, regularly reflecting on my teaching with an eye toward improvement, and having ongoing conversations with friends and colleagues help make more concrete my beliefs about how learning happens. A ninth grade student of mine made the insightful statement, "Learning is natural." I believe learning is natural when the learner has interest and a voice as a participant within the learning environment of school.

Sara Davis Powell

learning for our students. He advises us to continue to develop as professionals in his *Teaching in Focus* feature.

Now let's look inside schools in the United States to examine both their commonalities and some of their differences, beginning with what may seem like an intangible but actually can be sensed in every aspect of schooling: the culture of a school.

What Is the Culture of a School?

School culture is the context of learning experiences; it's the prevailing atmosphere of the school. As places where people work together and learn together, schools function according to their cultures. Noted educator Roland Barth (2001) tells us, "A school's culture dictates, in no uncertain terms, 'the way we do things around here.' Ultimately, a school's culture has far more influence on life and learning in the schoolhouse than the state department of education, the superintendent, the school board, or even the principal can ever have" (p. 7).

A school's culture can be a positive force for learning or a negative influence that interferes with learning. It is important to recognize elements of a school's culture, both the forces that created it and those that perpetuate it. If the culture is positive, acknowledging the influential forces and then reinforcing them keeps the culture vibrant and growing. If the culture is negative or apathetic, altering it begins with looking closely at the influential forces and finding ways to begin the change process.

From a new teacher's standpoint, a positive school culture may be evident when experienced teachers consistently ask how things are going and offer to help with lessons, materials, managing student behavior, paperwork, and so on. Hearing teachers talking and laughing together, sharing what works in their classrooms, and speaking of students with caring and concerned attitudes demonstrates positive culture. On the other hand, when a school seems to have a territorial atmosphere with cliques of teachers criticizing other teachers and the principal, when offers of assistance are few, when students are spoken of primarily in critical terms, a new teacher will likely sense a negative culture. Because most of the adults in a school are teachers, their influence on school culture is immense.

Schools

TEACHERS AND SCHOOL CULTURE

Teachers' instructional skills and professionalism either improve a school's culture or keep it stagnant or negative. The level of respect teachers engender among their colleagues and in the community either builds a positive culture or serves to drag it down. This level of respect has much to do with the relationships that exist among a school's adults, which, in turn, influence the ways teachers relate to students. Because all teachers, experienced and new, have considerable influence on school culture, they must be instrumental in maintaining a positive culture or helping to change a negative culture into a more positive one.

CHANGING SCHOOL CULTURE

A school's culture can change. Can it change quickly or easily? Definitely not when improvement is the goal. Positive culture shifts require strong leadership, ownership of the problems and potential solutions by the adults in the school, and a steady, conscious influx of both attitudes and actions that produce the desired results. In contrast, changes in a school culture from positive to negative may only require apathy and neglect.

All components of American education discussed in this text influence a school's culture. For instance, what is taught in a school can be dynamic and challenging, or mediocre and boring. Not only *what* is taught, but *how* it is taught, influences culture. The level of respect teachers and students have for one another influences school culture as does the level of teacher expectations for student success. Remember that the context of schools is complex; schools are living systems. Because students, teachers, parents, communities, policies, and politics all potentially influence school culture, many variances exist among schools, even those with the same basic structure.

How Do School Venues Differ?

U.S. schools vary greatly, from the traditional neighborhood public school to the ultimate private school: the home. This section looks at **school venues,** the variety of ways American students are educated in the more than 130,000 schools in the United States (National Center for Education Statistics [NCES], 2010).

PUBLIC SCHOOL VENUES

The vast majority of educational settings in the United States are public schools, with most of the funding to support them coming from some form of taxation. Public schools are accountable to the community through elected or governmental officials who have policy and oversight responsibilities.

Public schools come in all shapes and sizes. They are not only open to every student regardless of socioeconomic status, disability, race, or religion, but in fact they must provide a school setting for every child—that's part of being public.

TRADITIONAL PUBLIC SCHOOLS. The traditional, or **neighborhood, school** is still the predominant form of public schooling in the United States. **Traditional public schools** have no admission criteria, other than perhaps residency in a particular attendance zone. Their educational programs are designed to meet the needs of almost all students, with the possible exception of some with severe physical or mental disabilities. Most of the more than 55 million students in grades K to 12 in the United States attend traditional public schools (Snyder, Dillow, & Hoffman, 2009).

A traditional public school that provides a comprehensive program of education and includes student and community services, such as after-school and family-education programs, may be considered a **full-service school**. Many of the components of a full-service school are made possible through community partnerships with businesses, health-care providers, foundations, and government agencies. These services help students and their families cope with a variety of dilemmas. The goals of a full-service school may include the following:

- Meeting students' needs, both academic and nonacademic, through extended-day programs, counseling groups, homework assistance, and the like
- Increasing family stability through parent education
- Creating a safe haven for the community
- Providing role models for all family members
- Responding to physical and psychological needs
- Providing easy access to government services
- Involving community members from all walks of life in public education

Three particular venues of public schools draw specific groups of students. Each has a structure that uniquely matches the needs and interests of its student population.

MAGNET SCHOOLS. A school with a specific emphasis or theme may be known as a **magnet school**. The curriculum and/or instructional program of a magnet school is tailored with unique opportunities that attract certain students. A magnet school's focus may be math or science (or both), performing arts, technology, or high academic expectations and student qualifications. For example, a magnet school with an emphasis on preparation for a career in the trade arts, sometimes called a vocational magnet, would attract students interested in careers in construction, mechanics, cosmetology, culinary arts, and so on.

Magnet schools are more expensive to operate than traditional neighborhood schools. Their special programs may require funds for career-related equipment, performance studios, staff with specific expertise, smaller teacher-to-student ratios, and transportation beyond immediate neighborhoods More and more magnet schools are opening and drawing specific groups of students out of the traditional neighborhood schools as parents and students seek more specialized environments. Magnet schools account for about 2% of public schools, with approximately 3% of students enrolled in public schools attending them.

CHARTER SCHOOLS. A **charter school** is a public school that is freed in specific ways from the typical regulations required of other public schools. For instance, teachers and administrators in charter schools usually have more control over how they spend their funds and the kinds of classes they offer than their counterparts in traditional public schools. Charter schools are open to all students within a school district and must attract students to stay in operation. They must get the word out to the public, convince parents that they can better meet the learning needs of their children, and then follow through with their plans and promises to keep students coming back year after year.

Charter schools are created by people who see a need or an opportunity to fix a problem, such as declining student achievement, or to enhance a particular area, such as student ability in the arts. They may be started from scratch or converted from preexisting schools. Themes may revolve around a subject area, particular teaching techniques, a social problem, specific grade levels, or anything else the creators imagine, propose, and get approved by a state board of education. Once approved and in operation, charter schools are usually governed through **site-based management,** meaning that the school is in the hands of those closest to it, generally teachers, administrators, and parents. There are more charter schools than magnet schools in the United States, but only about 1.2% of students in the United States are enrolled in them.

ALTERNATIVE SCHOOLS. Magnet and charter schools are both alternative forms of school organization. However, in public education, the term *alternative school* takes on a unique meaning. If a school is called an **alternative school,** more than likely it is a school designed for students who are not successful in a traditional school setting. Because school districts can't exclude students and attendance is compulsory until age 16, alternative settings have emerged that may be categorized in two ways: remedial and last chance.

Schools

In The News abc NEWS

One Last Chance

Ted Koppel and ABC news correspondent Michelle Martin introduce us to a unique charter school. The Seed Public Charter School is the only public urban boarding school in the United States. Located in Washington, D.C., Seed provides housing, meals, a safe and clean environment, and an education for seventh through twelfth grade students chosen by lottery. Believing that millions of students are being shortchanged, the founders of Seed created an educational structure that allows students previously thought to be destined to drop out of school because of their environment an opportunity for success.

Watch the video to learn more about Seed and the students and teachers who learn together there by visiting the **In the News** section of Chapter 2 on your

MyEducationLab for this course. Respond to these questions and prompts.

1. Why do the founders of Seed claim that the students they serve need an "entirely new environment" to succeed in school?

2. The math teacher says it takes courage for the students to move forward academically. What are two things the Seed students must overcome to be successful in school?

3. What are the purposes of "gates" at Seed? Is the success rate related to them higher or lower than you would have anticipated? Why?

4. What caused Jonathan to say, "You may think because you know my neighborhood that you can judge me for who I may become"?

Students who need more focused attention to be successful than what the traditional school can provide are in need of remediation: academic, social, emotional, or some combination of the three. Once remediation is completed, a student may return to a more traditional setting. Often students who are characterized as being **at risk**—those in serious danger of not completing school and who may be heading toward nonproductive or counterproductive

TABLE 2.1 Public School Venues				
Venue	Definition	Admission Criteria	Advantages	Disadvantages
Traditional	Neighborhood school	None	Close to home; sense of ownership	May not have programs of interest or that meet specific student needs
Full-service traditional schools	School that offers student and community services that go beyond academics	None	Draws families in; provides services such as health promotion and community education	None
Magnet	School with specific emphasis or theme	Interest; talent; academic achievement	Specialized curriculum or instruction	May exclude some students; requires more funding
Charter	School freed from some regulatory control of district or state	None; generally first come, first admitted	Site-based decision making; specialized curriculum or instruction	May lack sufficient oversight; danger of "ends justify means" mentality
Alternative	Usually a school for students who are not successful in other public school settings	Behavioral or academic problems	Can provide specialized assistance for students who need it most	May neglect some aspects of school while targeting specific needs; may stereotype or stigmatize students

lifestyles—are strongly urged to attend remedial alternative schools. Students who are not successful in a remedial setting may attend public alternative schools that are considered last-chance schools. In most cases the students have gotten into significant trouble in a traditional or remedial school, have been suspended multiple times, have consistently been disruptive in the classroom, or generally have not benefited from other, less intrusive programs. A school that qualifies as both a charter school because of its vision and unique structure and an alternative school because it was developed to meet the needs of students at risk of not succeeding in traditional public schools is the Seed Public Charter School in Washington, D.C., featured in this chapter's *In the News*.

The wide variety of public schools provides opportunities and choice. Table 2.1 summarizes the commonly available public school options. This chapter's *Letter to the Editor* deals with the possibility of public schools in Tulsa, Oklahoma, reverting to all neighborhood schools, an interesting proposition.

Points of Reflection 2.2

Did you attend public schools? Were they traditional neighborhood schools, magnet schools, charter schools, or alternative schools? If you attended a variety of public school venues, what differences among them did you experience?

Letter to the Editor

This letter appeared in the Tulsa, Oklahoma, newspaper, *The Tulsa World*. It was written by a citizen responding to recent local budget deliberations and the possibility of returning to a system of neighborhood schools.

DECEMBER 17, 2009

FOR NEIGHBORHOOD SCHOOLS

With the continuous hand-wringing that has been publicized almost daily with budget cuts and potential budget cuts to Tulsa Public Schools, it appears the proposal to make some of the schools community centers has gone underground. Not one mention of the first remedy many school districts nationwide, including Seattle, implemented prior to this school year: returning each child to a neighborhood school. I have not seen the costs TPS spends in transporting children outside neighborhood schools but it must be large. Not only would this cut costs, but it would give the impetus to returning school pride and a sense of ownership to local neighborhoods/ communities, students and parents. Most children could then walk or ride their bikes to and from schools providing exercise each day. This would allow Tulsans to volunteer in local schools surrounded by neighborhood children and their parents. Where extra emphasis or resources are needed it would be much easier to implement before and after school programs with travel and time distances reduced. It is time to pool resources and combine programs such as health initiatives, library, career counseling, and academic programs. Quit whining about potential budget cuts that are based on economic realities and get to work. Tulsans deserve the quality public school options that existed prior to 1980 when neighborhood schools were the norm!

Roger Hilst

Tulsa

Now it's your turn. Write a letter to the editor from the perspective of a future teacher expressing your views on this issue and any broader issues you feel it invokes. You may comment on any, or all, of the writer's expressed opinions. The following questions may help you frame your thinking but should not limit nor determine what you write.

1. Do you agree that changing most or all of the Tulsa schools to neighborhood schools is a good idea? If so, why? If not, why not?

2. The issue of the budget led to this letter, but what else about neighborhood schools appeals to many people and would justify changing schools to this format?

3. What does the writer mean by community centers, and would elaborating this point be helpful?

4. Would consolidating services and placing them in schools be helpful? Why or why not?

5. Although it's not directly addressed in this letter, changing school formats will likely mean doing away with magnet and/or charter schools. Do you agree or disagree with this? Why?

6. What recommendations do you have for Tulsa officials as they consider reverting to neighborhood schools they once had? Are there studies they might do or research that could help them decide if this would be the best move for Tulsa?

7. Do you agree or disagree with the letter writer about the relative importance of the issue? Is there a larger issue here that needs to be addressed?

Write your letter in understandable terminology, remembering that readers of newspaper Letters to the Editor are citizens who may have limited knowledge of school practices and policies.

PRIVATE SCHOOL VENUES

The two elements that make schools public—public funding and public accountability—are both absent in **private schools**. About 10% of students in the United States attend private schools (NCES, 2010). Families choose private education for a variety of reasons. Some choose private schools for potential benefits such as smaller class size, specific instruction to meet the needs of students with learning disabilities, or travel and extracurricular opportunities. Still others may choose private education because of family history. Perhaps generations of family members have attended a particular private school.

Some families choose private schools because of negative perceptions about local public schools. They may consider public schools inferior or inadequate. Still others want their children to have religious instruction or believe that their children's specific mental or physical needs require a private setting. Then there are other families who perceive that a private school may be more prestigious than the public schools available.

In most instances, public and private schools exist side by side in a community with little rancor. Yet there may be differences in underlying philosophy that cause friction. Unlike their public school counterparts, private schools are not obligated to educate all students but are able to choose and dismiss students. Thus their classrooms typically have fewer behavior problems, a smaller teacher-to-student ratio, and stronger parental support. Some private school teachers see this as a trade-off because most of them are paid less than teachers in public schools.

PAROCHIAL SCHOOLS. Most private schools are affiliated with a particular religious sect (denomination) and are often called **parochial schools**. Most religion-affiliated schools are aligned with the Catholic faith.

Private schools that are not aligned with a religious group exist in many forms and cater to a wide spectrum of student and family needs and wants. They may resemble charter schools with themes and areas of emphasis, but they are free from all government regulation because they are privately funded.

SINGLE-GENDER SCHOOLS. Some private schools are **single gender**, enrolling either all boys or all girls. Because **Title IX of the Education Amendments Act of 1972** prohibits government money from being used for programs that discriminate on the basis of gender, most single-gender schools are private.

HOMESCHOOLING. Students who receive most of their academic instruction in their homes are considered to be **homeschooled**. Although it's hard to pinpoint an exact number, we know there are over 1 million homeschooled students in the United States (NCES, 2004). This figure represents less than 3% of the total U.S. student population. The reasons for parents choosing homeschooling vary but are similar to parental reasons for choosing private over public school venues.

Homeschooling has become a social movement, with parents as political activists, organizers of national networks, and developers of curriculum and instructional materials. As you can imagine, the quality of the education received in the home varies widely. However, on standardized academic achievement tests homeschoolers tend to score 15 to 30 percentile points higher than students in public schools (Ray, 2006). How students fare socially has not been measured, only openly speculated about. A concern is that children who are homeschooled may miss out on the civic perspective and experiences gained only through going to school with students who are not like themselves in religious beliefs, racial or cultural background, socioeconomic status, or academic aptitude.

Homeschooling has always been part of the human experience. Some notable homeschooled students include Florence Nightingale, Thomas Edison, Margaret Mead, Charles Dickens, Benjamin Franklin, Orville and Wilbur Wright, Woodrow Wilson, and former U.S. Supreme Court justice Sandra Day O'Connor.

FOR-PROFIT SCHOOLS. Nonreligious private schools are often **for-profit schools**. These schools are managed by some entity that receives a percentage of the money generated. Even some public schools may be for-profit. While for years public schools have contracted with private companies to provide aspects of schooling such as transportation, custodial work, and food services, when companies contract with states or districts to take over all aspects of schooling and make money by doing so, then it's capitalism in the schoolhouse. These for-profit schools are given the federal, state, and local money per pupil that a public school receives and are referred to as **Education Maintenance Organizations, or EMOs** (the educational equivalent of health care's HMOs). Public schools run by private companies are controversial.

The largest EMO is managed by EdisonLearning, Inc., with the schools called Edison Schools. In 2008–2009, Edison Schools served over 350,000 students in 24 states and the United Kingdom (EdisonLearning, Inc., 2010). Although they make claims of increased student learning, EdisonLearning, Inc. data calculations are often questioned by those who oppose privatization. Another controversial claim made by opponents of privatization is that when profit is the bottom line, services to the students with special needs may be neglected. More research is needed to determine the efficacy of for-profit companies managing public schools.

As you consider the variety of schools in Table 2.2, keep in mind that what some may view as advantages may be considered disadvantages by others, and vice versa.

Both public and private schools create choices for families. Let's explore how school choice is manifested in U.S. schools.

SCHOOL CHOICE

School choice—letting parents and students decide which schools meet their needs—has a very democratic feel, doesn't it? Increasing parental involvement, providing learning environments more suited to individual students, attempting broader integration, accommodating particular interests and talents, and affording more desirable settings to at-risk or underprivileged students are just a few of the reasons for choice among schools.

Points of Reflection 2.3

Did you attend private schools? If so, were they religiously affiliated? If you attended more than one venue of private school, what differences did you experience? Did you attend a combination of public and private schools? If so, what differences did you experience between public and private schools?

TABLE 2.2 Private and for-profit school venues

Venue	Definition	Admission Criteria	Advantages	Disadvantages
Religious	School with a religious affiliation	Agreement to either uphold or not interfere with the principles of the affiliation	Allows parents and religious groups to include their traditions and beliefs	Not accountable to any government agency
Nonreligious	School without a religious affiliation	Interest; can afford tuition; students may be rejected for any reason	Specialized curriculum or instruction	Not accountable to any government agency
Single gender	School for boys only or girls only	Must be gender of school; generally first come, first admitted	May better meet specific learning styles of either boys or girls	Not accountable to any government agency; may not mirror reality of the coed world
Homeschooling	Students are taught at home or in a home environment	Family member	Provides very specific one-on-one instruction in a manner desired by parents	Not accountable to any government agency; may isolate student from other cultures and viewpoints; may neglect some aspects of what is commonly agreed upon as necessary curriculum
For-profit	Schools run by individuals or corporations that make and keep monetary gain	Any criteria set by school managers	Can be very specialized	If private, not accountable to any government agency

Schools

55

Figure 2.1 School choice options supported by government funding

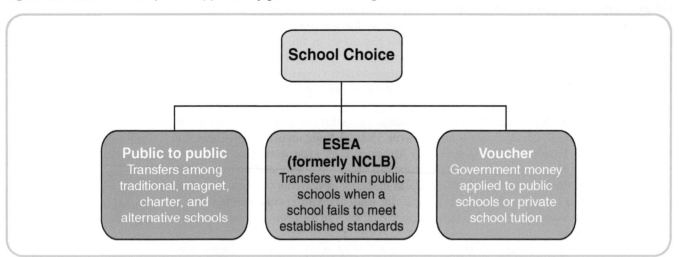

Let's consider school choice in the context of competition. Marketplace theory says that competition leads to improvement. But does this apply to schools competing for student enrollment when more students mean more money? If all schools were high performing and differed only in theme or focus, then competition would simply mean appealing to student interests or learning preferences. But when schools gain enrollment while others lose because of real or perceived failure to meet the needs of students, the failing school is left in an even more untenable situation. If we close them down, we may be eliminating the possibility of improving the predominant public school setting, the neighborhood school. However, no child should be in a school that is not making progress toward improved levels of learning. Answering the question, "And how are the children?" becomes even more complex and important.

For any choice plan, there are two key ingredients for success: information and transportation. Without provisions for both, a choice plan only gives choices to families who seek out information and have the capability to provide transportation out of their neighborhoods. Figure 2.1 illustrates three ways that public school choice may be manifested.

PUBLIC-TO-PUBLIC SCHOOL CHOICE. Allowing for choice among public schools occurs in a variety of ways. The option of attending magnet, charter, and alternative schools versus a traditional neighborhood school within a district is by far the most common manifestation of school choice. Taking this option a step further, **open enrollment** allows students to choose from among all the schools in a school district with a few exceptions, such as magnet schools with specific student qualifications and alternative schools with student enrollment controlled by the district. Open enrollment may extend across district lines as well.

ELEMENTARY AND SECONDARY EDUCATION ACT. In 1965 President Lyndon B. Johnson proposed, and Congress passed, the **Elementary and Secondary Education Act** (ESEA) as a part of the "War on Poverty." The ESEA emphasizes equal access to education and establishes high standards and accountability (U.S. Department of Education, 2010). From 2001 to 2010, the ESEA was reauthorized as the No Child Left Behind Act (NCLB). One provision of the act is that parents and students have school choice under certain conditions. The act includes guidelines for grading schools based on their progress toward reaching designated goals dealing with, among other factors, student achievement on standardized tests and attendance. Schools are evaluated and given report cards called **Adequate Yearly Progress,** or simply AYP reports. After 2 years of failing AYP, students at schools with a high percentage of students in poverty may transfer to schools with passing AYP reports. The school district has the responsibility to provide at least two designated recipient schools that passed AYP for each student and to make transportation available for students.

TABLE 2.3 Advocates' and critics' views of school choice

Advocates	Critics
Competition raises the standards, and consequently the performance, of all schools.	Competition destroys cooperation among teachers, schools, communities.
Competition gives parents decision-making power to choose for their children.	Only parents who are vocal advocates for their children will take advantage of options.
Competition forces low-performing schools to go out of business.	Students remaining in low-performing schools suffer.
Choice better accommodates diversity.	Choice leads to the possibility of further segregation.
Choice provides equal opportunities.	Choice exacerbates inequities.

Are parents and students likely to take advantage of the choices provided by ESEA? Maybe, maybe not. More will if they are informed of the options in a timely fashion, if they are comfortable that long bus rides won't be necessary, and if the students are not socially committed to staying with their neighborhood friends who opt not to move. These are powerful "ifs." Here's another to consider: *If* their parents do not explore options, students will likely remain in schools designated as failing.

VOUCHERS. Perhaps the most controversial of current efforts to provide school choice is the **voucher,** a government-issued form that represents part of the state's financial contribution for the education of a student. Parents choose a school and present the voucher, and the government allocates funding accordingly to the school.

Some vouchers are only for students living in poverty, allowing them to choose a school that perhaps better meets their needs. Other vouchers are awarded to any student within a designated area to use within a school district, or even across district lines. Some vouchers may be used only in public schools, whereas others may be applied to private school tuition or even to schools with a religious affiliation. The viability of voucher plans often sparks debates in state legislatures.

Consider this. Private schools are free to admit or refuse any student. They can decide not to take vouchers from students who don't fit in for any reason, including gender, race, past or potential achievement, or disability. Likewise, they can recruit and admit the most motivated, highest achieving students. Public money in the form of vouchers thus has the potential to become a tool of discrimination.

The use of vouchers to attend schools with a religious affiliation is perhaps the most controversial aspect of the program. Many people consider it a violation of the separation of church and state, and this obstacle may lead to the demise of vouchers as school choice alternatives.

ADVOCATES AND CRITICS OF SCHOOL CHOICE. School choice, regardless of the format, has its advocates and its critics. If we simply pose the question, "Should parents have the right to choose a school that best meets the needs of their children?" most Americans would say yes. Table 2.3 lists several opposing views of school choice.

Points of Reflection 2.4

Does a particular school venue appeal to you? If so, what elements of the particular type of school make it a possible career choice?

What Is School Like at Different Levels?

U.S. schools are organized and structured in four basic levels: early childhood, elementary, middle, and high school.

Summit Primary School,
Summit Station, Ohio
Sara Davis Powell

STRUCTURE AND ORGANIZATION OF EARLY CHILDHOOD EDUCATION

Early childhood education is commonly divided into three basic age spans: preschool, kindergarten, and primary grades. Educators tend to agree that early childhood settings should be characterized by warmth, sensitivity, and nurture. Learning through play, with healthy doses of experimentation and discovery, describes a commonly held and balanced early childhood philosophy. Let's briefly explore some of the structural and organizational components of early childhood educational settings.

PRESCHOOL. Experiences of 3- and 4-year-olds in the United States vary enormously. Some children stay home with a parent; some are provided simple child care. Others have a more structured **preschool** environment housed within a primary or elementary school. In this setting, often designated as a prekindergarten for 4-year-olds, care is enhanced by exposure to basic educational concepts. Preschool education may follow many different models.

The **Montessori** approach to early childhood education, with mixed-age grouping and self-pacing, is growing in popularity and has the reputation of being high quality when faithfully implemented (Morrison, 2008). Teachers in a Montessori setting are primarily guides, with children acting independently to choose learning activities. The **High/Scope** approach, widely used in preschool through early elementary settings, is built on consistency and few transitions during the day as children construct meaning for themselves in problem-solving situations within learning centers. The **Reggio Emilia** approach to early childhood education for ages 3 months to 6 years is based on relationships among children, families, and teachers. Close long-term relationships are built because the teachers in each classroom stay with the same children for up to 3 years (Kostelnik, Soderman, & Whiren, 2004). **Head Start** is the largest provider of government-funded preschool education, employing 1 of every 5 preschool teachers in the United States (Barnett, 2003).

KINDERGARTEN. Once considered an optional bridge between preschool, or no school at all, and the beginning of formal education in first grade, **kindergarten** (meaning "chil-

Some children enter kindergarten with many readiness skills; others do not. Cody White

dren's garden") has become part of almost every 5- to 6-year-old child's educational experience, some for half a day and others for the entire day. However, kindergarten is mandatory for 5-year-olds in only 12 states, with 42 states requiring that kindergarten be offered in every school district (Morrison, 2008).

What occurs in both whole-day and half-day kindergarten classrooms across the country varies. In some kindergarten classrooms children are involved in literacy-building activities; in others there's little evidence of any emphasis on literacy. Some kindergartens are housed in K–5 or K–6 elementary schools, while others are in primary school settings that may include prekindergarten or kindergarten through grade 2 or 3. Figure 2.2 displays a possible schedule for half-day kindergarten, with teachers following a similar schedule twice a day. The step from kindergarten to first grade is a giant one, so it is crucial that the term *readiness* has become a major part of the vocabulary of early childhood education.

Schools

Figure 2.2 Sample half-day kindergarten schedule

9:25–9:40	Arrival, morning exercises
9:40–10:40	Learning centers
10:40–10:50	Cleanup
10:50–11:10	Outdoor or gym play/snack
11:10–11:30	Whole group instruction
11:30–11:45	Small group time, cooperative activity
11:45–12:00	Art projects
12:00–12:15	Closing exercises/dismissal
Repeat with another group of children 1:20–4:05	

PRIMARY GRADES. Teachers in primary classrooms, grades 1 through 3, are faced with the challenge of meeting the needs of children with widely varying levels both of readiness for learning and of acquired knowledge and skills. Imagine a first grade classroom with 5 children who have received very little home encouragement for learning and did not attend kindergarten, 10 children who attended three different kindergartens that varied widely in their approaches, and 4 students who are reading independently. The challenge is to engage them all in learning based on where they are, with a view of unlimited potential. Figure 2.3 shows a general schedule for a primary classroom.

Our early childhood focus school, Summit Primary, does not have a preschool program. Children must be 5 years old to enter one of Summit's three levels of kindergarten. The *Boost* class is for children who need more basic guidance and instruction. The *Average* class is for most of the children. The *Enrichment* class is for children who have already mastered some of the typical kindergarten skills, such as recognizing and writing the alphabet, reading one-syllable and often-used sight words, recalling a story orally in correct sequence, counting to 100, and making and explaining simple graphs. Some children go directly from one level of kindergarten to first grade, and others have the opportunity to stay in kindergarten for another year to build a stronger foundation for first grade. In addition to kindergarten, Summit Primary offers first and second grade.

To learn more about the structure and organization of Summit Primary School, where Brandi Wade and Renee Ayers teach, take a school tour and watch an interview with principal Laura Hill in the Teaching in Focus *section for Chapter 2 in MyEducationLab for this course.*

Points of Reflection 2.5

Now that you know more about early childhood education, can you envision spending your days with the youngest students in American schools? What aspects appeal to you? What aspects do not appeal to you?

STRUCTURE AND ORGANIZATION OF ELEMENTARY EDUCATION

Elementary classrooms may be **self-contained**, meaning that one teacher has responsibility for one group of children most of the school day. In some schools, teachers may share responsibility for a group of children, each specializing in one or two subject areas. A sample schedule for a third grade self-contained classroom is provided in Figure 2.4. A sample

Figure 2.3 Sample primary grade schedule

8:50–9:10	Arrival, daily business, opening activities
9:10–9:30	Whole group instruction in literacy
9:30–10:30	Small groups rotate through reading and writing centers
10:30–10:45	Recess
10:45–11:45	Math instruction
11:45–12:15	Lunch
12:15–12:30	Read aloud
12:30–1:15	Science (physical education on Tuesday and Thursday)
1:15–1:30	Silent reading
1:30–2:15	Social studies (art on Monday; music on Wednesday)
2:15–2:45	Center Time
2:45–3:10	Whole group review of day, clean-up, dismissal

Schools

Rees Elementary School,
Spanish Fork, Utah
Sara Davis Powell

To learn more about the
structure and organiza-
tion of Rees Elementary,
where Brenda Beyal,
Chris Roberts, and Tim
Mendenhall teach, take a school
tour and watch an interview with
principal Mike Larsen in the
Teaching in Focus section for
Chapter 2 in MyEducationLab for
this course.

Points of Reflection 2.6

Does teaching all subjects to
the same group of elementary
children sound like something you
would enjoy? Elementary schools
provide opportunities for professionals who are guidance
counselors, media specialists,
and teachers of students with
special needs. Do these fields
interest you?

schedule for a fourth grade classroom with a team of three teachers, each teaching a core subject area, is provided in Figure 2.5. A team of three teachers would accommodate three classes of fourth graders.

Our three focus teachers at Rees Elementary School, Utah, have **multiage,** or multigrade, **classrooms,** where children in three grade levels learn together. Chris Roberts, Brenda Beyal, and Tim Mendenhall each have homeroom classes made up of third, fourth, and fifth graders. They teach all four **core subjects**—language arts, math, science, and social studies—to their own classes, but each specializes in a fine arts area. Chris teaches movement and dance, Brenda teaches visual arts, and Tim teaches theater to all three classes. Let's consider Brenda's class as an example of a multiage classroom. In the beginning of the school year, she has third graders who are new to her class, fourth graders who have already been in her class 1 year, and fifth graders who have already been in her class 2 years. At the end of the school year, the fifth graders move on to middle school after having been in Brenda's class for 3 years, and a new group of children who have finished second grade will be assigned to their first year with Brenda. One third of her class will be new each school year.

Another possible elementary school teacher-student configuration with benefits similar to those of multiage grouping is **looping,** which occurs when a teacher stays with a particular group of students for more than 1 year. As the students go, for instance, from first to second grade, the teacher moves with them. Among the many positive reasons to loop are the following (Roberts, Kellough, & Moore, 2006):

- A consistent relationship develops between teacher and students and lasts for 2 or 3 years.

- Student learning styles, strengths, weaknesses, interests, behavior patterns, potential, family circumstances, and the like, are well known to the teacher.

- The last few weeks of the school year are often used more productively, with summer reading and project assignments more meaningful.

- The beginning of the school year requires fewer getting-acquainted and routine-practicing experiences.

Figure 2.4 Sample third grade schedule (self-contained)

8:50–9:15	Whole class morning meeting
9:15–9:35	Small group reading
9:35–9:55	Whole class instruction in writing/spelling
9:55–10:20	Reading and writing activities
10:20–10:40	Recess and snack
10:40–11:15	Whole group math instruction/activities
11:15–12:00	Alternating physical education (M), art (T), physical education (W), music (Th), physical education (F)
12:00–12:35	Lunch, recess
12:35–1:15	Alternating social studies and science
1:15–1:45	Alternating computer and library time
1:45–2:00	Read aloud
2:00–2:30	Free choice centers
2:30–2:50	Reading and writing activities
2:50–3:10	Whole group class meeting
3:15	Dismissal

Schools

Figure 2.5 Sample fourth grade schedule (three-teacher team)

8:50–9:05	Whole class meetings in homerooms
9:05–10:10	Block time:
	Group 1: Math
	Group 2: English language arts
	Group 3: Science/social studies
10:10–10:30	DEAR (Drop Everything And Read) in homeroom
10:30–10:50	Journal writing in homerooms
10:50–11:10	Recess and snack
11:10–12:15	Block time:
	Group 1: English language arts
	Group 2: Science/social studies
	Group 3: Math
12:15–12:35	Lunch
12:35–1:00	Computer or library time
1:00–2:05	Block time:
	Group 1: Science/social studies
	Group 2: Math
	Group 3: English language arts
2:05–2:40	Physical education
2:40–3:00	Alternating art and music
3:00–3:10	Whole class meetings in homerooms
3:15	Dismissal

STRUCTURE AND ORGANIZATION OF MIDDLE SCHOOL EDUCATION

Some schools that serve sixth, seventh, and eighth graders are **departmentalized,** with teachers teaching their own subjects and meeting occasionally with other teachers who teach the same subject. With departmentalization, a teacher who, for instance, has Jamal in math does not collaborate with Jamal's social studies or science teacher. The math teacher may not even know who Jamal has for social studies or science.

According to the **National Middle School Association** (2010), the preferred organizational structure for middle level education is the student-teacher team, known as an **interdisciplinary team**. A team generally includes four core subject area teachers and the 80 to 100 or so students they share. If Jamal is on a team, all his teachers know exactly who teaches him each core subject. The team of teachers meets at least three times a week to plan together and discuss student progress and concerns. This kind of teaming is developmentally appropriate for **young adolescents**.

In some **middle schools,** students attend six or seven classes a day, each 50 to 60 minutes long. These classes include the core subjects, as well as other subjects that are considered **exploratory** or **related arts**. These may include art, music, physical education, industrial arts, languages, drama, and computer education, among others. Figure 2.6 shows both a traditional six-period student schedule and a schedule allowing for longer class periods, commonly called a **block schedule**.

Teaming is successfully implemented at Cario Middle School, where focus teachers Traci Peters and Deirdre Huger McGrew teach. At Cario, each core class is taught for 70 minutes. The students also have one class period for a variety of special classes that are rotated every 9 weeks. They have

Cario Middle School, Mt. Pleasant, South Carolina
Sara Davis Powell

To learn more about the *structure and organization of Cario Middle School, where Traci Peters and Deirdre McGrew teach, take a school tour and watch an interview with principal Carol Bartlett in the* Teaching in Focus *section for Chapter 2 in MyEducationLab.*

Figure 2.6 Middle school student schedules

Traditional schedule (5 minutes to change classes)

8:00–8:10	Homeroom
8:15–9:10	Math
9:15–10:10	English language arts
10:15–11:10	Band/art/foreign language/drama (9 weeks each)
11:15–11:45	Lunch
11:50–12:45	Science
12:50–1:45	Computer education/physical education (one semester each)
1:50–2:45	Social studies
2:50–3:00	Homeroom
3:00	Dismissal

Block Schedule

8:00–8:15	Homework
8:20–10:00	English language arts block
10:05–10:55	Related arts rotation
11:00–11:30	Lunch
11:35–1:15	Math block
1:20–2:10	Science and social studies (rotating days)
2:15–3:05	Related arts rotation
3:05	Dismissal

Points of Reflection 2.7

Does teaching young adolescents on an interdisciplinary team in a middle level setting appeal to you? Would you prefer teaching a core subject area or perhaps a special area such as a foreign language, art, or choral music? Does working as a guidance counselor, media specialist, or teacher of students with special needs interest you?

a 30-minute lunch period and 5 minutes to go from class to class. Cario teachers provide a rich array of clubs and after-school activities from which students may choose.

STRUCTURE AND ORGANIZATION OF HIGH SCHOOL EDUCATION

High school may be a very recent experience for you, or it may have occurred decades ago. Virtually everyone agrees that high school represents a unique time of life. The 4 years of 9th, 10th, 11th, and 12th grade provide vivid memories that many of us choose to relive every 10 years or so as we make our way back to reunions to reminisce, to see what and how our classmates are doing, or perhaps to show off or embellish our own accomplishments. Then there are those of us who would rather forget that time of our lives. Regardless of our feelings or memories from both an academic and a social perspective, high school experiences have a significant and long-lasting impact on most of us.

High school teachers typically specialize in one major subject and teach different areas or levels of that subject. All teachers of a subject form a department and meet periodically to discuss issues such as course materials, innovations and dilemmas in the subject field, and professional development opportunities. Departmentalization is the primary organizational structure of high schools.

Some high schools adhere to a traditional schedule of six or seven classes a day, each about an hour long. Students attend these classes for two semesters to earn a credit in each. However, alternative schedules are gaining popularity. Some schools are choosing to use blocks of 90 to 100 minutes per class that allow for more complete cycles of learning, such as completion of labs, reading and reflecting on literature, and proving as well as applying math theories.

Block schedules take one of two forms. Each has benefits. One form is composed of four classes per day of 90 to 100 minutes, every day, thus

Roosevelt High School, Fresno, California
Sara Davis Powell

allowing four courses to be completed in a semester. One of the major benefits of this type of schedule is that students have only four subjects to study at a time, rather than six or seven. With four courses per semester, students have the opportunity to earn 32 credits in 4 years of high school. The other basic form of block scheduling is the alternating-day model. With this schedule, students also receive credit for eight courses a year, but each course meets for 90 to 100 minutes every other day for two semesters.

As an urban high school, Roosevelt is actually two high schools in one. Most of the students (about 2,100) attend the comprehensive program, and about 500 students attend the arts magnet school, Roosevelt School of the Arts. The student population of Roosevelt High School, primarily Hispanic and Asian, is not typical of most high schools in the United States but is more common in California, Texas, and Florida. Most of you did not attend high schools that mirror Roosevelt. Most of you will not teach in high schools like Roosevelt, but some of you will. The majority of Roosevelt's students are from low-income homes. The majority of you are not. So why is Roosevelt our focus high school? There are several reasons. First, you need to see that effective teachers engage students in interesting and relevant lessons in all schools, regardless of the student profile or school setting. Second, because the high school so fresh in many of your memories is most likely a rural or suburban high school with families in middle- to upper-income brackets, you need to be exposed to a high school that's outside most of your zones of awareness and comfort. And, perhaps most important, adolescents are adolescents. Similarities outweigh elements of diversity.

In this chapter's *Diversity Dialogue,* we read about Advanced Placement (AP) classes and the dilemma surrounding the lack of minority students in them. This issue exists in many high schools across the country.

To learn more about the structure and organization of Roosevelt High School, where Craig Cleveland, Derek Boucher, and Angelica Reynosa teach, take a school tour with assistant principal John Lael and watch an interview with principal Maria Romero in the Teaching in Focus *section for Chapter 2 in MyEducationLab.*

Points of Reflection 2.8

Does teaching in a high school appeal to you? Is there a teacher who had a profound influence on the direction of your life that you would want to use as a model for your own teaching?

DIVERSITY DIALOGUE

Derek Boucher, social science and reading teacher, Roosevelt High School, California

Jessica O'Rourke

Roosevelt is a dual-purpose school campus, with both a comprehensive high school and an arts magnet program housed on the same campus. Looking at the student populations side by side reveals an out-of-balance picture with regard to race. Roosevelt's general population is predominantly of Hispanic ethnicity, with a growing population of students from countries such as Laos and Cambodia. The arts magnet is a healthy mix of a number of races; about half of the students are white.

When inequities are evident, or suspected, programs in schools may become controversial. The difference between the two high school populations is not unusual, but the discrepancies are much more pronounced in the AP classes, which are the most academically challenging in any school and designed for students who have mastered foundational content. At the end of an AP course students take a rigorous exam, with passing scores resulting in college credit. AP classes are often more expensive to run than others because they are typically smaller, with teachers required to attend special institutes to qualify to teach the courses. Some research studies show that students who take AP classes, regardless of how they do on the exam, fare better in college.

Derek Boucher acknowledges that opportunities to be part of AP classes are available to all Roosevelt students because they cross the regular/magnet barrier. He also knows that walking into an AP class reveals a visible gap regarding which students actually enroll in these advanced courses. They are mostly, and some are exclusively, white. Derek is aware that this is a controversial and complex issue with no easy remedies.

Respond to these dilemmas by writing one well-developed paragraph for each.

1. Because doing well in AP classes requires students to have foundational knowledge and skills, how might Derek and his colleagues go about beginning the process of increasing diversity in AP classes at Roosevelt?

2. When students are chosen for AP classes, would adding several minority students who come close to qualifying have a positive effect on them? If you believe this to be true, explain your reasoning. If, on the other hand, you think this would not be good for the students who do not actually qualify, explain your reasoning.

We return to discussions of school levels as we address various aspects of the teaching profession. Each time the information will build on previous topics so you will have a view of the big picture of what teaching is like in each level. Regardless of the level you decide to teach, your school will be in one of three settings.

What Are the Three Principal Settings of U.S. Schools?

When it comes to schooling, geography has a major impact. Sometimes a mile or two is significant with regard to educational experiences. The commonly accepted categories of rural, suburban, and urban schools that exist in all 50 states probably conjure up images in your mind, generalized impressions of what each embodies. This section refines those images.

An in-focus view will reveal some generalities about the context of schooling in each of three areas: rural, suburban, and urban. The day-to-day realities of children both in and out of school within these three settings may be vastly different in terms of home, socioeconomic circumstances, and school opportunities. These differences may reflect the expectations held by parents, community, and educators of what children can do and be. Most teachers can do little to alter the out-of-school realities faced by schools and schoolchildren. However, what teachers can alter are the ways they view students and their potential. It's a matter of values—both teachers' and students'.

RURAL SCHOOLS

About a third of schools across the United States are in **rural** communities. In Montana, over 70% of the state's schools are rural. Twenty percent of Alaska's schools employ three or fewer teachers each (Carter, 2003).

Most rural schools are smaller than urban and suburban schools. However, some draw students from an area that may encompass hundreds of square miles and have large student populations. A single primary school, elementary school, middle school, and high school, each with more than 800 students, may serve such a large geographic area.

Geographic isolation often means that students may have few of the opportunities and experiences found in more populated areas, such as museums and performing arts. Even basic services that people in suburban and urban areas take for granted, such as hospitals and large libraries, may not be readily available.

A high school of 100 to 200 students that is over an hour away from a medium-size town may have difficulty offering ample opportunities for what's commonly viewed as a well-rounded education. Think about it. To offer adequate coursework, a high school must employ certified subject-area teachers. Supporting an algebra II class of 6 costs just about as much as supporting a class of 28. Regardless of class size, the course requires a teacher and a classroom. Small high schools face similar constraints in offering extracurricular opportunities. It may be difficult to offer French club, debate team, football and basketball teams, and orchestra.

Hiring and retaining qualified teachers in small or large rural schools is a significant problem, even though the schools may be community oriented centers in safe, scenic places. However, the benefits that may accompany a rural area such as ready access to recreation and natural beauty may outweigh any perceived drawbacks.

SUBURBAN SCHOOLS

Suburban schools most often serve students who live in single-family homes with grassy yards in areas dotted with shopping centers, places of worship, and recreational facilities. Apartment complexes and townhouses are scattered among the well-lit paved streets. Every few miles or so, there's a school.

Many people who live in the suburbs are likely to be in the middle-class to affluent socioeconomic spectrum. Their communities are basically safe places with adequate public services that provide a generally comfortable lifestyle. The schools, even in tight state budget situations, generally continue to operate at acceptable levels with tolerable class sizes, textbooks for each child in most subjects, and satisfactory building maintenance. Within suburban schools

Points of Reflection 2.9

Did you live in a rural area, a suburb, or an urban setting? How would you describe the setting(s) of your PreK–12 experiences? If you had the opportunity to live in more than one setting, what do you recall about the differences?

Points of Reflection 2.10

When you graduate with teacher certification, would you consider moving to an isolated rural area where you may be needed, but where there are no shopping malls, no theaters, and few single people under age 50? Does this lifestyle appeal to you? If so, why?

students generally experience organization and order, extracurricular opportunities, and some degree of community participation and approval. These factors don't necessarily mean that students are learning at optimal levels, but there are some obvious advantages.

Many families choose to live in the suburbs and in small- to medium-size towns primarily because of what the schools offer their children. Real estate agents have long known that the public school options for specific residential areas have much to do with property appeal. Families desire stability and a satisfactory free education. If they can afford it, they buy homes in locations that will fulfill these desires. Do they get what they pay for? Most would probably say yes.

Points of Reflection 2.11

Did you grow up in a suburban area? Do you enjoy the conveniences these areas generally afford? Is this type of location where you want to spend your teaching career? If so, why? If not, why not?

URBAN SCHOOLS

Most **urban** school settings are in sharp contrast to those of suburban schools. The facilities tend to be older, part of the fabric of downtowns that may or may not continue to be vibrant community areas. While architecturally appealing, the older buildings are generally more expensive and difficult to maintain and may be in a state of disrepair more often than suburban school buildings.

Urban schools are likely to serve many students who live in low-income settings. Although funding differences certainly exist between some urban and suburban areas, as poignantly related by Jonathan Kozol in *Savage Inequalities* (1991), some urban schools actually receive more funding per student than do suburban schools. One reason for this is that the federal government has programs that provide extra money for schools with

A few miles can make a significant difference in the school experience of students. At Wells High School in San Francisco, students look out the window to see Alamo Hill and the city skyline. Just 30 miles north of the city, students look out the window of Bolinas-Stinson Elementary at sea lions in Bolinas Lagoon. Sara Davis Powell

Schools

TABLE 2.4 Comparison of schools in rural, suburban, and urban settings

Setting	Definition of Setting	Percentage of All Public Schools	Advantages	Challenges
Rural	Designated area with fewer than 2,500 people	31%	Smaller schools; community ownership	Inadequate tax base for funding; difficulty hiring qualified teachers; geographic isolation
Suburban	Neighborhoods and small- to medium-size towns located on the fringes of large cities	44%	Families with higher socioeconomic status; relative ease of hiring qualified teachers	Satisfying various factions in the community; making continuous improvements
Urban	Cities that have large downtowns and a dense population	25%	Possibility of making large gains in student learning	Low socioeconomic status of many families; problems associated with low expectations; low levels of parental/family education

Source: National Elementary and Secondary School Enrollment Model, National Center for Education Statistics, 2003.

Points of Reflection 2.12

Is this the kind of challenge you might want to tackle? Can you see yourself nurturing and guiding students who may depend on you for encouragement to see beyond their current circumstances?

student populations living below certain economic levels. Research supports the assertion that students from low-income families require more resources to perform at the same levels as students from middle-income families.

Many urban school settings present some unique challenges. The students in urban schools more often come to school with greater needs than can be met by the curriculum alone (Scherer, 2005).

Table 2.4 illustrates some of the general distinctions among rural, suburban, and urban schools. Keep in mind that there are exceptions in every setting and that schools in every setting can make effective teaching and learning connections.

What Is an Effective School?

Effective schools meet the learning needs of the students who attend them. What are the characteristics of an effective school? Theorists and practitioners have attempted to measure schools' effectiveness for decades. Grappling with what elements characterize effective schools keeps the conversation alive. The minute we say, "Okay. This is it. If a school does this list of things in these ways, it is effective," we will box in our thinking and become stagnant. Still, although characteristics may vary in many ways, we need a picture of what effective schools may look like and what students and teachers do in them.

CHARACTERISTICS OF EFFECTIVE SCHOOLS

The Equal Educational Opportunity Survey in 1966, commonly referred to as the **Coleman Report,** concluded that family and community factors, such as poverty and parental levels of education, prevented some children from learning; that no matter what schools did, some children would not be successful. Appalled by this assertion, many in

Schools

the education community adopted the mantra "All children can learn." President Lyndon B. Johnson responded in the late 1960s with landmark legislation, the Elementary and Secondary Education Act, which, among other things, provided extra funding for schools with high numbers of children from low-income homes, called **Title I funding**. In the 1970s, President Gerald Ford expanded equal educational opportunity by signing **Public Law 94-142,** making special education services a right, not a privilege.

In the 1970s, the **Effective Schools Movement** was initiated based on the belief that all children can learn. This movement was designed to locate schools deemed effective for all children and to identify common characteristics among these schools. The basic tenets of these identified schools included the following:

- All children can learn.
- Schools control enough of the variables to make it happen.
- Schools should be accountable for measuring achievement to be certain that all children, regardless of gender, race, ethnicity, or socioeconomic status, are learning.
- All schools require qualified and capable people to ensure that all children learn.

Effective Schools research, led primarily by Ronald Edmonds and Lawrence Lezotte, concluded that there are seven elements relating to effective schools. These elements, or correlates, listed in Figure 2.7, are all associated with improved student learning. Examining schools in light of these elements reveals areas of needed improvement.

In 2010 the Bill and Melinda Gates Foundation accepted the challenge to determine what characteristics effective teachers possess that translate into effective schools. Designating six large school districts across the United States for participation in the study, the Gates Foundation pledged over $500 million to the task. Educators and the general public await the results of this largest study to date on teacher and school effectiveness.

Effective schools may be found in rural, suburban, and urban areas. They may be early childhood, elementary, middle, or high schools. They serve any range of colors, classes, and ethnicities of students. School effectiveness exists where students are learning and experiencing positive personal growth, facilitated by teachers who make a difference.

WE MAKE A DIFFERENCE

We make a difference when we ask ourselves and one another "And how are the children?" in conjunction with our best efforts to facilitate learning. According to Kati Haycock, director of The Education Trust, what schools do makes a huge difference in whether students learn. She asserts that what matters most is good teaching (Haycock, 2003). Quality teachers

Figure 2.7 The seven correlates of effective schools

1. *Clear and focused mission.* The school staff shares a commitment to instructional goals, priorities, and accountability, and they accept responsibility for students learning their curricular goals.
2. *High expectations for success.* The school staff believes, and demonstrates that belief, that all students can master essential content and skills.
3. *Instructional leadership.* The principal is the instructional leader who persistently communicates the school mission to staff, students, and parents.
4. *Frequent monitoring of student progress.* Student academic progress is measured frequently in a variety of ways. The results are used to improve instruction and student performance.
5. *Opportunity to learn and student time on task.* Students are engaged in learning essential content and skills for a significant amount of the school day.
6. *Safe and orderly environment.* Schools are orderly, purposeful, and free from threat of physical harm. The climate is conducive to learning.
7. *Positive home-school relations.* Parents understand and support the school's mission and have opportunities to play important roles in helping to achieve the school's mission.

Source: Lezotte, L. W. (1991). *Correlates of effective schools: The first and second generation.* Okemos, MI: Effective Schools Products.

for every student will enhance a school's effectiveness. The education of quality teachers, the hiring and retention of quality teachers, and the continuing professional growth of quality teachers are key elements of effective schools, where a balance exists between students' academic achievement and personal development.

CONCLUDING THOUGHTS

George Albano, 25-year veteran principal of Lincoln Elementary School in Mount Vernon, New York, can answer "And how are the children? Are they all well?" by stating that 99% of his school's fourth graders made it over the New York state achievement bar in English, math, and science even though more than 50% are eligible for free or reduced-price lunch and 60% are African American or Hispanic. He leads an effective school where the achievement gap is nonexistent, and students are in the care of competent teachers who make them feel valued. Albano puts it this way, "Success comes down to hard work; great and dedicated teachers; an integrated curriculum; lots of art, music, and physical education; the willingness to bend and break rules occasionally; and the complete refusal to let any child fail to learn" (Merrow, 2004, p. 456).

Your challenge is clear. Be the generation of teachers who figures it out—the teachers who bring us closer to quality, effective education for all students.

After reading the *Chapter in Review,* interact with Brandi Wade in this chapter's *Developing Professional Competence*.

Chapter in Review

What are the purposes of public schools in the United States?

- Although often used interchangeably, there are distinctions between education and schooling. Education happens continually through all of life's experiences, whereas schooling is the formal structure of teaching and learning.
- Transmitting and reconstructing society are two complementary purposes of U.S. schooling.
- Teaching students how to participate positively in society while facilitating academic learning are two complementary purposes of U.S. schooling.
- There is no conflict between meeting individual student needs and collective student needs.
- Although schooling in the United States sustains students for today, it also prepares them for tomorrow.

What is the culture of a school?

- The culture of a school is the context of the learning experiences, as well as adult and student behaviors and attitudes.
- A school's culture can be a positive force for learning, or a negative influence that interferes with learning, and all shades in between.
- Teachers have an enormous impact on a school's culture.

How do school venues differ?

- There is a great variety of schools in the United States, from the traditional neighborhood public school to the ultimate private school, the home.
- Traditional public schools have education programs that suit most students.
- Full-service schools attend to the academic, health, and social service needs of students and families, and, in many cases, of the community.
- A magnet school is a public school with a specific theme or focus.
- A charter school is a public school that operates under a contract negotiated between the initiator of the school and an oversight agency to which the school is accountable. Charter schools are free from many of the regulations that apply to other public schools.
- Alternative schools are schools designed to meet the needs of students who are not successful in traditional schools.
- Private schools may or may not be affiliated with a religious organization.
- Single-gender schools, almost all of which are private, are schools for boys only or for girls only.
- Homeschooling is a growing trend in the United States.

- For-profit schools are run by management companies. The concept is controversial when applied to public schools.
- School choice plans provide students and parents with options in both the public and private sectors.

What is school like at different levels?

- Early childhood education spans birth through age 8, or roughly through third grade.
- Elementary education may include a variety of grade levels, with K–5 or 6 as the most common. Early childhood and elementary overlap on the low end; elementary and middle overlap on the high end.
- Middle school education usually includes grades 6 to 8.
- High school education includes grades 9 to 12.

What are the three principal settings of U.S. schools?

- Urban settings are cities with large downtowns and a dense population. Urban schools are likely to have a high percentage of minority students from low-income homes.
- Suburban settings are distinct locations that include neighborhoods and small- to medium-size towns that have grown up on the fringe of cities. Suburban schools are likely to have a lower percentage of minorities, with most students coming from middle- or upper-income homes.
- Rural settings are areas with population under 2,500 and few retail stores and services. Rural schools may be all white, all minority, or integrated to some extent, depending on the area.

What is an effective school?

- Effective schools are those that meet the learning needs of the students who attend them.
- Effective schools may have a variety of characteristics, with quality teaching as the most important common element.

Developing Professional Competence

Visit the Developing Professional Competence section on Chapter 2 of the MyEducationLab for this text to answer the following questions and begin your preparation for licensure exams.

You first met Brandi Wade in **Meet the Focus Teachers and Students**. Then in the beginning of this chapter you learned more about Brandi and Summit Primary School.

Brandi enjoys the fact that as a kindergarten teacher she benefits from having all the other district kindergarten teachers in her building. Recall that as a K–2 school, Summit Primary houses all the kindergarten, first grade, and second grade classes in the Licking Heights, Ohio, school district. However, as the district grows and diversifies, community members and individuals on the school board are talking about creating neighborhood schools, five for grades K to 5, three for grades 6 to 8, and two high schools for grades 9 to 12.

Think about this dilemma from the perspectives of a variety of **stakeholders,** or those who have legitimate involvement and stand to gain or lose from the situation. Answer the following multiple-choice questions:

1. Brandi and the other kindergarten teachers think their teaching is more effective because of their collective expertise. They want to stay together. All of the following support the teachers' desire to stay together except
   a. They can share ideas among nine teachers, rather than two or three that would result from structure changes.
   b. If there is a problem student, they have more options for classrooms for him or her.
   c. New programs are easier to implement because they can help each other.
   d. Materials are easier to manage.

2. Teachers of grades 3 to 6 in the intermediate school next door see the value of smaller schools that would be created if the county divides into school zones and also moves grade 6 to the middle school. With

Schools

four grade levels, they have over 1,000 children in one building, with projected growth to 1,300 by next fall if nothing changes. Which rationale is the least important to their desire to see the district change grade-level configurations?

   a. There is no place large enough to gather all the students for special events.

   b. Research shows there is more violence and bad behavior in large schools than in small schools.

   c. Research shows that children feel a greater sense of belonging in a small school than in a large school, regardless of class size.

   d. Having grades K to 5 in one building may lend to more family stability, especially for those with several children in the grade range.

3. Teachers in the current middle school that now includes grades 7 and 8 think that participation in after-school activities would increase if kids lived closer to the school they attend. It's very difficult to have after-school clubs and sports when most students are bused to school from all across the county. From a student's standpoint, which of the following would be the least important reason for creating schools that are physically more accessible to all students who attend?

   a. A school with fewer students, based on a smaller geographic area, will allow students more opportunities to be involved in a variety of activities.

   b. The schools would be more ecologically friendly because more students could walk to them.

   c. Students could go to school with others in their immediate vicinity, making it more likely that their friends live close enough to socialize on weekends or after school.

   d. In smaller schools students tend to know each other and their teachers better.

4. Many community members, including parents, believe that smaller schools with wider grade bands located throughout the county will be best for the Licking Heights district. In the plan, Summit High School, which is now a full-service school with a health clinic and adult education classes, would be divided into two smaller schools. Why might two high schools, strategically located in the county, benefit students and their families more?

   a. High school sports teams would have competition within the district, allowing for more playing time for athletes.

   b. Competition between the two high schools would increase enthusiasm in the community.

   c. Research has shown that higher percentages of students in small schools get involved in activities more than students in larger schools.

   d. A full-service school with a health clinic in a central location at the large school has not proven to be useful.

5. Some parents and alums are opposed to breaking up Summit High School into two schools. Which of the following may explain some of their reasons?

   a. A large county high school has a better chance of having an excellent record of athletic championships.

   b. A larger school provides more curricular opportunities for students.

   c. Both a and b.

   d. Neither a nor b.

Now it's time for you to respond to two short essay items involving the scenario. In your responses, be sure to address all the dilemmas and questions posed in each item. Each response should be between one half and one double-spaced page.

6. Brandi and several other kindergarten teachers plan to present their case for keeping the district schools in their current configuration at a school board meeting. What do you think their three strongest arguments will be?

7. Do you predict the district will reconfigure the schools? If so, explain why. If not, explain your reasons for thinking the schools will remain in their current configuration.

Where
DO I Stand NOW?

In the beginning of this chapter you completed an inventory that gauged your interest in teaching students in a particualr level, the teaching setting you prefer, and your preference for either public or private schools. Now that you have read the chapter, completed exercises related to the content, engaged in class discussions, and so on, answer the following questions in your course notebook.

1. What have you learned about the four levels of school that has affected your choice of students with whom you want to work? Did you learn something that confirmed your original choice? If so, what? Did you learn something that has made you change your preference or at least consider another level? If so, explain.

2. With which setting are you most familiar? What did you learn through this chapter about rural education? How about suburban schools? What did you learn about urban schools? Has your original preference changed? If so, how?

3. If you originally had a preference for either public or private schools, have your experiences through this chapter confirmed your preference or changed your mind? Explain.

MyEducationLab

The MyEducationLab for this course can help you solidify your comprehension of Chapter 2 concepts.

- Explore the classrooms of the teachers and students you've met in this chapter in the Teaching in Focus section.
- Prepare for licensure exams as you deepen your understanding of chapter concepts in the Developing Professional Competence section.

- Gauge and further develop your understanding of chapter concepts by taking the quizzes and examining the enrichment materials on the Chapter 2 Study Plan.
- Visit Topic 2, Schools and Society, to watch ABC videos, explore Assignments and Activities, and practice essential teaching skills with the Building Teaching Skills and Dispositions unit.

References

Barnett, W. S. (2003). Preschool: The most important grade. *Educational Leadership, 60*(7), 54–57.

Barth, R. S. (2001). *Learning by heart*. San Francisco: Jossey-Bass.

Carter, G. R. (2003). *NCLB and the diverse needs of rural schools*. Retrieved September 26, 2004, from www.ascd.org/cms/index.cfm

EdisonLearning, Inc. (2010). About us. Retrieved March 15, 2010, from http://www.edison learning.com/about_us

Eisner, E. W. (2004). Preparing for today and tomorrow. *Educational Leadership, 64*(6), 6.

Goodlad, J. I. (1984). *A place called school*. New York: McGraw-Hill.

Haycock, K. (2003). Toward a fair distribution of teacher talent. *Educational Leadership, 60*(4), 11–15.

Kostelnik, M. J., Soderman, A. K., & Whiren, A. P. (2004). *Developmentally appropriate curriculum: Best practices in early childhood education* (3rd ed.). Upper Saddle River, NJ: Merrill/Prentice Hall.

Kozol, J. (1991). *Savage inequalities: Children in America's schools*. New York: Crown.

Lezotte, L. W. (1991). *Correlates of effective schools: The first and second generation*. Okemos, MI: Effective Schools Products.

Merrow, J. (2004). Meeting superman. *Phi Delta Kappan, 85*(6), 455–460.

Morrison, G. S. (2008). *Fundamentals of early childhood education* (5th ed.). Upper Saddle River, NJ: Merrill.

National Center for Education Statistics [NCES]. (2003). *National elementary and secondary school enrollment model*. Retrieved August 2, 2005, from http://www.nces.ed.gov/pubs2003

National Center for Education Statistics [NCES]. (2004). *National household education survey*. Retrieved March 16, 2007, from http://nces.ed.gov/quicktables/result.asp? SrchKeyword=national+household+education+ survey&topic=All&Year=2004

National Center for Education Statistics [NCES]. (2010). *Digest of education statistics, 2009*. Washington, DC: U.S. Department of Education.

National Middle School Association. (2010). *This we believe: Keys to educating young adolescents*. Westerville, OH: Author.

Roberts, P. L., Kellough, R. D., & Moore, K. (2006). *A resource guide for elementary school teachers* (6th ed.). Upper Saddle River, NJ: Merrill/Prentice Hall.

Scherer, M. (2005). Our cities, ourselves. *Educational Leadership, 62*(6), 7.

Snyder, T. D., Dillow, S. A., & Hoffman, C. M. (2009). *Digest of education statistics, 2008* (NCES 2009-020). National Center for Education Statistics, Institute of Education Sciences. Washington, DC: U.S. Department of Education.

U.S. Department of Education. (2010). Elementary and Secondary Education Act (ESEA). Retrieved July 31, 2010, from www2.ed.gov/policy/elsec/leg/ esea02/beginning.html

Curriculum and Instruction

Sara Davis Powell

In this chapter we explore what is taught in U.S. schools, along with a variety of teaching and learning strategies. Here are the questions we focus on in this chapter:

✦ What is the formal curriculum?

✦ What other curricula do we teach in U.S. schools?

✦ How is instruction implemented in U.S. schools?

✦ How do teachers match instruction to school levels?

It's time to move from the "who" of school—the students and teachers—to the "what" and "how." **Curriculum** is the educational term for what students experience in schools, and **instruction** encompasses the strategies used to convey the curriculum and achieve the desired end result of student learning. Curriculum and instruction are interdependent in the sense that content (curriculum) is meaningless without methods (instruction) to convey it, and those methods are useless without the content of the curriculum. Explore your stance on curriculum and instruction by completing this chapter's *Where Do I Stand?*

Shutterstock

From Chapter 4 of *Your Introduction to Education: Explorations in Teaching*, 2/e. Sara Davis Powell.

Where DO I Stand?

The purpose of this inventory is to determine where you stand concerning what is taught and how it is taught in PreK–12 schools. After reading an item, indicate your level of agreement by choosing a number and placing it in the blank before the statement. Following the inventory are directions for how to organize your responses and what they may indicate in terms of where you stand.

4   I strongly agree
3   I agree
2   I don't have an opinion
1   I disagree
0   I strongly disagree

_____ **1.** What students learn in school is basically what the school plans for them to learn.

_____ **2.** Teaching in ways that meet the needs of students with differing aptitudes is important.

_____ **3.** Much of what is learned in schools is unintentional on the part of teachers.

_____ **4.** Most of what is taught in school should be stable and not swayed by society.

_____ **5.** If only English language arts, math, science, and social studies were taught, schools would still fulfill their primary purposes of educating children and adolescents.

_____ **6.** Basing learning on real-world situations is an excellent way to teach.

_____ **7.** Projects provide ideal learning opportunities.

_____ **8.** Teacher-led class discussion is one of the most effective teaching strategies.

_____ **9.** The expectations of society should guide what is taught in schools.

_____ **10.** Although interesting, classes that don't directly address English language arts, math, science, and social studies are not important in fulfilling the primary purposes of U.S. schools.

_____ **11.** After-school clubs and organizations are important to the education of students.

_____ **12.** The teacher should be the focus of attention in the classroom.

_____ **13.** We teach who we are in the classroom.

_____ **14.** Our vision of the future should heavily influence what is taught in U.S. schools.

_____ **15.** Some students should be allowed to go through some topics more quickly than other students.

_____ **16.** Music, visual arts, and dance should be part of a public school education.

_____ **17.** Teaching reading and writing is the responsibility of all teachers at all levels.

_____ **18.** Concentrating on one subject at a time is best for student learning.

_____ **19.** What is taught in schools should not be impacted by cultural diversity.

_____ **20.** Lecture is a preferable way to teach for maximum learning.

_____ **21.** There are benefits associated with student collaboration.

_____ **22.** It is more important to master the basic subjects than to learn how to think critically.

_____ **23.** There is a core of knowledge that should dominate what is taught in PreK–12 school.

_____ **24.** Student learning opportunities depend on what teachers teach.

Now let's analyze your responses. Remember, there are no wrong answers. _Find six sums, A to F, based on your responses to the numbered items as indicated._

ITEM #	MY VIEW	ITEM #	MY VIEW	ITEM #	MY VIEW	ITEM #	MY VIEW	ITEM #	MY VIEW	ITEM #	MY VIEW
1		3		2		8		4		6	
5		11		7		12		19		9	
10		13		15		20		23		14	
18		16		21		24		sum E		sum F	
22		17		sum C		sum D					
sum A		sum B									

**If sum A is larger than sum B,** _you believe there is a basic group of subjects that should dominate what is taught. The learning experiences are carefully planned and little is left to spontaneity. Courses or experiences other than what are planned are secondary._

**If sum B is larger than sum A,** _you believe in a broader scope of what should be part of student experiences. Teacher personality and demeanor figure into student learning, as do classes not considered basic and after-school activities._

**If sum C is larger than sum D,** _your preferred approach to teaching and learning is student centered._ _**If sum D is larger than sum C,**_ _your preferred approach to teaching and learning is teacher centered._

**If sum E is larger than sum F,** _you believe that what is taught in schools should be stable and not altered based on societal changes._

**If sum F is larger than sum E,** _you believe that at least some of what is taught in schools should be responsive to societal changes._

Now that you have explored your opinions, let's discuss curriculum and instruction in the United States, beginning with what we call the formal curriculum. _You will recognize the statements and ideas in Where Do I Stand? as you read._

Teaching in Focus

Chris Roberts is an adventurer. He travels extensively, climbs mountains, and rafts in white water. He could do lots of things with his life—and he does. But his career choice is teaching 9-, 10-, and 11-year-olds at Rees Elementary School, Utah.

It takes only a few minutes in Chris's multiage classroom to recognize how his energy and wide range of interests influence how he interacts with students. He teaches all the core elementary subjects, as well as the dance component of the arts emphasis at Rees. When asked what he gets out of teaching, Chris says, "I like to play, I love these kids, and learning is the most exciting thing in the world."

You won't find references to the fascinating displays in Chris's classroom in his lesson plans. Nor will you find "Tell the kids about my last dive off the Yucatan" or "Let my students know that life is a wonderful adventure." When Chris infuses his hobbies, interests, and travel into his classroom, he is teaching what we define later as the informal curriculum—lessons that aren't in a curriculum guide. The cartoons with philosophical messages, the inspirational stories and poems, the giant topographical map of Utah, the newspaper and magazine clippings about people who triumphed over unimaginably difficult circumstances, and the personal family photographs—all of it speaks to who Chris is and what he values.

As you look around his classroom during the room tour in the Teaching in Focus section for Chapter 4 in MyEducationLab for this course, Chris Roberts's personality, interests, and philosophy of life are evident.

What Is the Formal Curriculum?

The **formal curriculum** encompasses what is intentionally taught within the stated goals for student learning. The formal curriculum, sometimes referred to as the **explicit curriculum,** is what teachers are expected to teach, what students are expected to learn, and what society expects of schools. The formal curriculum is based on three foundations: the needs of the subject, the needs of students, and the needs of society (Gunter, Estes, & Mintz, 2007). These three needs align with what John Dewey conveyed in two of his most important books, *School and Society* (1900) and *The Child and the Curriculum* (1902). The titles speak volumes, as does the text, about the interconnectedness of society, students, and the subject matter itself. Dewey (1938) also emphasized that formal curriculum is dynamic, meaning that it is continually changing and evolving. Later in the chapter we explore three other kinds of curricula that contribute to the experiences of students in schools: informal, extra, and null.

As we consider the formal curriculum, we must acknowledge the guiding contributions of Ralph Tyler (1949), one of Dewey's students. Tyler developed what is now called the **Tyler Rationale,** proposing four questions that should be asked throughout the stages of curriculum development. Each question is examined in this text as indicated.

1. What educational purposes should the school seek to attain?
2. What educational experiences can be provided that are likely to attain these purposes?
3. How can these educational experiences be effectively organized?
4. How can we determine whether these purposes are being attained?

Before about 1990, broad guidelines for what to teach were developed primarily by state planning committees and were based largely on textbook content, federal educational goals, and a "this is the way it's always been" attitude. Individual schools and teachers refined the state or school district guidelines to suit their particular circumstances. However, in 1989 curriculum development moved abruptly into what might be called the **era of standards** when the National Council of Teachers of Mathematics (NCTM) published math standards for grades K to 12, the first official set of standards written for a core subject area (NCTM, 2000).

Curriculum and Instruction

STANDARDS INFLUENCE WHAT WE TEACH

Very simply put, **content standards** define what students should know and be able to do relative to subject areas at specific grade levels. Standards help organize and guide teaching and learning in the classroom.

Following NCTM's lead, the professional organizations of other core subject areas developed subject-specific content standards. Each professional organization is quick to say that its standards are not the curriculum but should be used to develop a cohesive plan for what is taught. When we discuss the individual subjects of the formal curriculum, we'll learn more about professional organizations and the standards that guide what teachers teach and students learn within specific disciplines.

Two other types of standards influence curriculum. **Performance standards,** or **benchmarks,** designate the level of the knowledge or skill that's considered acceptable within a particular grade level. Some standards documents also include **process standards** that support content learning by explaining both how the content might best be learned and how to use the content once it is acquired. For example, the five broad areas of NCTM content standards—number and operations, algebra, geometry, measurement, data analysis/probability—are accompanied by five process standards: problem solving, reasoning and proof, communication, connections, and representation.

STATE STANDARDS. Because the Constitution does not specifically address education, what is taught and learned in U.S. schools is largely left up to individual states. By the beginning of the 21st century, virtually every state had content standards in place, leading to what may some call the **standards-based reform movement,** another way of expressing the era of standards.

Although most state standards are based on professional organization standards, there are variations among them. When the 2001 reauthorization of the Elementary and Secondary Education Act, the No Child Left Behind Act, required accountability, state standards and the associated standards-based testing became key to meeting this mandate. The pressure was on to show student achievement and improvement. The competitive nature of states, with their test results stacked up against one another, inevitably lead to comparisons between state-determined results and results from the National Assessment of Educational Progress (NAEP). This comparison revealed major discrepancies, indicating that some state standards and tests are not as rigorous as others. Some states report high levels of proficiency among their students only to have NAEP results imply that the state's students are not measuring up. In other words, it's easier to look good with regard to test results when standards are lower and tests are easier.

In part because some states appear unwilling to raise standards even in light of their apparent lack of rigor, there is increasing momentum to adopt common standards to which all states adhere.

NATIONAL STANDARDS. In this second decade of the 21st century, efforts aimed at the adoption of national standards are in full swing. Interestingly, the push for national standards, which would mean in a practical sense a national common curriculum, comes from two organizations that are made up of representatives from all of the states: the **National Governors Association** (NGA) and the **Council of Chief State School Officers** (CCSSO). These organizations have joined together to work on the **Common Core State Standards Initiative**.

With mounting research indicating state-to-state differences in standards and testing, the federal government is putting funding on the line. President Obama and Secretary of Education Arne Duncan are spearheading **Race to the Top,** an initiative that challenges states to make bold efforts to improve teaching and learning. Over $4 billion in federal money was awarded to 11 states in 2010, with one of the four required specific areas of improvement for individual states linked directly to alignment with common, internationally competitive standards and testing.

The debate over whether content standards should be state specific or uniform for the entire United States, and, if so, what those standards should be, will no doubt continue for a number of years. As we more closely examine the issues, objections to the standards currently in place in individual states surface.

Curriculum and Instruction

Points of Reflection 4.1

Did your teachers refer to standards in your PreK–12 experiences? Do you think individual states should be allowed to develop standards based on state needs and priorities? Why or why not? Do you think we should have the same standards for all students in the United States? Why or why not?

OBJECTIONS TO STANDARDS. Although grade-level-specific, subject-based standards have brought unprecedented organization to what is taught and when, they are not perfect documents. Some of the most noted flaws of state content standards include:

- excessive coverage—the sheer volume of standards in any content area may be overwhelmingly impractical
- fragmentation of learning—isolated bits and pieces of knowledge and skills may not be connected and therefore lose context and meaning
- details that obscure major ideas—too many details may keep students and teachers from "seeing the forest for the trees"
- broad concepts that are too nebulous—standards written in broad generalities can be open to many interpretations
- lack of consistency—state standards, and subsequent standards-based testing, are uneven with some more demanding than others
- a less flexible way of teaching—many experienced teachers find adherence to sets of standards inhibiting when compared to a curriculum that gives more choices
- high-stakes accountability—standards lead to testing, the results of which determine student grade-level retention, school status, teachers' jobs, and availability of funds, among other major consequences
- decisions influenced by disagreeing factions—liberals and conservatives, religious and nonreligious all battle for inclusion and exclusion of content, making standards "political footballs"

All of these objections and more are to be expected because any reform measure that changes the way teachers teach and students learn is bound to be controversial. The debate is healthy and keeps the process alive and dynamic. Regardless of the controversy, standards give teachers information about what students should have learned in the past and must learn in the future. Using grade-level-specific standards for planning helps teachers fit their expectations into the bigger picture of student learning over time. Along with standards, another major factor impacts what is taught on a daily basis: the textbook.

TEXTBOOKS

One of the most influential determiners of what we teach has historically been the *textbook*. Now that adherence to standards in the content areas is mandated by states, textbooks may have lost a little of their power to shape curriculum. However, if a textbook publisher responds to the standards movement by aligning content and skills with state standards, textbooks are likely to guide teaching on a daily basis.

TEXTBOOKS IN THE CLASSROOM. Quality textbooks help organize and sequence course content. They provide a logical progression of topics, with content and skills that build on prior understanding and skill mastery. For instance, a social studies text will be organized chronologically so learners see how events impact subsequent events. A math textbook helps learners build on prior knowledge and skills in logical ways as they move, for instance, from recognition of geometric shapes to finding perimeter and then area in elementary geometry.

Teachers base up to 90% of classroom assignments and homework on textbooks and the accompanying supplements (Jones, 2000). Supplementary materials may provide options for enrichment, remediation, extension, application, and practice of skills, as well as lesson plans to guide teachers, online assistance, workbooks, tests, and a variety of other resources for both students and parents. These options allow teachers to more easily tailor content to student needs and readiness.

HOW TEXTBOOKS ARE SELECTED. About half the states have a statewide textbook adoption process, meaning that a committee at the state level chooses several books for each subject/level from which school districts may choose particular texts for use in local schools. In other states, school districts choose their texts directly. Whatever the process or at whatever level of governance, citizens are generally invited to give input. Teachers, as citizens, are encouraged to provide input, but few choose to do so, either indicating a level of trust in those who ultimately make the choices or a lack of time to become familiar with possible books.

Textbook publishing is big business. It would not be economically feasible for publishers to tailor textbooks to every state's standards. Textbook publishers often customize content to more closely align with the content standards of large states with a statewide adoption process such as Texas, California, Florida, and North Carolina.

LIMITATIONS OF TEXTBOOKS. We should be aware that while textbooks can be powerful, and generally positive, influences on what we teach and students learn, they may also pose the following problems:

- Textbook content may not match standards.
- Textbooks may include too many topics and few in adequate depth.
- There may be readability issues as the textbooks attempt to be readable for a range of abilities.
- Textbook authors may avoid interesting but controversial topics to please constituent groups.
- Textbooks may lack content or be of poor quality, problems perhaps masked by concentration on making the books colorful and appealing.
- Textbooks may exhibit bias related to conservative or liberal ideology, culture, race, gender, and the like, either overtly or by omission.

You probably will not have much choice when it comes to textbooks available for your use. Be conscious of both their value and their limitations, knowing that textbooks have a significant impact on what we teach and what students learn in the subject areas of the formal curriculum. But although standards and textbooks have considerable influence on what we teach, the various levels of government also have influence because our public schools are precisely that—public.

GOVERNMENT INFLUENCES WHAT WE TEACH

Because most everyone in the United States has attended school, most of us think we know a lot about what should be taught, as well as how to teach it. This attitude, in part, leads to influence of levels of government on education.

Local government generally has little to do with standards and textbooks, but involved local citizens serve on school boards and, as such, have some say in how schools function. The state level of government, however, exerts a good deal of influence because most standards and other curricular decisions are made at the state level. Governors, legislators, and officials within state departments of education influence what is taught and learned in public schools.

The federal government, although not directly dictating standards, has significant influence on how schools educate students through laws that have been passed, most notably since the Russian launch of *Sputnik* in 1957 that created a sense of urgency in terms of improving U.S. education in a competitive world. Once the National Defense Education Act of 1958 created math, science, and foreign language priorities, other federal legislation was passed in rapid succession that continues to influence what we teach and how we teach it, including the following:

- Economic Opportunity Act of 1964 made vocational training a priority.
- Civil Rights Act of 1964 prohibited discrimination, with the stated goal of equal access to quality education.
- Elementary and Secondary Education Act of 1965 established Title I status, intended to increase funding in schools with large populations of economically disadvantaged children.

Points of Reflection 4.2

What do you remember about using textbooks in your PreK–12 experiences? Were they major determiners of what was taught and learned? Were they interesting to read? Did they help increase your understanding and skills?

- Bilingual Education Act of 1968 ensured the teaching of the curriculum in native languages as students learned English.
- Title IX legislation of 1972 provided for more girls to participate in athletics.
- Individuals with Disabilities Education Act of 1975 made participation in public education of students with disabilities a right rather than a privilege.
- No Child Left Behind Act of 2001, one of several reauthorizations of the Elementary and Secondary Education Act of 1965, required states to maintain curricular standards, test all students on the standards' knowledge and skills, and report on student achievement in disaggregated ways (separating various groups so their scores may be compared).

ADDITIONAL INFLUENCES ON CURRICULUM

In addition to those we have discussed, other groups and ideologies influence the formal curriculum.

PARENTS AND THE COMMUNITY. Every community has a unique identity by virtue of the citizens who live within it, including parents who send their children to public schools. While the inclusion of core subject areas in the curriculum is rarely questioned, some of the topics addressed within the core subjects may be. Even more community impact may be exerted on topics addressed in related arts subject areas. What gets the attention of the community is often a controversial issue that strikes a dissonant chord among community members. What may be considered mainstream in Miami, Florida, could be controversial in Boise, Idaho. What is taught in school seems only to grab community and parental attention when it is considered objectionable.

Parents and community members can exert influence on curriculum in a variety of ways including voicing opinions to school personnel and school board members or local media, refusing to allow children to participate in certain activities, suggesting alternative curricular approaches, and serving on textbook adoption committees.

PARTNERSHIP FOR 21ST CENTURY SKILLS. As we have already discussed, the knowledge and skills made explicit in the P21 documents are not necessarily new, but when packaged in this organization's format they make a compelling case for inclusion in the curriculum. The states that have officially become partners are all working toward including the P21 framework of knowledge and skills in their state standards. Even with the development of national curriculum standards, the Partnership for 21st Century Skills will likely continue to impact what is taught and learned in U.S. schools.

CORE KNOWLEDGE. The organization **Core Knowledge** proposes that there is a body of lasting knowledge that should determine the curriculum in PreK–8 schools. Proponents of Core Knowledge believe that this body of knowledge, sometimes referred to as cultural literacy, motivates students to learn more about topics because they grasp foundations of subjects. (Note that in this case, *cultural* refers to what some consider a culture unique to the United States.) For schools and school districts, those who align with Core Knowledge believe their prescribed curriculum provides a coherent, sequential plan for learning that isn't swayed by current events and technology innovations. Core Knowledge doesn't necessarily discount the value of current events and technology in the curriculum but rather sees them as add-ons to a base that remains relatively stable from year to year (Core Knowledge, 2009).

A stable core of knowledge is certainly not something new or innovative in the history of curriculum in U.S. schools. However, as with P21, the very fact that an organization has formed to promote a common core of knowledge in schools leads to a greater impact on curriculum.

COLLEGES AND UNIVERSITIES. Students enter the doors of colleges and universities with knowledge and skills determined by the PreK–12 curriculum. Simultaneously, colleges and universities affect the direction of what is taught and learned in schools primarily through the preparation of teachers, research conducted by faculty, and faculty involvement in standards development. Because of this, higher education is in the unique position of being both a recipient and a molder of curriculum.

SUBJECTS OF THE FORMAL CURRICULUM

We generally consider English language arts, math, science, and social studies as the core subject areas. In early childhood and elementary settings, classes outside the core curriculum are built into the day either within the individual classroom or in special classes that meet perhaps weekly. Most middle and high schools require students to take a specific number of courses that are not part of the core. These courses, known as **related arts, exploratory,** or **encore,** are valuable components that enhance the formal curriculum and include physical education, technology, world languages, music, home arts, theater, and more.

Points of Reflection 4.3

Before reading further, think about your own experiences with English language arts, math, science, and social studies. Which content area appealed to you most? How did the teacher's level of enthusiasm and teaching strategies influence the appeal of the subject for you?

CORE SUBJECT AREAS. The subjects designated as core have basically been the same for over a century. Of course much of the content has changed, but English language arts (ELA), math, science, and social studies are consistently taught in early childhood, elementary, middle, and high schools. The emphasis in early childhood and elementary is on ELA and math, with the degree of attention given to science and social studies sometimes dependent on the teacher's level of knowledge about, and interest in, these subject areas. All four core subject areas are prominent in the curriculum of middle and high school.

English Language Arts. The National Council of Teachers of English (NCTE) and the International Reading Association (IRA) tell us that language development includes reading, writing, speaking, listening, viewing, and study of media. In early childhood, elementary, and middle school, much of the ELA curriculum focuses on skills, including reading, grammar, spelling, mechanics of punctuation and capitalization, editing, and basic research. Reading consists mainly of fiction (short stories and simple books) through fourth grade. In middle school, the focus begins to shift toward a variety of literary forms and writing. High school ELA is primarily literature based, with continued emphasis on writing skills and research. Communication skills such as oral presentation and persuasive speech have figured more prominently in ELA classes at most levels in recent years.

Mathematics. According to the National Council of Teachers of Mathematics (NCTM, 2000), the need to understand and use math in everyday life has never been greater. From making purchasing decisions to interpreting tables and graphs, math is a vital part of the present and will be increasingly important in a more complex future. Children in early childhood settings now explore concepts of algebra, geometry, and data analysis. Elementary and middle school students are asked to write about problem-solving strategies involving scenarios with multiple variables. An increasing number of high school students are taking advantage of advanced placement math courses for college credit.

By viewing math as something students do and connect to real life, NCTM standards ushered in a shift in math education from memorizing procedures to understanding concepts, and from emphasizing isolated mechanical ways of finding solutions to problem solving (NCTM, 2000).

Science. The vision of the National Science Teachers Association (NSTA) is for all students to regularly experience science that revolves around unifying themes such as order, organization, models, change, measurement, and function. To do this, teachers emphasize that science is a process involving observation, inference, and experimentation. This is a major shift from content-specific facts to understanding concepts through process and inquiry (more on inquiry later in this chapter). For instance, when science is taught through themes, young children learn what it means to measure and how to use measurement tools. In middle and high school, they examine how and why measurement is important in every aspect of science (NSTA, 2005).

Social Studies. The National Council for the Social Studies (NCSS) tells us that the "primary purpose of social studies is to help young people develop the ability to make informed and reasoned decisions for the public good as citizens of a culturally and demographically

Science comes alive for students like Amanda at Rees Elementary when they are encouraged to observe and experiment. Sara Davis Powell

diverse society in an interdependent world" (2005, p. 1). This is a definite shift from the way social studies was approached for much of the last century. Before the influence of NCSS and the curricular changes prompted by standards, social studies was dominated by names and dates to be memorized, with little or no application of concepts to local, national, or international dilemmas.

The NCSS standards are based on 10 themes that are addressed in all school levels but approached differently based on the developmental level of the students. For instance, for standard 1 (culture), students in early childhood and elementary settings may explore food, clothing, and shelter in places that represent the ethnicities of students in a class. In middle grades a unit on the culture of a country may involve examining the lifestyles of the people and the environment and completing comparative writing exercises. A high school social studies class may address culture through a unit on religious expression in schools in which students consider different faiths, examine relevant case studies, argue opposing views, freely voice opinions, and develop supporting rationales (NCSS, 2005).

RELATED ARTS. Related arts courses complement and enhance the core curriculum. Let's take a look at some that are frequently offered.

Technology. The International Society for Technology in Education (ISTE) is a professional organization whose mission is to provide "leadership and service to improve teaching and learning by advancing the effective use of technology in education" (ISTE, 2005). The standards for technology are organized into categories such as basic operations, communication tools, and ethical issues. Almost all schools have computer labs used for classes in **information literacy,** a broad phrase involving recognition of when information is needed, knowing how to access information, and judging information credibility. In these labs, designated technology teachers teach whole classes of students at a time.

Foreign Language. The statement of philosophy of the American Council for the Teaching of Foreign Language (ACTFL) tells us that "the United States must educate students who are linguistically and culturally equipped to communicate successfully in a pluralistic American society and abroad" (2005, p. 2). To accomplish this mission, high schools and most middle schools offer courses in a variety of world languages, most commonly Spanish and French. Because of the recognition that young children acquire a second language more readily than do young adults, many early childhood and elementary schools offer opportunities to learn a second language.

The Standards for Foreign Language Learning are organized according to five goals that ACTFL calls the "Five C's of Foreign Language Education": communication, cultures, connections, comparisons, and communities (ACTFL, 2005, p. 2).

Physical Education and Health. Leaders of physical education (PE) and health education strongly advocate for more time spent in physical activity and health-related instruction. Supporting standards are provided by the National Association for Sport and Physical Education (NASPE) and the American Association for Health Education (AAHE).

In early childhood and elementary schools PE may be unorganized play time, often the responsibility of the classroom teacher, or there may be a designated PE teacher who conducts whole class sessions two or three times a week for each grade level. In middle school PE and health are likely to be rotated courses, perhaps covering 9 weeks each year, with health taught by the PE or science teacher. In high school, students are usually required to take only one or two courses in PE and even fewer in health. Given the health risk factors associated with adolescence in society today, implementation of the NASPE and AAHE standards is especially important for teenagers.

Arts. The National Standards for Arts Education define what students should know and be able to do in the four arts disciplines: music, dance, theater, and the visual arts. Essentially, the standards state that by the end of high school students should be able to communicate at a basic level in the four disciplines and be proficient in at least one art form. The availability of art experiences in music, dance, theater, and visual arts in PreK–12 schools varies tremendously. In early childhood and elementary schools, the classroom teacher may be responsible for the art curriculum or the school may have an art specialist. In middle and high schools, students usually have a variety of arts classes from which to choose and perhaps a limited number of arts activities.

It is an unfortunate fact that when the budget is tight in schools and districts, the arts are often the first to go. After all, standardized tests don't even mention forms of dance, genres of paintings, composers and their works, or elements of drama.

Career and Tech-Prep Courses. Career and tech-prep cover a broad category of courses usually offered in high school. Some courses are of general interest, such as basic industrial or home arts classes, while some are career oriented, such as auto mechanics and cosmetology. The federal government supports a program called **School-to-Work,** initiated to bring real-world work-related skills and understanding to students through courses that introduce them to career possibilities.

Before discussing the remaining types of curricula, let's look briefly at three aspects of the formal curriculum that cross subject-area boundaries: integrated curriculum, culturally responsive curriculum, and arts-infused curriculum.

IMPORTANT CONCEPTS THAT ADD VALUE TO CURRICULUM

There are some important concepts to consider as we explore curriculum. If we think of the formal curriculum as a cloth that covers the school day with learning opportunities, these concepts may be thought of as threads that weave in and out of the subjects and add value, as illustrated in Figure 4.1.

INTEGRATED CURRICULUM. Continuing the cloth analogy, the strength of cloth comes from weaving the threads in different directions so the cloth holds together. When teachers include content and skills from a variety of subjects in lessons, and weave them together in meaningful ways they are incorporating **integrated,** or **interdisciplinary,** curriculum. An integrated curriculum basically involves approaching a concept from different perspectives to create learning opportunities based on connections. This is often accomplished through the use of a unifying topic or theme. Early childhood and elementary teachers do it all the time. Second grade teachers may weave a study of farm life throughout the year, aligning core and related arts subjects with the theme whenever possible. Math problems may deal with farming scenarios and science may revolve around light, rain, and soil, along with zoology. The history of farming and literature about farming and farmers may be taught.

Figure 4.1 Integrated curriculum

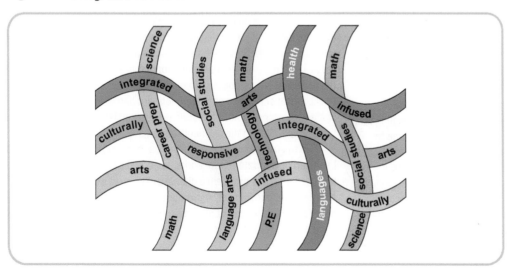

In middle school, teams of teachers may weave whole days, or even weeks, around a theme that brings together research of real-world events and phenomena. Curriculum integration is least common in high school. Although high school teachers are usually organized into subject-area departments, this in no way prevents an ELA teacher from teaching about literature through short stories, poems, and novels that reflect a topic addressed in the social studies curriculum for the grade level. For instance, if U.S. history is a course taken by most sophomores, the sophomore ELA teachers could incorporate period literature that coincides with the progressive history of the United States as taught by the history department faculty.

Connecting subjects of the formal curriculum can occur at a variety of levels of complexity. From merely mentioning in a geometry lesson that the word *symmetry* is also important in art, then showing a painting that exhibits the concept, to a well-planned series of lessons with subject-area boundaries blurred by real-world context, our efforts to make connections within the curriculum pay big dividends in terms of student interest and learning.

Points of Reflection 4.5

What do you recall about your teachers' efforts to connect subject areas? Did you experience thematic units of study? If so, describe what you remember.

CULTURALLY RESPONSIVE CURRICULUM. As diversity in U.S. schools increases, the importance of, and demand for, a culturally responsive perspective grows. When we approach curriculum in **culturally responsive** ways, we incorporate a **multicultural curriculum** that purposefully includes contributions and viewpoints from the perspectives of different cultures, ethnicities, races, genders, socioeconomic levels, or any other way we may differ. At its best, a multicultural curriculum is accurate, timely, and sensitive while avoiding tokenism or a sense of forced inclusion (Banks, 2003).

The methods used to demonstrate cultural responsiveness and infuse a classroom with a multicultural curriculum will depend on the grade level and subject area. In early childhood and elementary settings, celebrating historical events and holidays of a variety of cultures helps create awareness of values and traditions within various cultures. In middle and high school, making a variety of perspectives part of your classroom discussions, and asking students to research and report on issues of interest to them that include various perspectives, can help forge an understanding of people of different cultures. One of the most effective tools for including a variety of perspectives is an emphasis on current events.

Considering our cloth analogy, think of culturally responsive curriculum as adding texture to the cloth, and perhaps a tapestry effect, as connections are made among subject

Teaching in Focus

Sara Davis Powell

Derek Boucher, History and Reading, Roosevelt High School, California. *In his own words. . . .*

After 12 years working in an urban, public high school in the Central Valley of California, I still firmly believe that teaching is a noble profession. Allow me to share the components that have made the biggest difference in my life as a teacher.

Love your content area. Engage in reading, writing, research, discussions, and even travel in your content area. The passion these activities generate comes across to students and changes lives.

Developing a philosophy of education will serve you better than learning multiple strategies. From a rich philosophy, great strategies emerge. Strategies apart from a philosophy come and go. In 1995 my teacher education program pushed me to think deeply about my philosophy of teaching and learning. For example, I believe that curriculum should be relevant and meaningful to students as often as possible. Humans are innately curious. I believe that faith in the learner is imperative.

Go to graduate school. After 5 years in the profession, I enrolled in graduate school and studied in the area of reading/language arts. This experience changed my life as a professional and benefited me infinitely more than school district training has ever done. Find the most progressive graduate program around and go for it! You'll never regret it.

Curriculum and Instruction

areas. Read focus teacher Derek Boucher's philosophy about a teacher's relationship to the curriculum, making curriculum relevant, and furthering our knowledge and skills in *Teaching in Focus*.

ARTS-INFUSED CURRICULUM. Including arts in the curriculum requires awareness of opportunities, along with purposeful determination to include music, theater, dance, and the visual arts when possible. You don't need to be an artist or musician to display art or play music in the classroom. Encouraging students to create their own works of art to enhance a project takes exactly that—encouragement.

"The arts are the great equalizer in education. Regardless of native language, ability or disability, music, art, and drama are accessible to all" (Gregoire & Lupinetti, 2005, p. 159). As an equalizer, the arts can provide both expression and success for all students, regardless of the diversity they may display. Consider these four reasons for integrating the arts:

- Arts provide a natural view into the contributions and perspectives of other cultures.
- Arts are primary means of communication.
- Arts provide opportunities for achievement that may not otherwise be available.
- Arts may focus on alternative ways to assess and evaluate (Cornett, 2003).

Brenda Beyal, the multiage teacher at Rees Elementary in Utah who infuses both visual arts and drama into the curriculum, encourages her students to express themselves in unique ways through what she calls a squiggle, a randomly drawn curvy line that forms the basis for artistic expression. Each student is given a piece of paper with the same squiggle on it and is asked to use imagination and creativity to fashion a drawing around the basic structure. While they work on their masterpieces, music plays in the classroom. Does this activity distract from the formal curriculum? Brenda views experiences such as the squiggle as enriching her classroom by creating a sense of ownership on the part of her students that ties them more closely to the formal curriculum they will encounter during the day.

Although it's hard to imagine objections to infusing arts into the curriculum, there are groups who oppose arts on the grounds that their inclusion detracts from the core subjects. Controversy and curriculum are never far apart.

CONTROVERSY AND CURRICULUM

In a society that values opposing views and encourages diversity, the curriculum is sure to be debated. The dynamic nature of debate is healthy, but it can also be frustrating at times for educators. Religious beliefs, censorship for a variety of reasons, and philosophical differences all influence what's included in the formal curriculum. Here are a few examples of issues that are controversial in some school districts and states with regard to what is taught in public schools.

- There is an ongoing debate over the exclusive teaching of evolution to explain the origin of human beings. **Intelligent design,** proposed by some parents and community members who practice Christianity and oppose the teaching of evolution, includes a belief that certain features of the universe and of living things are best explained by an intelligent being (God), not by the process of natural selection espoused by evolution. Some people argue for an evolution-only curriculum; others argue for intelligent design only. Still others propose the teaching of both as theories, incurring the disapproval of many in the scientific community, including most colleges and universities, where evolution is considered factually based.
- Earlier we discussed multicultural curriculum, or the purposeful inclusion of contributions of persons of diversity and traditions that are not considered

Points of Reflection 4.6

What do you remember about your teachers' efforts to be culturally responsive? Were various holidays acknowledged or did you study contributions of a variety of people of different races and ethnicities? If so, what do you recall? How did you experience the arts as part of your PreK–12 experiences?

To see some of the multiple ways the arts are infused at Rees Elementary, view Mike Larsen's school tour and Brenda Beyal's room tour by visiting the Teaching in Focus *section for Chapter 4 in the* MyEducationLab *for this course.*

mainstream America (a loosely conceived concept). One of the arguments for more cultural responsiveness is that U.S. curriculum is too **Eurocentric,** meaning that contributions and traditions that do not originate in Europe are underrepresented. For instance, in 2010 there was ongoing debate in the Texas legislature about whether or not Hispanics should be added as historic characters to the public school curriculum now that about 40% of the Texas population is Hispanic. Some proponents of a core knowledge curriculum argue there is enough to learn about basic ideas, classic literature, scientific knowledge, and so on, without efforts to be culturally responsive that may take away valuable classroom time.

• Whether schools should teach sex education, and, if so, what should be taught, and when should topics be introduced, are questions about which many in the United States feel strongly. The whole issue of sex education is value laden and emotionally charged. Many believe that the responsibility to teach children and adolescents about sex falls squarely on the home and religious organizations, while others contend that the school is the appropriate venue because it impacts the most students over a long period of development. With the goal of reducing teen pregnancies and sexually transmitted diseases, courts generally uphold the rights of schools to provide sex education. But the mere legality of a controversial issue such as this does not equate with widespread benign acceptance, nor does it alleviate the burden of deciding what to teach and when to teach it. This chapter's *Letter to the Editor* addresses the issue of sex education.

Letter to the Editor

This letter appeared in the Fort Wayne, Indiana, newspaper, *The Journal Gazette*. It was written by a citizen responding to recent local controversy over sex education in schools.

SEPTEMBER 10, 2009

There have been several letters lately from concerned parents who have embraced their right and responsibility to educate their children about sexuality. They are all adamant that schools should not be teaching sex ed. But what about the millions of children who obviously aren't getting "the talk" at home? What happens to them? They are the ones who will go out, have babies, ready or not, and continue the cycle of failing families. Don't those children deserve to be educated about the consequences of sexual activity?

It would be great if all parents would accept the responsibility for the education of their own children. But clearly they are not doing so. If we really want to do something about teen pregnancy and reduce the spread of sexually transmitted diseases, we have to educate as many children as possible. This self-congratulatory attitude of "I'll educate my own and to heck with everyone else" only perpetuates the problem. Biological

facts can and should be taught in schools. The preaching and moralizing can be done somewhere else.

Brad Huff

Now it's your turn. Write a letter to the editor from the perspective of a future teacher expressing your views about the role of schools in sex education. The following questions may help you frame your thinking, but should not limit nor determine what you write.

1. Who has responsibility for teaching children and adolescents about sex-related issues? Why? Are there multiple parties, or is responsibility limited to a specific group?

2. If sex education is appropriate in schools, who should decide which topics and issues should be taught in a classroom setting?

3. If sex education is appropriate in schools, who should teach it and why?

4. At what point in the PreK–12 curriculum might some form of sex education be appropriate?

Write your letter in understandable terminology, remembering that readers of newspaper letters to the editor are citizens who may have limited knowledge of school practices and policies.

What Other Curricula Do We Teach in U.S. Schools?

We've learned what goes into creating the formal curriculum for U.S. schools. Now let's look at other kinds of curricula that are part of what teachers do. Although not as obvious in many ways, and certainly not as regulated by standards and policies, the informal, extra, and null curricula nonetheless impact teachers and students.

INFORMAL CURRICULUM

The **informal curriculum** is what teachers and schools teach and what students learn that is not part of a lesson plan, a curriculum guide, or standards. It encompasses what is learned by students through attitudes, values, and various types of informal teaching situations, such as in the hall between classes, at recess, and on field trips when conversations are casual. This informal learning may be positive or negative and is sometimes unintentional. When the formal curriculum is referred to as the explicit curriculum, the informal curriculum may be called the **implicit curriculum,** meaning that often it is implied and subtle. You may also hear informal curriculum and **hidden curriculum** used interchangeably. There is a distinction, however, because the informal curriculum has positive connotations, while the hidden curriculum has more of a negative sense, implying there may be teacher motivations that are somehow less than positive.

Another phrase equated with the informal curriculum is **wayside teaching**. John Lounsbury (1991), a noted middle-level educator and advocate for young adolescents, tells us that wayside teaching is the teaching we do inside and outside the classroom through our attitudes, values, habits, interests, and creation of classroom climate. Regardless of what students learn in terms of content and skills through the formal curriculum, they learn *us*. They watch us, listen to us, and notice their surroundings; they learn more than we imagine. If we are positive, caring, excited about learning, fair, and organized, students learn that

- optimism is more productive than pessimism
- cooperation and empathy matter
- structure and enthusiasm enhance learning
- responsibility is personal and valuable (Powell, 2010)

On the other hand, if we are negative, lack interest in students and subjects, and exhibit a general disdain for our work, students are likely to mirror these qualities. If our classrooms are a mess, if the school building is dilapidated, and if the community is unsupportive, students learn that they may not matter very much.

The informal curriculum is all about relationships. Purposefully using wayside teaching involves taking advantage of teachable moments, accepting students for who they are rather than what they do, teaching to student strengths, and building a sense of belonging among students (Powell, 2010). When students sense they are valued, they are more willing to cooperate and engage in the classroom (Jensen, 2005). Students who sense they belong have more inner resources to use to be successful (Osterman, 2002). Nel Noddings, a highly respected teacher and researcher, tells us that caring about students leads to their sense of belonging. Moreover, Noddings (1992, p. 27) maintains that "Care is the bedrock of all successful education." In this very important way, the informal curriculum complements the formal curriculum. Building relationships leads to increased student engagement and achievement (Stipek, 2006).

A middle school science teacher wrestling with the "What should I teach?" question decided to ask her former students what they remembered about her class and what they believed were the most important lessons. She developed a survey and received responses

Renee Ayers at Summit Primary develops caring relationships with her students. Here she and Sherlonda share secrets in the positive environment Renee maintains for her students. Sara Davis Powell

from students she taught in each of her 9 years in the classroom. These responses included the following:

> "The most important things I learned from you weren't in class, but during the Science Olympiad . . ."
>
> "The [finest] things I learned from you have nothing to do with science."
>
> "The most important thing I learned from you would have to be the ability to be nice to people even if you feel like screaming. . . . The way you acted toward our class and the compassion you showed to our class [taught me this]."
>
> "Self-confidence and how important it is."
>
> "How important science is to society."
>
> "How you encouraged everyone to do their best."

Points of Reflection 4.7

Think about how the informal curriculum affected you. What did teachers say and do that impacted you most? What attitudes did they display that spoke volumes to you as a learner? What informal lessons do you remember most from grades PreK–12?

Several students responded that the books she read aloud to them (in science class!) changed their opinions on diversity (Little, 2001, pp. 62–63). What a powerful example of positively teaching the informal curriculum!

EXTRACURRICULUM

Activities sponsored by the school but outside the limits of the formal curriculum are considered extracurricular. Although some elementary schools offer extracurricular activities, such as jump rope and craft clubs, most extracurricular opportunities begin in middle school and expand in high school.

Extracurricular activities provide opportunities for active involvement for students, and for sponsorship and coaching for teachers. Examples include

- Odyssey of the Mind, math and book clubs
- debate, chess, and photography clubs
- band and choral activities
- athletics of all kinds, including cheerleading
- school newspaper, student government, and honor society

Recently there has been renewed interest in the factors that contribute to **school connectedness,** or student bonding and engagement. Lack of school connectedness may lead to disruptive behavior, substance abuse, emotional distress, absenteeism, and dropping out. The importance of doing what it takes to foster connectedness is magnified when we consider that approximately half of all high school students, whether urban, suburban, or rural, feel "chronically disengaged" from school (Klem & Connell, 2004, p. 262). A major factor that influences school connectedness is participation in extracurricular activities (Blum, 2005). Researchers have found that extracurricular activities "provide all students—including at-risk and gifted students—an academic safety net" (Holloway, 2000, p. 88). This chapter's *Diversity Dialogue* addresses connecting students to school in culturally responsive ways, with extracurricular possibilities.

Points of Reflection 4.8

In what extracurricular activities did you participate? What did participation mean to you? In which activities did you want to be involved but for some reason were not?

Curriculum and Instruction

Watch Angelica's interview in the Teaching in Focus *section for Chapter 4 in MyEducationLab for this course.*

One of our focus teachers, Angelica Reynosa, has taught Folkloria as one of her five classes each year for 5 years. Through her section of Folkloria students explore their genealogical roots and the history of Hispanic cultures. Students at Angelica's school may register for one section of Folkloria each semester as their related arts choice. Other Folkloria classes concentrate on visual and craft art of Hispanic origin, or music and dance of Hispanic cultures. When it is announced that the Folkloria program will no longer be offered during the school day, Angelica is quite distressed.

Angelica sees the reasons given for discontinuing Folkloria as a credit-bearing experience as reasonable but only if the students aren't considered. The school budget is tight and the teachers who have Folkloria as part of their teaching loads are needed to teach core subject areas now that there is a hiring freeze (no one can be hired for a period of time). Angelica would be happy to pick up an additional World History class, but she also feels strongly that the Folkloria program meets needs that the regular classes do not. Her fear is that if Folkloria is completely eliminated at her school, aspects of the Hispanic culture will be relegated to the null curriculum that she has read about in education journals.

Sara Davis Powell

Think about Angelica's beliefs concerning Folkloria. Respond to these items by writing one well-developed paragraph for each.

1. What is a possible way Angelica can continue offering a program similar to Folkloria at her high school? What would be involved? What are two possible benefits?

2. From what we know about Angelica, what strengths does she bring to Folkloria?

NULL CURRICULUM

The **null curriculum** is what *isn't* taught—those concepts and skills that perhaps simply haven't been considered or are not considered important enough. The way certain subjects are taught is simply based on tradition. "We teach what we teach largely out of habit" (Eisner, 2002, p. 103). The null curriculum also includes topics considered controversial, including almost anything dealing with religion, abortion, homosexuality, and other topics that are controversial in some areas but not in others.

The null curriculum may not be as important as the formal curriculum, the informal curriculum, and the extra curriculum, but it is certainly worth thinking about. What's *not* part of the school curriculum may never be considered by students and therefore may have little to do with their futures. For instance, if we neglect to incorporate a culturally responsive curriculum, failing to acknowledge and celebrate differences may contribute to prejudice and exclusionary attitudes in students.

The Partnership for 21st Century Skills promotes the teaching of some concepts that are not currently in most curricular plans. On the P21 Web site we are told that the challenge is to purposefully incorporate the broad literacies they

The poster behind Mayra and Roosevelt Assistant Principal John Lael lists some of the extracurricular possibilities at RHS.
Sara Davis Powell

support. A **literacy** involves the ability to analyze and apply knowledge and skills necessary to solve problems within a discipline. The Partnership recommends that schools promote financial, economic, business, entrepreneurial, civic, health, wellness, information, and communication literacies. In many schools these broad disciplines are not addressed

Curriculum and Instruction

Points of Reflection 4.9

Did you gain insight concerning any of Wolk's missing curricular pieces when you were in PreK–12 school? If so, through what part of the curriculum? What do you wish would have been included in your PreK–12 experiences?

and are part of the null curriculum. When schools incorporate them, they will become part of the formal curriculum.

Wolk (2007) tells us there are important concepts typically missing from school curriculum, thereby relegated to the null curriculum. He contends that students and society as a whole would benefit from the inclusion of, and emphasis on, knowledge of self; love of learning; caring and empathy; environmental literacy; social responsibility; global awareness; and money, family, food, and happiness.

How Is Instruction Implemented in U.S. Schools?

Just as curriculum is the *what* of teaching, instruction is the *how*. Without effective instruction that meets the needs of learners, "the most elegant curriculum in the world . . . would fall short of its promise" (Tomlinson & McTighe, 2006). We know there is not one single approach to instruction that works for every student in every subject all the time. Differing student intelligences, learning styles, abilities, societal contexts, and so on, make using a variety of instructional approaches necessary to meet students' needs. Therefore, building a repertoire of instructional strategies is vital. No need to worry—instructional possibilities are practically limitless.

A teacher provides learning opportunities that fall within a spectrum from teacher centered to student centered, depending on the topic or skill, the level of students, the time frame in which instruction must occur, and the teacher's instructional style. There are circumstances when lecture (perhaps the most teacher centered of all strategies) is appropriate, and other circumstances when student exploration with guidance works best. You may hear the phrases *sage on the stage* and *guide on the side* as you continue your teacher preparation. When a teacher is a *sage on the stage*, there is a lot of telling and demonstrating going on. Strategies such as lectures and **mini-lectures** (shortened, focused versions of the lecture) and teacher demonstrations are examples of *sage on the stage* teaching. These can be effective strategies as part of a teacher's broader repertoire of teaching techniques. When a teacher is a *guide on the side,* the teacher is setting expectations, providing instructions, and serving as a resource while students do the work and exploration that lead to learning. Guiding, or facilitating, student learning leads to increased active engagement.

BIG IDEAS OF INSTRUCTION

Now let's explore some of the big ideas of instruction, along with some supporting instructional strategies that allow teachers to apply the big ideas in their classrooms. Each of the big ideas of instruction deserves, and indeed has had, entire books written about it. What you read here is an overview so you will be aware of some of the ideas that will likely be emphasized during your teacher preparation program.

PROMOTING CRITICAL THINKING. **Critical thinking** involves observing, comparing and contrasting, interpreting, analyzing, seeing issues from a variety of perspectives, weighing variables, and then making decisions and solving problems based on these thinking skills. Can we really teach children and adolescents to think critically as they learn the standards of the formal curriculum? The answer is *yes*. Teaching critical thinking and **problem solving** is not an addition to the curriculum but rather a way of approaching the knowledge and skills we teach.

Benjamin Bloom and others at the University of Chicago first published what is now referred to as **Bloom's taxonomy** of thinking skills in 1956. Simply put, **thinking skills** are those skills that aid in processing information. These skills grow in complexity and sophistication as they progress from level I to level VI of the taxonomy that has become a tool used by teachers as they plan and organize learning experiences. All the levels, as

TABLE 4.1 Bloom's taxonomy

Categories	Key Verbs		Question Stems
Knowledge (Remembering)	Recognize Identify Recall Memorize	Retrieve List Define Duplicate	When did _____? Who was _____? Where is _____? Why did _____? Can you list four _____?
Comprehension (Understanding)	Interpret Summarize Infer Illustrate	Classify Compare Explain	How would you compare _____ to _____? What is the main idea of _____? What is meant by _____?
Apply	Implement Use Operate	Dramatize Illustrate Solve	How would you use _____ to _____? What approach would you use to _____? Can you _____ by _____?
Analyze	Organize Integrate Focus	Categorize Differentiate Examine Test	What evidence can you find to conclude that _____? What does _____ have to do with _____?
Evaluate	Check Critique Judge	Monitor Defend Support	How would you change _____ to form _____? Can you propose a different way to _____? How would you design _____ to _____?
Synthesis (Creating)	Generate Plan Design	Construct Produce Develop	What is your opinion of _____? How valuable is _____ for _____? Why would you recommend _____?

Source: From *Introduction to Middle School*, 2e (p. 206), by S.D. Powell, 2011, Boston: Allyn & Bacon. Copyright 2011 by Pearson Education, Inc.

illustrated in Table 4.1, are necessary, and none should be neglected. Designing learning experiences that call only for knowledge and comprehension is cheating the minds of students who need to apply and analyze what they know, synthesize or create something new, and evaluate ideas and events. When planning lessons and assessments, teachers should use Bloom's taxonomy and the action verbs associated with each level. Questioning, as an important strategy to promote student thinking, is enhanced by using the question stems, or question beginnings, in Table 4.1. In 2001 Anderson and Krathwohl revised Bloom's taxonomy by, among other things, using different words to describe some of the levels and designating synthesis (creating) as a higher thinking level than evaluation.

TEACHING THROUGH INQUIRY. When students pursue answers to questions posed by others or developed on their own, they are involved in **inquiry learning**. Observation, questioning, hypothesizing, and predicting are all part of inquiry-based learning, which requires students to move beyond rote memorization to become independent thinkers and problem solvers. Teaching and learning through inquiry may involve real-world contexts and discovery, and it can be accomplished in such simple ways as providing scenarios for students to explore or objects for students to manipulate.

Inquiry-based instruction is not new. All discoveries have come about as the result of questioning and answer seeking. Before students can formulate questions on their own or search for answers, they need knowledge and skills as building blocks. Once these building blocks are in place, then students are ready to inquire and look for answers. Inquiry-based instruction is an effective way of teaching and learning because the ideas we create ourselves are the ones we tend to retain (Renzulli, Gentry, & Reis, 2004).

Curriculum and Instruction

A common way of implementing inquiry-based teaching is to design experiences that require students to engage, explore, explain, elaborate, and evaluate. This is commonly called the **5-E lesson plan**. For instance, an elementary teacher can tell third graders the conditions necessary for bean plants to sprout and grow. The students can be tested and many will be able to recite the conditions, at least for the test. Using the 5-E plan, here's how the teacher might guide children through a cycle of inquiry learning:

- Take students outdoors and ask them to observe the plants in the schoolyard (engage and explore).
- Have students discuss with each other what they observed as the conditions for plants to grow and thrive (explain).
- Talk with students about the possibility of an experiment involving some beans given the conditions the students think are needed for plants to thrive, as well as other beans deprived of the conditions (elaborate).
- Assist students as they work together to create the desirable and undesirable conditions using real beans (elaborate).
- Guide students as they observe and record bean growth and come to conclusions about what contributes to bean plants thriving, and whether their predictions were correct (evaluate).

An important element of inquiry learning is the thinking skill of questioning. Asking students appropriate questions helps them examine concepts and phenomena in in-depth ways. When a teacher asks thoughtful questions, students also learn how to frame questions that lead to meaningful learning.

DIFFERENTIATING INSTRUCTION. Approaching instruction in a variety of ways provides multiple paths for students to learn the knowledge and develop the skills of the curriculum. In 1999 Carol Ann Tomlinson gave this philosophy and practice a name: **differentiation of instruction**. Tomlinson tells us that teachers who differentiate instruction strive to do whatever it takes to diagnose student strengths and weaknesses in terms of readiness, interests, and learning profiles. Then they provide an array of content, a variety of processes, and choices of products when possible. The *content* is what the students should know, understand, and be able to do. *Process* consists of the ways students make sense of content, typically through activities and practice. A *product* shows what students know and are able to do; it may be, for example, a project, demonstration, test, or display.

Tomlinson wisely cautions against trying to differentiate too much, too quickly. She advises us to start slowly by recognizing one need in our classroom, changing one part of a lesson (content, process, or product), and implementing this differentiated strategy followed by reflection on the results. As our comfort level grows with diagnosing the readiness, interests, and learning profiles of our students, we can incorporate more and more instructional practices to meet their needs. Tackling too many differentiated strategies too soon in a career can lead to doing activities for activity's sake and the sacrifice of solid, well-designed teaching (Tomlinson, 1999). Great advice.

Taking Tomlinson's advice and starting small may involve simply incorporating **manipulatives,** or objects, to represent numbers or concepts into a lesson on fractions. Differentiating may involve letting pairs of students complete an assignment together, allowing students to teach each other. Or perhaps differentiation will be giving students choices about how they want to work on the week's vocabulary words, with some individually writing definitions and others quizzing each other quietly in a corner of the room. In Figure 4.2 you'll read Tomlinson's view, in general terms, of what teachers do in differentiated classrooms.

INCORPORATING STUDENT COLLABORATION. When students collaborate in a learning environment there are benefits. Students may share responsibility for a project, discuss a question or prompt given by a teacher, tutor each other, help each other study for a quiz, or participate in a planned group activity. Most often student collaboration in schools is referred to as cooperative learning.

Curriculum and Instruction

Figure 4.2 Differentiation of instruction

When teachers differentiate instruction they . . .

- begin where students are
- accept and build upon the premise that learners differ
- engage students through different learning modalities
- ensure that a student competes against himself more than he competes against other students
- believe that students should be held to high standards
- ensure that each student realizes that success is likely to follow hard work
- use time flexibly
- are diagnosticians who prescribe the best instruction for their students

Source: Tomlinson, C. A. (1999). *The differentiated classroom: Responding to the needs of all learners.* Alexandria, VA: Association for Supervision and Curriculum Development.

Loosely defined, **cooperative learning** refers to any instance of students working together. It was, however, more strictly defined in the 1980s when Roger and David Johnson designed the following cooperative grouping patterns:

- informal groups that meet together for a variety of tasks as needed
- formal groups that complete designated, often long-term, tasks
- base groups whose members support one another with remembering and completing assignments, studying, and sharing resources (Johnson & Johnson, 1999)

The Johnson brothers devised five requirements for effective student grouping practices:

1. Positive interdependence—setting group goals for which all members must work to achieve; shared rewards; roles for each member including facilitator, recorder, materials gatherer, timekeeper, and encourager
2. Face-to-face interaction—students work together to explain, complete assignments, solve problems, and so on
3. Individual accountability—students must complete individual tasks that contribute to the group
4. Interpersonal skills—students learn to work together in socially acceptable ways
5. Group processing—students reflect on how well they worked together and how effectively they accomplished their goals; students give teacher feedback on group functioning (Johnson & Johnson, 1999)

Cooperative learning is a big idea of instruction that can be successfully implemented in early childhood, elementary, middle, and high school. It's likely that you have been a member of many cooperative groups during your school experiences. Table 4.2 contains some ways teachers group and regroup students for learning.

USING TECHNOLOGY. Today's students are referred to as the "Media Generation," digital learners in "techno-drenched atmospheres" that are "gizmo-intensive" (McHugh, 2005, p. 33). "No generation has ever had to wait so little to get so much information" (Renard, 2005, p. 44). Using technology in instruction that enhances learning is imperative. **Educational technology** is any technology-based device that assists teachers in teaching and students in learning. As educators we have the responsibility to guide students in ways that will help them excel in our technology-rich society.

The International Society for Technology in Education (ISTE) provides detailed descriptions of the knowledge and skills related to technology use appropriate for children and adolescents. Virtually all major subject-area organizations join ISTE in promoting technology use in the classroom, as do professional organizations representing the various levels of PreK–12 education.

Points of Reflection 4.10

Think about the cooperative learning experiences that were productive and pleasant for you in school (including college), as well as those that either failed or were not enjoyable. What made them successful? What contributed to problems with group functioning?

Curriculum and Instruction

TABLE 4.2 Cooperative learning strategies	
Strategies	Description
Think-Pair-Share (T-P-S)	T-P-S involves all students in nonthreatening ways. Teachers expose students to information, give a prompt, ask a question, or provide an experience and then challenge them to think about it in a particular way and perhaps record their thoughts on paper (T). Students then choose a partner (P) and share their thoughts with another student (S).
	Pyramid T-P-S involves multiple pairs of students discussing the question/prompt.
Jigsaw	This strategy involves students becoming experts on particular topics within *expert groups* and then teaching those topics to the other students in their *base groups*. Jigsaw is a powerful tool that actively involves students both in their own and other people's learning.
Role play	Getting students up and moving as they dramatize a scenario can make a point or prompt students to think in divergent ways. Role playing becomes more effective with practice.
Tableau	Similar to role play, tableau involves students assuming a freeze-frame position that illustrates an event in a short story, book, or historical event. While students pose, another student in the tableau group reads a narrative that is being dramatized.

In looking at technology available in schools, the two broad categories to consider are teaching tools and tools for teachers. Technology *teaching tools* are resources that enhance curriculum, instruction, and assessment when used by teachers to teach and by students to learn. Some of the available technology teaching tools are in Table 4.3. Technology *tools for teachers* are those that expedite and/or enhance the work of teachers and, consequently, curriculum, instruction, and assessment in the classroom. Examples include software that helps with lesson planning and electronic gradebooks. Many technologies accommodate both categories.

Handheld computers may be used to share information commonly referred to as *beaming.* Sara Davis Powell

INTEGRATING READING AND WRITING ACROSS THE CURRICULUM. Reading and writing are vital skills, without which life is difficult and limited in many ways. Regardless of the subject or grade level, all teachers need to be teachers of reading and writing. Infusing the curriculum with reading and writing is often referred to as *reading across the curriculum* and *writing across the curriculum*.

Reading. An old adage says that children learn to read through third grade and read to learn from then on. If only that were true. Emphasis is placed on emergent literacy (getting ready to read) and beginning reading (letter/word recognition, story patterns) in early grades when teachers expect to be teachers of reading, and often their efforts are supported by reading specialists whose sole responsibility is teaching children to read.

Many students are not proficient readers by the end of third grade. Even if they are proficient, reading expectations become more stringent and complex, creating the need for specific literacy instruction beyond third grade. In middle and high school there is a devastating

Curriculum and Instruction

TABLE 4.3 Technology teaching tools

Technology Tool	Value in the Classroom
Word processor	Built-in support for writing and publishing
PowerPoint	Popular presentation program used by teachers in their classrooms to deliver instruction and by students to demonstrate skills and display project products
Streaming video	Allows students to view video that is either stored on a site, or live, as it downloads on the computer
Instructional software	Used to learn about concepts and/or practice skills; five categorizes of instructional software: drill-and-practice, tutorial, simulation, instructional games, and problem solving (Roblyer, 2006)
Handheld computers	Pocket-sized computers with small folding keyboards give teachers and students flexibility to move around while using them; class sets are easily mobile; information and products may be shared simply by pointing one computer at another, commonly referred to as "beaming"
Internet	Most widely used network: World Wide Web (WWW)
Podcast	Like creating a radio program and then distributing it on the Internet; virtual publishing
Electronic books	e-media; iBooks
Distance learning	Acquisition of knowledge and skills through instruction delivered using technology; learning is not place based
Digital games	Attention getting and interactive; simulations

lack of reading proficiency. More than half of the ninth graders in the 35 largest cities in the United States read at the sixth grade level or below (Vacca, 2002). The average student in a high school classroom is reading below the level of content-area texts (Allington, 2002), and 25% of adults are functionally illiterate (Moats, 2001). Some ideas for promoting reading skills are in Figure 4.3.

Access to books, recreational reading, and silent reading all lead to improved skills in both decoding and comprehension (Krashen, 2002). Fluent readers have the skills to be fluent writers. Conversely, students who struggle to read will struggle to write as well.

Writing. Techniques for effective writing in multiple genres have not received as much attention or classroom time as reading instruction. Writing can be meaningfully integrated into all subjects at all grade levels and may be descriptive, creative, factual/informative, or expository. Teaching students to write involves many components, including sentence formation, punctuation, capitalization, word usage, style, and spelling.

Figure 4.3 Ways to promote reading skills

- Give students access to student-friendly, inviting, content-rich reading materials (books, magazines, newspapers, etc.).
- Read aloud to students at all grade levels to show them how to navigate through difficult text.
- Provide opportunities for silent, oral, and recreational reading.
- Use appropriate before (explain vocabulary, predict), during (graphic organizers, note taking, integrating prior and new knowledge), and after (summarizing, checking for understanding) reading strategies.
- Take a "textbook journey" as a class to help students understand the way the pages are set up, the purposes of the illustrations and data representations, the length and structure of the lessons and sections, the activities and exercises that follow sections, the glossary, and so on.

Curriculum and Instruction

Students may benefit from keeping notebooks or journals in any subject in which they take notes, record questions about content, reflect on their learning, and so on. Writing essays, biographical sketches, descriptions of events, stories, poetry, and answers to prompts fit naturally into ELA and social studies classes. Writing narrative explanations of science and math procedures deepens and extends understanding.

Now that we have considered some big ideas of instruction and some strategies that bring the big ideas to life in the classroom, we are ready to explore how teachers plan for instruction.

PLANNING FOR INSTRUCTION

In the beginning of the chapter we established that curriculum and instruction are interdependent, that curriculum is meaningless without instruction to convey it and instruction is useless without curriculum. **Assessment,** the gathering of evidence of student learning, is a third component of teaching and learning that is interdependent with curriculum and instruction. All three components are vital in planning learning experiences for children and adolescents.

BACKWARD DESIGN. In their 1998 book, *Understanding by Design*, Wiggins and McTighe introduced educators to a concept that links curriculum, instruction, and assessment in meaningful and interconnected ways. The approach to planning for teaching and learning to accomplish understanding is called **backward design**. The word *backward* is used because the approach is in contrast to the way many teachers approach planning, which is to think of activities before considering the desired results of using those activities. Backward design starts with deciding on the desired learning results (curriculum), then identifying how to collect the evidence necessary to know if the results have been achieved (assessment), and finally proceeding to choosing how to help students acquire the desired knowledge and skills (instruction). These three stages, as illustrated in Figure 4.4, constitute backward design. Although some teachers view backward design as revolutionary, others call the concept just plain common sense and say they have used some version of it to plan their work for years.

In addition to introducing the concept of backwards design and expanding our view of understanding, Wiggins and McTighe (2005) contend there is too much for teachers to teach and for students to thoroughly understand in state content standards. They advise us to prioritize the standards within three categories. The most vital knowledge and skills are in the first category and are referred to as the big ideas and core tasks, defined as those that give "meaning and connection to discrete facts and skills" (p. 5). The next category consists of the knowledge and skills that are important to know and be able to do. The third category, and the one where some content may simply be mentioned or possibly eliminated altogether, consists of the knowledge and skills that may be worthy of being familiar with but don't rise to the category of being important to know and do. This is good advice.

LEVELS OF PLANNING. In early childhood and elementary classrooms, a daily **lesson plan** may mean planning experiences involving reading and math, with perhaps some social

Figure 4.4 Stages of backward design

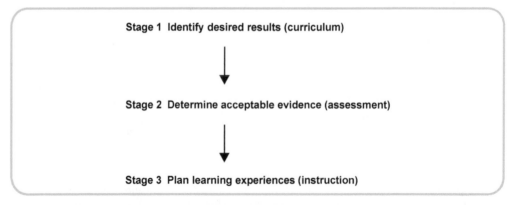

Source: Wiggins, G. P., & McTighe, J. (2005). *Understanding by design* (2nd ed.) (p. 18). Alexandria, VA: Association for Supervision and Curriculum Development.

Curriculum and Instruction

studies and science, a little art and maybe some music and physical activity. In middle and high school, a daily lesson plan may mean planning for two English classes and two literature classes. Daily lesson planning is the planning that links teaching and learning every day in U.S. schools.

A daily lesson plan should build on the lessons of previous days in cohesive ways. To assure this, daily lesson plans should be conceived within weekly plans or unit plans. A weekly lesson plan is just that, 5 days of sequential lessons. A **unit of study** usually involves a theme, with daily plans within the unit addressing aspects of the theme. Weekly and unit plans should be conceived within **long-range plans** that may encompass a 9-week time frame, a semester, or a year. The best way to plan is with the entire school year's worth of standards in focus. Many schools and school districts provide **pacing guides** that outline what should be taught and when it should be taught, designating the order of concepts and skills. There are online resources to assist in all levels of planning. Figure 4.5 lists helpful Web sites.

COMPONENTS OF A LESSON. There are many lesson plan formats, with a common one shown in Figure 4.6. Subject-area organizations recommend specific components and particular formats that you will learn about as part of your teacher preparation program. Regardless of the lesson format, there are lesson components that are usually considered necessary for effective instruction. Keep in mind that not every lesson will include each component, but over the course of a week, teachers generally incorporate the components in Figure 4.6 in some way.

Here is a brief explanation of each of the lesson components in Figure 4.6.

- Standards—As we have discussed, standards basically set the curriculum and determine what teachers teach and students learn.

- **Objectives**—This is a concise statement about what students are expected to learn and be able to do as a result of the lesson.

- Lesson opening—The lesson should begin in a way that captures students' attention and creates interest. The opening can be a time to figure out what students already

Figure 4.5 Internet sources to assist with lesson planning

- Education World
  www.education-world.com/
  Includes many subjects, professional development,
  technology integration, multiple resources

© Copyright EducationWorld .com, reprinted with permission.

- Eisenhower National Clearinghouse
  www.enc.org
  Multiple math and science resources for all grade levels

- Lesson Planet
  www.lessonplanet.com
  Resources, tools, lessons in many subjects

- Ed Helper
  www.edhelper.com/
  All grades, seasonal lessons, includes special education

- Teachers.net Lesson Bank
  http://teachers.net/lessons/
  Allows you to search, submit, or request lessons;
  covers multiple subject areas and grade levels

- A to Z Teacher Stuff
  http://atozteacherstuff.com/
  Lesson plans, thematic units, teacher tips,
  discussion forums for teachers, downloadable
  teaching materials

- The Educator's Reference Desk
  www.eduref.org/
  Resource guides Lesson plans in all subject areas,
  including foreign language and vocational

Curriculum and Instruction

Figure 4.6 Sample lesson plan format

Standard(s) to be addressed:
Lesson objective(s):
Lesson opening:
Procedures:
Plan for differentiation:
Opportunities for guided practice with feedback:
Independent practice:
Assessment of learning:
Closure of lesson:
Materials and resources:

know about the lesson content (their prior knowledge). The information teachers gather requires them to be flexible as they adapt the lesson based on student knowledge and skill.

- Procedures—This is the step-by-step plan for how students will learn/explore a topic and/or skill. Procedures may include a variety of models including cooperative learning, inquiry-based instruction, technology integration, and more, with combinations of strategies that include reading and writing and contribute to project- and problem-based learning. Class discussion, questioning, note taking, demonstration, and so on, are traditional teaching genres that may be part of the lesson procedures.

- Plan for differentiation—All of the ways previously discussed for differentiating instruction and more provide choices for meeting the needs of students.

- Opportunities for **guided practice** with feedback—It's important for students to have opportunities to work independently on applying knowledge in a nonthreatening setting (without being graded). Feedback from the teacher (or as part of an online program) as to whether the student is on the right track will prevent students from practicing incorrectly.

- Independent practice—This can be in or out of class and often takes the form of **homework**.

- Assessment of learning—How do we know if students have learned what we have articulated in the lesson objective? There are multiple ways of assessing student learning that we will explore in the next chapter.

- Closure of lesson—Providing a way for students to summarize what has been learned is a good way to close a lesson. The bell should not end the class period; there should be a plan to logically draw the class session to a close.

- Materials and resources—Planning a lesson includes gathering everything necessary for the lesson to proceed.

Planning for instruction is a vital part of what teachers do. Knowing our students and their developmental levels allows us to plan our teaching appropriately to facilitate their learning.

How Do Teachers Match Instruction to School Levels?

Not every instructional strategy is appropriate for every grade level. Early childhood is not the place for note taking, and high school is not the place for graphing solely with pictures. Some strategies, however, are appropriate for all levels of school. For instance, demonstration and cooperative learning can be used effectively in early childhood, elementary, middle, and high schools.

Each of our focus teachers uses instructional strategies that are level appropriate. As we discuss the strategies of the teachers, note that concepts we have discussed are in italics.

To watch sample lesson segments in the classrooms of Brandi, Brenda, Traci, and Craig, go to Chapter 4 in MyEducationLab for this course.

Curriculum and Instruction

EARLY CHILDHOOD INSTRUCTION

Active engagement is absolutely necessary in early childhood classrooms. Early childhood teachers need to be masters of engaging children in meaningful activities and providing an environment for creative and cooperative play. In PreK, children learn prereading strategies and the meaning of numbers, among other basic concepts. In kindergarten through third grade, children *learn to read* and perform basic *problem solving.*

In Brandi Wade's kindergarten class at Summit Primary, Ohio, the lesson *objective* is for students to make judgments about the concepts of less than, greater than, and equal to as they manipulate objects. Because Brandi works with the children every day, she knows that their *prior knowledge* includes awareness of the symbolism involved with the concepts and how to count to at least 20 by assigning a number to an object (one-to-one correspondence). Brandi uses what the students already know to engage them in an activity. Here are some strategies Brandi uses in her lesson:

- *demonstrates* counting, sorting, writing numbers, choosing correct symbols
- uses *manipulatives* (M&Ms)
- encourages children to work at tables where they can observe and help each other (*cooperative learning*)

Brandi uses the natural social nature of children to encourage them to work together with real objects to accomplish the lesson objective.

Sara Davis Powell

ELEMENTARY INSTRUCTION

For students in elementary classrooms, reading takes on new purposes beyond learning to decode words and reading fiction. Reading becomes a tool for acquiring new knowledge in language arts, math, social studies, science, and other subjects. Although *active engagement* remains vital, elementary children can be expected to read, study, and complete assignments with some measure of independence for brief periods of time.

In Brenda Beyal's multiage class at Rees Elementary, Utah, the students experience *tableaus*, discussed earlier in Table 4.2. Here are some strategies Brenda uses to support the tableau lesson:

- delivers *mini-lecture* on author Eve Bunting
- *reads aloud* portions of *Smoky Night*
- uses a graphic organizer to explain what a *tableau* involves
- incorporates *cooperative group work* as a vital part of the tableau
- *facilitates* work of groups

Sara Davis Powell

Brenda knows that her students would have been able to read *Smoky Night* silently and answer questions about its content. However, she wanted her students to be more deeply involved with the book and, among other things, understand the author's motivations, become knowledgeable about the period of history in which the story takes place, understand the societal implications of the story, and experience some of the emotions of the characters. She chose the tableau strategy to accomplish her instructional *objectives.*

MIDDLE-LEVEL INSTRUCTION

Young adolescents typically respond positively to *active learning* opportunities. They are eager to be involved in meaningful experiences that require *inquiry* and creative *problem solving.* They also respond to more traditional strategies such as *mini-lectures* and *note taking* if they have been taught to actively listen, record, and organize what they learn. Variety and frequent shifts in strategies are key to engaging middle-level students.

In Traci Peters's seventh grade math classroom at Cario Middle School, South Carolina, the students are reviewing topics. They complete a worksheet and are both responding to *teacher questions* and *taking notes.* The new learning in this lesson involves students

Sara Davis Powell

Curriculum and Instruction

discovering the sum of the measures of the angles of a triangle, then writing generalizations about what they have learned. Here are some strategies Traci uses to support the day's lesson:

- begins class with checking *independent practice (homework)* to support and review concepts
- *demonstrates* and *questions* using overhead projector
- uses *manipulatives* to discover concept
- facilitates *cooperative learning* to check for understanding
- requires *written explanation* of learning
- *facilitates* small group work

Traci knows the value of *inquiry-based learning.* She knows that if her young adolescents *discover* the sum of the angles of a triangle they will understand the concept and remember what they learn.

HIGH SCHOOL INSTRUCTION

Students in high school respond to *active learning* opportunities. They work best when the content interests them and when they interact with the subject or topic in ways that require them to be *problem solvers.*

Craig Cleveland's U.S. History class at Roosevelt High School, California, engages in thought-provoking class discussion after he reads a picture book to them about discrimination. The students then read a series of Jim Crow laws, with the purpose of developing role plays that illustrate a particular law. The students act out their role-play scenarios, and then the class discusses what they have seen. This kind of active involvement is excellent for promoting *critical thinking.* Here are some of the strategies Craig uses in his lesson:

- *reads aloud* to students
- facilitates *class discussion*
- delivers *mini-lecture*
- uses quotation to provoke *critical thinking*
- assigns *role play*
- incorporates *cooperative groups*

Craig knows his students well. He understands that the study of discrimination through Jim Crow laws will appeal to them because of the *real-world context.* He also knows that language barriers in his classroom may be partially bridged through *role play.*

CONCLUDING THOUGHTS

John Goodlad, following his landmark study of American high schools, wrote that the typical classroom is a site where "boredom is a disease of epidemic proportion" (1984, p. 9). What a devastating indictment.

Can you picture a classroom full of students deeply immersed in learning rather than entrenched in boredom? Asking, "And how are the children? Are they all well?" leads us to make engaging teaching that leads to optimum student learning our ultimate goal. Now that you know more about curriculum—what it is and where it comes from—you understand the importance of both knowing content and being enthusiastic about it. Now that you know more about instruction—its limitless variety and potential—your ability to envision student engagement has increased.

We began this chapter by considering Chris Roberts and his classroom at Rees Elementary in Utah. Now as the chapter comes to an end, we join Chris as he uses his knowledge of curriculum and instruction to support multiage grouping. Read through ***Chapter in Review*** to help refresh your memory of what we have discussed. Then interact with Chris as he confronts a challenge in ***Developing Professional Competence.***

Sara Davis Powell

Points of Reflection 4.11

Can you imagine being the teacher in Brandi's classroom? Brenda's classroom? Traci's classroom? Craig's classroom? Which lesson and style appeal to you most?

To watch Chris Roberts's interview, visit the Teaching in Focus section for Chapter 4 in the MyEducationLab for this course.

Chapter in Review

What is the formal curriculum?

- The formal curriculum is what is intentionally taught and stated as student learning goals.
- Standards, defined as what students should know and be able to do, serve as the framework for much of the formal curriculum.
- Textbooks have a great deal of influence on the school and classroom curriculum.
- Various levels of government influence the formal curriculum.
- The formal curriculum includes both core and related arts subjects.
- An integrated curriculum involves linking curricular areas as their contents complement one another.
- A culturally responsive curriculum includes contributions and ways of viewing the world from perspectives of different cultures, ethnicities, races, genders, and socioeconomic levels.
- Infusing arts (music, theater, dance, visual arts) into the curriculum provides opportunities for expression that motivate and engage students.
- There are multiple points of controversy related to curriculum.

What other curricula do we teach in U.S. schools?

- The informal curriculum is what teachers teach and students learn that is not part of the planned curriculum or standards.

- The extra curriculum consists of activities that are sponsored by the school but outside the formal curriculum.
- The null curriculum is what isn't taught.

How is instruction implemented in U.S. schools?

- Backward design is an approach to planning for teaching and learning that starts with deciding on the desired learning results, then identifies how to collect the evidence, and concludes with choosing appropriate instructional strategies.
- Content priorities include first, vital knowledge and core tasks; then, what is important to know and do; and finally, what is worth being familiar with.
- There are big ideas of instruction that serve to ground and provide a framework for teaching and learning.
- Multiple strategies of instruction allow for variety in how the curriculum is taught.
- Thoughtfully planning for instruction is vital for effective teaching and optimal student learning.

How do teachers match instruction to school levels?

- Some instructional strategies are appropriate for students of all levels.
- Choosing instructional strategies for each of the four levels of school requires thoughtful consideration.

Developing Professional Competence

Visit the Developing Professional Competence section in Chapter 4 of the MyEducationLab for this text to answer the following questions and begin your preparation for licensure exams.

The district school board where Chris Roberts teaches is considering doing away with multiage classrooms. We know from the interviews with Chris and his teammates Brenda and Tim that they have successfully taught for years in classrooms occupied by third, fourth, and fifth graders. We hear Chris admit in his interview, however, that he doubts he gets to all the content standards of the three grade levels as he teaches in a multiage setting each year.

Chris believes strongly in exposing students to the world through a variety of means. His extensive travels, his love of the arts, and his selection of books for the classroom provide opportunities for him to infuse teaching and learning with real-world context. Through this context Chris knows that his students are learning valuable lessons.

It will be difficult to defend multiage grouping to the school board, but Chris is convinced the configuration works for his teaching team.

Think through this scenario and answer the following multiple-choice questions:

1. Chris states that he probably doesn't get to all the state standards in his classroom. He may be able to clarify which, if any, of the standards he doesn't address by
   a. reading summaries of the standards provided in the state document
   b. matching the textbooks he uses to the standards
   c. taking the time to look very closely at the standards for each grade level and create one document that sequences the standards
   d. asking someone from the state to observe his classroom

2. Chris knows that he will be questioned about the range of ages in his classroom. Which of the following statements is least appropriate for making a case for multiage grouping?
   a. My teaching style work because kids will learn what interests them.
   b. Chronological age does not necessarily determine learning readiness.
   c. Sometimes students learn much from each other and the age disparities often work in favor of peer teaching.
   d. In multiage classrooms teachers can guide learning over a 3-year period to make sure there is consistency and continual progress.

3. All of the following will likely be helpful to Chris as he prepares to make his case before the school board except for which one?
   a. Brenda and Tim
   b. parents of students in his class
   c. Mike Larsen, the principal
   d. Utah Superintendent of Education

4. What information might be most convincing if he had time to research it?
   a. the number of other schools using multiage grouping
   b. a comparison of the success of the students in multiage grades 3–5 settings in sixth grade and the students in self-contained classes in grades 3 to 5
   c. a survey of parents of children in grades K to 2 to see how many will request a multiage setting when their children reach third grade
   d. a comparison of how Utah fares relative to other states on the NAEP exam

5. Which combination of big ideas of instruction should Chris emphasize as the most powerful justification

for having third, fourth, and fifth graders in one classroom?
   a. promoting critical thinking and differentiating instruction
   b. incorporating student collaboration and promoting critical thinking
   c. differentiating instruction and incorporating student collaboration
   d. teaching through inquiry and using technology

Now it's time for you to respond to two short essay items involving the scenario. In your responses, be sure to address all the dilemmas and questions posed in each item. Your responses should each be between one half and one double-spaced page.

6. Chris has decided that he will attend the next school board meeting and present his reasons for continuing multiage grouping. This item is about his preparation. Who should he speak with to help him prepare to do this? What elements of his classroom practice should he emphasize? About what should he be very knowledgeable before addressing the board? Consider the following INTASC Standards and how Chris might use them as he prepares to address the school board:

Principle #2: The teacher understands how children learn and develop, and can provide learning opportunities that support their intellectual, social and personal development.

Principle #3: The teacher understands how students differ in their approaches to learning and creates instructional opportunities that are adapted to diverse learners.

Principle #4: The teacher understands and uses a variety of instructional strategies to encourage students' development of critical thinking, problem solving, and performance skills.

Principle #5: The teacher uses an understanding of individual and group motivation and behavior to create a learning environment that encourages positive social interaction, active engagement in learning, and self-motivation.

Principle #7: The teacher plans instruction based on knowledge of subject matter, students, the community, and curriculum goals.

Principle #9: The teacher is a reflective practitioner who continually evaluates the effects of his or her choices on others and who actively seeks out opportunities to grow professionally.

7. Chris knows how important his introduction is in terms of getting the board to listen to him and find him credible. What should he say in his opening remarks?

Where DO I Stand NOW ?

In the beginning of this chapter you completed an inventory that gauged where you stood on a variety of issues. Now that you have read the chapter, completed exercises related to the content, engaged in class discussions, and so on, answer the following questions in your course notebook.

1. If you discovered through this chapter's inventory that you favored a basic curriculum of ELA, math, science, and social studies to one that encompasses related arts while acknowledging the power of the informal curriculum and extracurricular activities before considering the chapter's content, have you changed your mind? If so, how?

   If, on the other hand, you began the chapter favoring a broad curriculum and now prefer a more basic curriculum, what changed your stance?

2. If you discovered that you prefer to approach instruction in a teacher-centered manner but now are leaning toward a more student-centered approach, what changed your mind?

   If, however, you now prefer a teacher-centered approach given what you have read, what convinced you that a teacher-centered approach will work better for you?

3. The debate involving a stable, not easily changed curriculum versus a curriculum that responds to societal circumstances is one that has existed for centuries. If you began this chapter with the opinion that curriculum should be a stable body of knowledge and skills but now think that societal changes should affect what is taught and learned, what altered your opinion?

   If, however, you began the chapter with the opinion that societal circumstances should influence teaching and learning but now believe that the curriculum should not be swayed by what's happening in the world, what changed your mind?

My Education Lab

The MyEducationLab for this course can help you solidify your comprehension of Chapter 4 concepts.

- Explore the classrooms of the teachers and students you've met in this chapter in the Teaching in Focus section.
- Prepare for licensure exams as you deepen your understanding of chapter concepts in the Developing Professional Competence section.

- Gauge and further develop your understanding of chapter concepts by taking the quizzes and examining the enrichment materials on the Chapter 4 Study Plan.
- Visit Topic 10, "Curriculum and Instruction," to watch ABC videos, explore Assignments and Activities, and practice essential teaching skills with the Building Teaching Skills and Dispositions unit.

References

Allington, R. L. (2002). What I've learned about effective reading instruction. *Phi Delta Kappan, 83*(10), 740–747.

American Council for the Teaching of Foreign Language. (2005). *Standards for foreign language learning.* Retrieved July 1, 2005, from http://www.actfl.org

Anderson, L. W., & Krathwohl, D. R. (Eds.). (2001). *A taxonomy for learning, teaching, and assessing.* New York: Longman.

Banks, J. A. (2003). *Teaching strategies for ethnic studies* (7th ed.). Boston: Allyn & Bacon.

Core Knowledge. (2009). About core knowledge. Retrieved November 20, 2009, from http://coreknowledge.org/CK/about/index.htm.

Cornett, C. E. (2003). *Creating meaning through literature and the arts: An integration resource for classroom teachers* (2nd ed.). Upper Saddle River, NJ: Merrill/Prentice Hall.

Dewey, J. (1900). *The school and society.* Chicago: University of Chicago Press.

Dewey, J. (1902). *The child and the curriculum.* Chicago: University of Chicago Press.

Dewey, J. (1938). *Experience and education.* New York: Macmillan/Collier.

Eisner, E. (2002). *The educational imagination: On the design and evaluation of school programs* (3rd ed.). New York: Macmillan College.

Goodlad, J. I. (1984). *A place called school*. New York: McGraw-Hill.

Gregoire, M.A., & Lupinetti, J. (2005). Supporting diversity through the arts. *Kappa Delta Pi Record, 41*(4), 159-163.

Gunter, M.A., Estes, T. H., & Mintz, S. L. (2007). *Instruction: A models approach* (5th ed.). Boston: Allyn & Bacon.

Holloway, J. H. (2000). Extracurricular activities: The path to academic success? *Educational Leadership, 57*(4), 87-88.

International Society for Technology in Education. (2005). *Mission statement*. Retrieved July 1, 2005, from http://www.iste.org

Jensen, E. (2005). *Teaching with the brain in mind* (2nd ed.). Alexandria, VA: Association for Supervision and Curriculum Development.

Johnson, D.W., & Johnson, R.T. (1999). *Learning together and alone: Cooperative, competitive, and individualistic learning*. Boston: Allyn & Bacon.

Jones, R. (2000, December). Textbook troubles. *American School Board Journal*, pp. 18-21.

Krashen, S. (2002). Whole language and the great plummet of 1987-1992. *Phi Delta Kappan, 83*(10), 748-753.

Little, C. (2001). What matters to students. *Educational Leadership, 59*(2), 61-64.

Lounsbury, J. H. (1991). *As I see it*. Columbus, OH: National Middle School Association.

McHugh, J. (2005). Synching up with the kids. *Edutopia, 1*(7), 32-35.

Moats, L. C. (2001). When older students can't read. *Educational Leadership, 58*(6), 36-40.

National Council for the Social Studies. (2005). *Curriculum standards for social studies: Executive summary*. Retrieved July 1, 2005, from http://www.socialstudies.org/standards/execsummary/

National Science Teachers Association. (2005). *National Science Education Standards*. Retrieved July 1, 2005, from http://books.nap.edu/html/nses/6a.html

Noddings, N. (1992). *The challenge to care in schools: An alternative approach to education*. New York: Teachers College Press.

Osterman, K. (2002). Schools as communities for students. In G. Furman (Ed.), *School as community: From promise to practice*. New York: State University of New York Press.

Powell, S. D. (2010). *Wayside teaching: Connecting with students to support learning*. Thousand Oaks, CA: Corwin Press.

Powell, S. D. (2011). *Introduction to middle school* (2nd ed.). Boston: Allyn & Bacon.

Renard, L. (2005). Teaching the DIG generation. *Educational Leadership, 62*(7), 44-47.

Renzulli, J. S., Gentry, M., & Reis, S. M. (2004). A time and place for authentic learning. *Educational Leadership, 62*(1), 73-77.

Roblyer, M. D. (2006). *Integrating educational technology into teaching*. Upper Saddle River, NJ: Merrill/Prentice Hall.

Stipek, D. (2006). Relationships matter. *Educational Leadership, 64*(1), 46-49.

Tomlinson, C.A. (1999). *The differentiated classroom. Responding to the needs of all learners*. Alexandria, VA: Association for Supervision and Curriculum Development.

Tomlinson, C.A., & McTighe, J. (2006). *Integrating differentiated instruction + understanding by design*. Alexandria, VA: Association for Supervision and Curriculum Development.

Tyler, R. (1949). *Basic principles of curriculum and instruction*. Chicago: University of Chicago Press.

Vacca, R.T. (2002). From efficient decoders to strategic readers. *Educational Leadership, 60*(3), 7-11.

Wiggins, G. P., & McTighe, J. (2005). *Understanding by design* (2nd ed.). Alexandria, VA: Association for Supervision and Curriculum Development.

Wolk, S. (2007). Why go to school? *Phi Delta Kappan, 88*(9), 648-658.

Student Similarities and Differences

Sara Davis Powell

In this chapter we explore the student population in the United States by looking at aspects of similarity as well as aspects of diversity. Here are some questions we focus on:

✦ How are we similar?

✦ How are gender differences manifested in schools?

✦ How are cultural and language diversity manifested in schools?

✦ What is the impact on students of family structure, religion, and socioeconomic status?

✦ How are learning differences manifested in schools?

✦ Who are students with exceptionalities, and how do we serve them?

This is not an exhaustive list of ways that diversity may be exhibited in your classroom, but it's a good start. These differences and more exist in early childhood, elementary, middle, and high school settings. Before we discuss how we are similar and how we are different, explore your own views about student development and diversity in this chapter's *Where Do I Stand?*

Fotolia

From Chapter 3 of *Your Introduction to Education: Explorations in Teaching*, 2/e. Sara Davis Powell.

Where DO I Stand ?

This inventory addresses two broad issues. One issue deals with your prior knowledge of diversity among PreK–12 students, and the other gauges the extent of your personal experiences with diversity. After reading an item, indicate your level of agreement by choosing a number and placing it in the blank before the statement. Following the inventory are directions for how to organize your responses and what they may indicate in terms of where you stand.

> 4 I strongly agree
> 3 I agree
> 2 I don't have an opinion
> 1 I disagree
> 0 I strongly disagree

_____ **1.** Some students have higher IQs than their teachers.

_____ **2.** The white student population is increasing at about the same rate as the Hispanic student population.

_____ **3.** I grew up in a home where I felt secure.

_____ **4.** Girls tend to use their emotions more aggressively than boys.

_____ **5.** Both those with disabilities and those with academic gifts are considered to be students with exceptionalities in public schools.

_____ **6.** I was in what were considered regular classes or advanced classes in PreK–12 school.

_____ **7.** Learning disabilities account for about 20% of those students receiving special services.

_____ **8.** Gender stereotyping occurs when perceived differences in attitudes, interests, and actions based on gender are assumed for all people.

_____ **9.** More people are designating themselves as multiracial now than ever before in the United States.

_____ **10.** I have very few acquaintances that are of a different race than me.

_____ **11.** It is possible for individuals to be smart in a variety of ways.

_____ **12.** Christianity is the religion with which I most relate.

_____ **13.** Studies reveal that about 5% of children in U.S. classrooms have attention deficit hyperactivity disorder (ADHD).

_____ **14.** Teachers tend to call on girls more often than boys.

_____ **15.** Girls are more likely to be inducted into the National Honor Society than boys.

_____ **16.** A diagnosis of ADHD qualifies a student for special education services.

_____ **17.** I don't know many people for whom English is not their first language.

_____ **18.** Immigrant students are spread evenly across the United States.

_____ **19.** About 1 of every 20 children in U.S. schools is an English-language learner.

_____ **20.** A person's ethnicity often reveals more about him or her than race.

_____ **21.** I spent all or much of my childhood in a two-parent home.

_____ **22.** Race is based primarily on a person's place of birth.

_____ **23.** In my K–12 school years, very few, if any, of my classmates were of races other than my own.

_____ **24.** Church services and church friends played a big role in my childhood.

_____ **25.** Boys tend to blame failure on lack of skill rather than lack of effort.

_____ **26.** About half of the people in the United States say their religion is based on Christianity.

_____ **27.** Most children in U.S. public schools who do not speak English fluently were born in the United States.

_____ **28.** I did not personally know students who received special education services when I was in PreK–12 school.

_____ **29.** Federal law states that all students with dis-abilities have a right to a free education in a regular classroom setting if parents decide it's appropriate.

_____ **30.** Race is based on physical characteristics people have from birth.

_____ **31.** Most of my friends had a mom, a dad, and siblings living together.

_____ **32.** I grew up knowing very few students who spoke a language other than English in their homes.

_____ **33.** Intelligence is a fixed attribute that can be accurately measured.

_____ **34.** My family had enough money for my needs, and most of my wants, to be fulfilled.

_____ **35.** When IQ is used to determine gifted status, the threshold number is about 125.

_____ **36.** Most children will only respond adequately to instruction after their need for security is met.

This inventory has addressed two broad issues:

- _To what extent do my personal experiences reflect exposure to diversity?_

- _How much do I know about diversity among PreK–12 students?_

To answer these questions, record your responses in three columns as indicated.

ITEM #	MY RESPONSE	ITEM #	MY RESPONSE	ITEM #	MY RESPONSE
3		1		2	
6		4		7	
10		5		13	
12		8		14	
17		9		16	
21		11		18	
23		15		19	
24		20		22	
28		27		25	
31		30		26	
32		35		29	
34		36		33	
Sum A		Sum B		Sum C	

To what extent do my personal experiences reflect exposure to diversity?

The closer your column A responses are to 4, the fewer experiences you have had with diversity. Divide Sum A by 12. If your mean is 3 to 4, you have not had significant experiences with diversity; if your mean is 0 to 2, you have had significant experiences with diversity.

How much do I know about diversity among PreK–12 students?

The closer your column B responses are to 4, the more you know about diversity among PreK–12 students. Divide Sum B by 12. If your mean is 3 to 4, you have significant knowledge of diversity among PreK–12 students.

The closer your column C responses are to 0, the more you know about diversity among PreK–12 students. Divide Sum C by 12. If your mean is 0 to 2, you have significant knowledge of diversity among PreK–12 students.

Take a few minutes to think about your responses and what you have learned from this exploration. Share your scores if directed by your instructor.

Teaching in Focus

As Craig Cleveland looks around his classroom at Roosevelt High School in Fresno, California, while his second-period U.S. History students are making their way to their seats, he sees 32 adolescents—7 sophomores, 21 juniors, and 4 seniors. They are chatting as they make themselves comfortable in the crowded second-floor room. Their primary languages tell much of their ethnic stories—15 speak Spanish, 10 Hmong, 6 English, and 1 Laotian. Thirteen of the 32 speak very little English and write even less.

All 32 students qualify for free or reduced-price meals. Craig knows that students from low-income families struggle more to achieve academically. When measured by standardized tests, over half are considered below basic, or far below basic, in both English language arts and math. In addition, 19 of the 32 have impairments of some kind that are recognized by the school and require special accommodations by teachers.

Craig's challenge today is to pique every student's interest in the question, "Is separate ever really equal?" To do this, Craig must find a way to define the issues, present background information and make it relevant to his heterogeneous class, and then facilitate an activity that engages every student.

The students in Craig's class are alike in many ways: They are all adolescents, most are from low-income homes in the same geographic area, and they have all gone through similar developmental stages to become 15-, 16-, 17-, and 18-year-olds. They also have many differences: Some are male, and some are female; some were born in the United States, whereas others are recent immigrants; some are Catholic, some Protestant, some Buddhist. When viewed as a group, Craig's students are a wonderful but challenging example of diversity in the American classroom.

Watch a segment of Craig's lesson, as well as his interview and room tour, in the Teaching in Focus section for Chapter 3 in MyEducationLab for this course.

How Are We Similar?

In the time it takes you to read about three pages of this text, a whole classroom of students will be born. That's right—statistically, every 8 minutes 30 babies are born in the United States. Your entire future kindergarten class, third grade class, middle school social studies class, or high school algebra class may be coming into the world right now.

Statistically, we can predict that of these 30 future students, 14 will be considered a racial minority, 8 will be born into poverty, and 9 will be born out of wedlock. Of these 30 children, 17 will have parents who divorce before the students graduate from high school, 5 will serve jail sentences, 5 will be victims of violence, 4 will commit a violent crime before age 16, and almost half will drop out before finishing high school (National Center for Education Statistics [NCES], 2004; U.S. Census Bureau, 2008). "And how are the children?"

Chances are your classroom won't mirror the statistics you just read. Classroom populations vary from little cultural or socioeconomic diversity to a challenging mix. You may teach in a school with students whose families are financially well off or one with families that move when the rent comes due. You may teach in a stable rural community with conservative values and lifestyles, or you may teach in a suburban area that affords a great variety of opportunities and educational options but where students tend to move often.

The 30 new lives that have begun in this 8-minute time frame may appear to be diverse, but they are actually more similar than they are dissimilar. They are individual beings with unique attributes and a variety of needs. But the most important thing to remember is that they are children, all worthy of our best efforts. Mark Twain said that every day children are born who could change the world. We just don't know who they are yet.

NATURE AND NURTURE

There has been much debate on the question of what has the greater influence in determining who we are—nature or nurture. These two concepts are generally presented as oppositional: nature *versus* nurture. **Nature** refers to genetically inherited influences. Not only are certain physical characteristics, such as eye color, skin tone, and adult height,

Figure 3.1 Maslow's hierarchy of needs

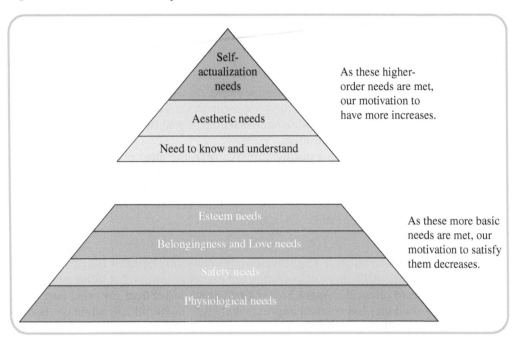

As these higher-order needs are met, our motivation to have more increases.

As these more basic needs are met, our motivation to satisfy them decreases.

Source: Maslow, A. H. (1999). *Toward a psychology of being* (3rd ed.). New York: Wiley.

determined by nature, but some aspects of our intelligence and personalities are established genetically as well. **Nurture** refers to the influences of our environment, encompassing everything that cannot be accounted for genetically. For instance, the people we meet, the schools we attend, and our economic status are all part of nurture.

Each child arrives in the world with predispositions, or tendencies, accounted for by nature and over which we have no control. Teachers do have some influence, however, over nurture. That's why we create classroom environments that stimulate growth—physical, intellectual, emotional, social, and moral. To more fully realize why we need to create this environment, let's examine the importance and relative priority of human needs that we all share.

MASLOW'S HIERARCHY OF NEEDS

Psychologist Abraham Maslow (1908–1970) proposed that human beings experience the same needs. Figure 3.1 shows his classic **hierarchy of needs,** which is widely accepted as an accurate depiction of the order, from bottom to top, in which needs have to be met for healthy and full human development.

Maslow proposed that basic needs for survival and safety must be met first. Once these needs are satisfied, humans are motivated to move up the pyramid toward higher-order needs.

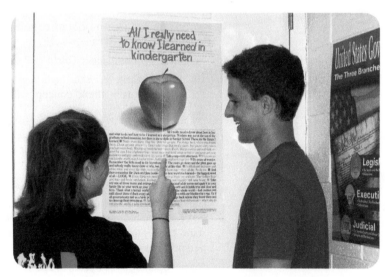

Many older students agree that what they learned during the rapid brain growth period before first grade continues to influence them. Sara Davis Powell

Makes sense, doesn't it? If students don't have food and shelter, or if they feel physically threatened, it's unlikely they will be concerned about understanding the Pythagorean theorem. Providing opportunities and support for needs fulfillment and promoting positive student development will help them ascend Maslow's pyramid and develop in positive ways.

STUDENT DEVELOPMENT

Most children progress through predictable age-related stages of development. The more we know about these developmental stages, the more empathy and support we can offer. Here we briefly consider five developmental areas.

Watch David McBeath's interview, including his mom, in the Teaching in Focus section for Chapter 3 in MyEducationLab for this course. You will see that David's physical development appears to have outpaced his other areas of development.

PHYSICAL DEVELOPMENT. Physical development involves how our bodies appear and how they function. Patterns of physical development are orderly in that the progression is generally predictable. Body parts mature at rates that make physical development the most obvious of the five areas of development.

Although each child follows a distinct growth curve, the most rapid growth occurs in early childhood, with steady growth through elementary school. In early adolescence there may be an explosive growth rate, leveling off in late adolescence. Girls often experience puberty as much as 2 years earlier than boys, but boys generally grow taller and heavier than girls by late adolescence (McDevitt & Ormrod, 2010).

COGNITIVE DEVELOPMENT. Cognitive (intellectual) development is considered the primary focus of school. Changes in cognition are just as profound, but often much more subtle, than outward physical changes. Yet the brain grows faster than any other part of the body. By age 5, the brain has reached approximately 90% of its full size while the body is only 30% developed (Feldman, 2008).

Jean Piaget (1896–1980) was one of the most renowned cognitive development theorists. Piaget recognized distinct differences in children's and adolescents' responses to questions that directly correlated to their chronological ages. This was the beginning of his research into the four **stages of cognitive development** encapsulated in Figure 3.2.

Although Piaget's work is still held in very high esteem, researchers have concluded that he based much of his theory on children's deficits rather than on their strengths. Children may be more capable at younger ages than Piaget believed. Teachers benefit from knowing about Piaget's stages but should never use them to limit how and when the intellectual capabilities of students are stretched.

Figure 3.2 Piaget's model of cognitive development

<u>Sensorimotor intelligence</u> (birth to 2 years of age)

Children primarily learn through their senses as their motor capabilities develop. Children in this stage don't actually "think" conceptually.

<u>Preoperational thought</u> (2–7 years of age)

Children begin to use symbols and their grasp of concepts develops rapidly. They begin to think about things and people outside their observable environment. Their viewpoint is generally limited because they have little ability to see things from different perspectives.

<u>Concrete operations</u> (7–11 years of age)

Children begin to think logically. They understand the concept of conservation, that quantities don't change because they are moved. Through manipulation of concrete objects they understand concepts such as number, space, and causality. They begin to see things from varied perspectives and draw conclusions.

<u>Formal operations</u> (11 years of age and on)

Adolescents progress from concrete thinking to the capability of thinking abstractly. They are able to make predictions, experience metacognition (thinking about thinking), and appreciate and use the structure and subtleties of language.

Source: McDevitt, T. M., & Ormrod, J. E. (2010). *Child development and education.* Upper Saddle River, NJ: Merrill/Pearson Education.

Student Similarities and Differences

Rather than looking at deficiencies, noted Russian psychologist Lev Vygotsky (1896–1934) advocated determining children's intellectual abilities and then providing opportunities for intellectual growth. He proposed that a child's cognitive development increases through exposure to new information and that learning takes place within the individual's **zone of proximal development**. This zone is the level at which a child can almost, but not completely, grasp a concept or perform a task successfully. As learning takes place, the zone widens. This theory is akin to **scaffolding,** a concept widely accepted within education that takes its name from the construction term for temporary supports placed around a structure to allow work to be completed. Vygotsky viewed learning scaffolding as the support given to children to help them move through progressive levels of learning.

Additionally, Vygotsky believed that children's learning is shaped by the culture and society around them. The more interactions, the greater the learning, as a child moves forward within an ever-expanding zone of proximal development (Feldman, 2008).

High school students' sense of identity develops during adolescence.
Sara Davis Powell

EMOTIONAL DEVELOPMENT. Human experiences are given meaning through emotions. Both our emotions and our responses to them become more complicated with time. Children and adolescents experience a wide array of emotions, including happiness, anxiety, anger, fear, sadness, shame, and pride. For young adolescents, all these emotions and more may be experienced in one class period. Teachers need to be able to identify emotions as well as know how and when to respond to them.

In 1995 Daniel Goleman wrote *Emotional Intelligence: Why It Can Matter More Than IQ,* in which he proposed that a person's **emotional intelligence quotient (EQ)** may be the best indicator of future success in life. Emotional intelligence quotient involves a set of skills that accompany the expression, evaluation, and regulation of emotions. A high-level emotional quotient indicates an ability to understand others' as well as one's own feelings, respond appropriately to them, and, in general, get along.

SOCIAL DEVELOPMENT. Learning to get along with others is a process that begins when young children sit next to each other in **parallel play,** agreeably sharing the same space but not communicating. When children begin to share toys and verbally communicate, they are engaged in **associative play**. Progressing to **cooperative play,** children actively coordinate ways to keep the interaction going. When you think about it, these stages of socialization describe how we relate to others regardless of our age. Relating to others and thinking about them (and ourselves) is called **social cognition**. Whether we are simply coexisting (parallel play), communicating when necessary (associative play), or actively engaging with others (cooperative play), we are social creatures.

Relationships matter to us; adolescents are, at times, consumed with them. Relationships are part of America's youth culture, much of which revolves around groups that inevitably form as adolescents search for their identities. It's quite easy to see which youth subcultures appear to fit most easily into the traditional school setting—generally it's the "cool kids," the "jocks," and the "preppies." Other students may exhibit different developmental patterns and be labeled "nerds," "stoners," "eggheads," "loners," "goths," and so on. The names may change, but subgroups live on. As teachers our challenge is to connect with all our students and let them know we care about them, regardless of their social affiliations. Helping students develop positive and productive relationships within society is a major aspect of what teachers do.

Watch Sherlonda Francis's interview, including her mom and dad, in the Teaching in Focus *section for Chapter 3 in MyEducationLab for this course. You will hear Sherlonda's parents talk about her very social nature. Her teacher, Renee Ayers, says that Sherlonda's social nature may be a source of difficulty in achieving academic success.*

Student Similarities and Differences

Teaching in Focus

Sara Davis Powell

Tim Mendenhall, grades 3–5, multi-age classroom, Rees Elementary School, Utah. *In his own words. . . .*

I would first encourage you to follow your heart. Trust yourself and do what you feel needs to be done for your students. Education is messy. You will try things and fail. That's how we learn.

Second, more than reading and math, teaching your students to be lifelong learners is your ultimate goal. Make your classroom fun. If you don't like a book or an activity, why do you think they will? Love what you are doing, and they will learn to love learning.

Finally, stay at teaching long enough to get the REAL pay. This could be a child bringing you a Cherry Coke (instead of an apple) every Friday. Or a former student running off the football field to talk with you when he is quarterback and supposed to be leading a play. Or a parent coming back and telling you that you are still their child's favorite teacher (even after all the years and they are now graduating from high school). The pay is great; you just have to wait for it sometimes.

Read focus teacher Tim Mendenhall's words about forming relationships, adjusting what we do in the classroom based on who our students are, and about making our classrooms fun in *Teaching in Focus*.

CHARACTER DEVELOPMENT. A discussion of character, or moral, development can easily become value laden, depending on particular religious or ethical beliefs. Even so, certain character traits are considered positive by almost everyone, including honesty, trustworthiness, fairness, caring, and citizenship (Gathercoal & Crowell, 2000).

Noted developmental psychologist Lawrence Kohlberg contends that people pass through **stages of moral reasoning** as illustrated in Figure 3.3. Kohlberg's stages are based primarily on observations of males in Western culture and have been criticized for not being more universal or sensitive to gender differences. A psychologist and colleague of Kohlberg, Carol Gilligan (1982) suggests that differences in the way girls and boys are raised (nurture) can lead to differences in how they view moral dilemmas. According to Gilligan, boys tend to view morality in terms of broad principles of justice, whereas girls tend to view morality in terms of responsibility to individuals. We look more closely at gender differences in the next section.

A brief summary of development stages is in Table 3.1. Now that we've established some of the ways we are the same, let's think about ways we may be different.

Figure 3.3 Kohlberg's stages of moral reasoning

Stage 1: A rule is a rule, and people obey rules to avoid punishment.

Stage 2: Rules are followed or disobeyed based on rewards.

Stage 3: People obey rules because it's what others expect of them.

Stage 4: Society's rules are what's right, and people conform to expectations.

Stage 5: People follow rules out of obligation to what is agreed upon behavior in their society. Laws and rules can be changed if society sees a compelling need.

Stage 6: People follow rules that agree with universal ethics. If a law doesn't, they feel free to disobey it.

Source: Adapted from Kohlberg, L. (1984). *The psychology of moral development: Essays on moral development.* San Francisco: Harper & Row.

Student Similarities and Differences

TABLE 3.1 Developmental characteristics by level

	Early Childhood	Elementary	Middle	High
PHYSICAL	-Dramatic changes in appearance and abilities -Boundless energy -Rapid brain growth -Healthiest time of life	-Coordination increases -Dexterity improves -Steady growth -Significant differences in size among children	-Onset of puberty -Sudden growth spurts may change appearance -Specialized gross and fine motor skills develop -Some risk-taking behaviors exhibited	-Sexual/reproductive maturity is reached -Girls complete growth spurt; boys continue to grow -High level of physical risk-taking activities exhibited
COGNITIVE	-Piaget's preoperational stage -Very intense brain activity -Increased ability to: speak with coherence, understand organization and patterns, learn prerequisites for reading	-Piaget's concrete operational stage -Increased ability to think logically, apply learning strategies, view multiple perspectives, decode phonetically, read aloud	-Beginning of Piaget's formal operational stage -Often self-absorbed -Increased ability to: reason, solve complex problems, use varied learning strategies	-Capacity for adult-like thought -Increased ability to: reason abstractly, make decisions with more realism, discern which learning strategies are effective
EMOTIONAL	-Self-concept develops and is influenced by family and society -self-conscious emotions such as guilt and pride develop	-Self-concept becomes more complex and differentiated -Coping skills develop -Emotional ties beyond family develop	-May be emotionally volatile -Drop in self-esteem -Strong emotional ties with friends develop -Frequent mood changes -Begin to establish a sense of identity	-Sense of being invulnerable -May be prone to depression -Seek independence and a sense of control -Sense of identity develops
SOCIAL	-Relationships with adults centered on direction, care, and protection -First friendships are developed -Types of play change from individual to cooperative -Become aware of other people's feelings	-Increasingly concerned with making and keeping friends -Becoming more assertive -Groups are generally same-gender -Capable of empathy -Awareness of social conventions and rules	-Conflicts with parents and other adults likely -Peers become more influential than adults -Popularity, or lack of it, becomes very important -Awareness develops of sexuality and gender-related relationships	-Identity crisis may lead to social dysfunction -Mixed-gender groups -Conformity with others decreases -Desire for self-reliance -Often overwhelmed with demands of relationships
CHARACTER	-Rules are rigid -Begins to understand intentionality -Aggression declines as language develops -Beginning awareness that actions may cause others harm	-Rules come from shared knowledge -Increased awareness of others' problems -Experience guilt and shame over moral wrong doing	-Strong sense of fairness -Desire to help those less fortunate -May value social approval over moral conviction	-Understand the need for rules to promote society -Increased concern about fulfilling duty to benefit others

Sources: Feldman (2008); Gallahue and Ozmun (2006); Goleman (1995); McDevitt and Ormrod (2010); Powell (2011); Richardson and Norman (2000).

How Are Gender Differences Manifested in Schools?

"It's a boy!" "It's a girl!" These are the exclamations heard in every delivery room in the United States. The anatomical differences between males and females determine sex; **gender** is the sense of being one sex or the other. Boys and girls, men and women—the differences

Student Similarities and Differences

are undeniable and are as fundamental as life itself. By age 2, children understand that they are either boys or girls, and they label others as well (Campbell, Shirley, & Candy, 2004).

It is common in U.S. households for girls to be encouraged to engage in what are considered gender-appropriate activities, such as playing with dolls and cooking on make-believe stoves; boys are encouraged to play with cars and throw balls. Household chores are often assigned by gender, with girls asked to wash dishes and boys asked to cut the grass. Boys and girls sense very quickly that there are expectations based on gender. **Gender stereotyping** occurs when perceived gender differences are assumed for all people, as in assuming that the play and chores described are always appropriate for one gender or the other. Generalizations about gender differences appropriately begin with phrases such as *tend to*. These two words indicate generalizing, as opposed to stereotyping. **Gender bias** is the favoring of one gender over the other in specific circumstances.

The federal government recognized gender bias in schools in 1972 when Congress passed Title IX of the Education Amendments Act, which states, "No person in the United States shall, on the basis of sex, be excluded from participation in, be denied the benefits of, or be subjected to discrimination under, any education program or activity receiving Federal financial assistance." Title IX has helped correct inequitable treatment of males and females in schools, most notably in athletic programs involving teams.

SOCIAL ASPECTS OF GENDER

During early childhood, children are friends with whoever is convenient, at day care, in preschool, or in the neighborhood. During the elementary school years children begin choosing friends of the same gender who have similar interests. With the advent of puberty, friends of the opposite gender begin to be included, and this trend continues through high school.

Boys tend to base their play on activities, whereas girls tend to base their play on talking. In group play, boys tend to play in more adventurous ways, such as acting out battles and physically challenging each other, whereas girls tend to take on roles that are calm, such as playing house or school. Research shows that boys tend to be more aggressive than girls, at least in physical ways. Boys most often show what researchers call **instrumental aggression,** or aggression based on attempting to meet a specific goal, such as grabbing a toy or establishing dominance in an activity. Girls may be as aggressive, but they usually learn to be so in more subtle ways that may be more emotional than physical. This type of aggression is known as **relational aggression** and may include name-calling, gossiping, or saying mean things just to be hurtful (Underwood, 2003).

ACHIEVEMENT AND GENDER

In general, researchers have found that boys tend to set higher goals than girls (Bandura, Barbaranelli, Caprara, & Pastorelli, 2001) and attribute their achievement to ability. When they fail, they tend to attribute their failure to lack of effort. In contrast, when girls meet their goals, they tend to attribute their success to effort. When they fail, they tend to attribute their failure to lack of ability (Vermeer, Boekaerts, & Seeger, 2000). This generalization, illustrated in Table 3.2, is significant for teachers to understand. It indicates that one gender may be conditioned to view failure as the result of a lack of effort, which is easily corrected. The other gender may see failure as the result of a lack of ability, which is not easily corrected.

Until recently it was generally held that boys scored higher than girls in almost every area tested. This academic gender gap has been closing in the last 20 years. Although girls

TABLE 3.2 Boys' and girls' perceived reasons for success and failure		
Perceived reason for	Boys	Girls
Success	High ability	High effort
Failure	Low effort	Low ability

Source: Vermeer, H. J., Bodkaert, M., & Seeger, G. (2000). Motivational and gender differences: Sixth-grade students' mathematical problem-solving behavior. *Journal of Educational Psychology, 92,* 308–315.

Student Similarities and Differences

In the News

abc NEWS

Boys in Crisis

This *World News Tonight* report raises the question of whether boys are really in crisis. Headlines are presented that seem to tell us that we need to pay particular attention to the plight of boys. A Harvard researcher says there is something inherently "sad" about boys and tells us that boys are much more likely to attempt suicide than girls and are not as enthusiastic about attending college. After examining test data, however, another researcher says that boys are fine. The Harvard researcher says there's more to the "sadness" of boys, elements that don't show up in test scores. In an interview of recent male high school graduates, we hear one young man say that boys simply don't feel as comfortable seeking help with the various stresses they may face.

To view this video, go to Chapter 3 in MyEducationLab for this course, click on In the News.

1. What do you think the researcher means when he says there is a "sadness" in boys? Do you agree with his characterization? If so, give an example of why. If not, why not?

2. Do you think boys are less inclined than girls to seek help with an emotional or social problem? On what do you base your opinion?

3. As a teacher, what could you do to help your male students not be "in crisis," as the headlines presented at the beginning of the video seem to indiate they are?

as a group may lag behind boys in some areas of science and upper-level math, they are outpacing boys in reading and writing, more likely to be inducted into the National Honor Society, and more likely to attend college (Glazer, 2005).

In classrooms many teachers call on boys more often than girls, allow boys to call out answers while scolding girls for doing so, give boys more encouragement to attempt difficult tasks, and generally have higher expectations for boys than for girls. This subtle discrimination is almost always unintentional, but it nevertheless has an effect on classroom participation (Gober & Mewborn, 2001).

This chapter's *In the News* addresses the perception that boys are in crisis. Some who study gender differences contend that boys have unique and previously unacknowledged problems dealing with school and achievement.

SEXUAL ORIENTATION

The sex to which a person is romantically or socially attracted determines a person's **sexual orientation**. Estimates of the percentage of Americans who are gay or lesbian (attracted to the same sex) range from 5% to 10%. It is reasonable to assume that these estimates apply to the American student population as well. Although it has achieved a measure of acceptance, homosexuality remains in many instances the basis of discrimination and focus of hateful attitudes and actions. The two places that we like to think of as safe and supportive—home and school—are often the very places where the most hurtful slurs and overt rejection of gay and lesbian students occur.

GENDER DIVERSITY: IMPLICATIONS FOR TEACHERS

As of January 2010, 91 of the 547 public schools offering single-sex education opportunities were completely either all-boy or all-girl settings. Note that when schools and classes are discussed by the National Association for Single-Sex Public Education, the label goes from *gender* to *sex*. The word *sex* is used rather than gender because it is a more readily definable attribute. When the National Association for Single-Sex Public Education (NASSPE) was founded in 2002, there were fewer than 20 single-sex education opportunities (NASSPE, 2010). You can see this is a growing trend. For more information, including a list of schools by state offering single-sex options, visit www.singlesexschools.org/home-introduction.htm.

Student Similarities and Differences

We can't deny that girls and boys are different in some ways, whether the differences stem from nature, from nurture, or from the inevitable combination. With awareness we can diminish gender-biased behaviors and attitudes in our schools. The most important contribution we can make toward alleviating gender bias in our classrooms is to treat our students as individuals, realizing that each is unique. In modeling this behavior we will help promote it in our students.

Our goal in creating **gender equity,** the fair and balanced treatment of boys and girls, is to provide learning environments where all students are free from limitations that might accompany gender stereotyping of what they can or should accomplish. Addressing the following questions will help foster gender equity in the classroom:

Points of Reflection 3.1

Have you ever felt discrimination based on gender? If so, explain. Are you aware of discrimination in a school setting based on sexual orientation? If so, explain. Have you considered teaching in an all-boy or all-girl setting?

- Do I use examples of males and females in all roles and occupations?
- Do I encourage girls as well as boys to explore science and math?
- Do I encourage boys as well as girls to read for pleasure and to participate in poetry writing and drama?
- Am I careful to include historical contributions of both males and females?
- Do I have a way of assuring that I call on boys and girls in equal numbers during class discussions?

How Are Cultural and Language Diversity Manifested in Schools?

Classrooms that were once populated with white students, black students, and perhaps a few students with other cultural identities are now filled with students of many races and ethnicities. Along with this diversity come more and more students whose first language is not English. Figure 3.4 shows projections for the changing student population ages 5 to 19 and represents more than 63 million children and adolescents in 2010. Note the trend of white students comprising diminishing percentages, with black and Asian percentages remaining relatively stable and the Hispanic percentage steadily increasing.

Figure 3.4 Projections of U.S. population, ages 5–19

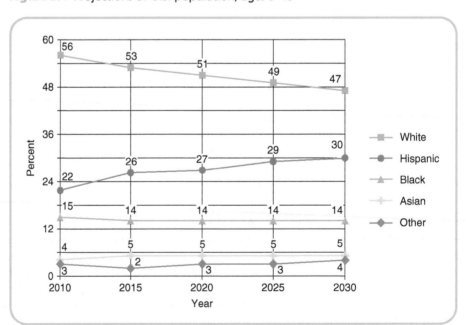

Source: U.S. Census Bureau, http://www.census.gov/population/www/projection/summarytables.html; 2000 census; 2008 prediction.

Student Similarities and Differences

Teachers in the United States are overwhelmingly white, with only about 5% black, and 5% Hispanic, Asian, and other races. Add this information to the fact that by 2025 less than half of children and adolescents in the United States will be white, and you can see that appreciating, acknowledging, and altering our curriculum and instruction to be responsive to the students in our classrooms will be increasingly challenging. Knowing our students well is imperative.

CULTURAL DIVERSITY

A widely accepted definition of **culture** states that it is a "dynamic system of social values, cognitive codes, behavioral standards, world views, and beliefs used to give order and meaning to our own lives as well as the lives of others" (Delgado-Gaitan & Trueba, 1991). Culture, and the complex combination of elements that compose it, should have a prominent place in any discussion of American education. Geneva Gay (2000) tells us that "culture is at the heart of all we do in the name of education" (p. 8).

Recent research suggests that culture affects perceptions of the characteristics of intelligence. In the study "Who Are the Bright Children? The Cultural Context of Being and Acting Intelligent," Sternberg (2007) tells us that "different cultures have different views of intelligence, so which children are considered intelligent may vary from one culture to another" (p. 148). He contends that teachers' acceptance and understanding of the differences can affect how well students learn. Intriguing idea, isn't it?

Gollnick and Chinn (2009) contend that culture has three primary characteristics. First, culture is *learned*. The language, the ways we behave, the social rules, the expectations, the roles—all these aspects of a culture are learned from family and others who influence our daily lives. The second primary characteristic of culture is that it is sustained and strengthened because it is *shared*. To learn how to "be" in a culture requires mentors, those who share the culture and, in doing so, perpetuate the culture. Third, a culture is *adaptive* to its environment. The culture of a large group of people changes, or adapts, over time in response to many variables.

The characteristics that apply to cultures of groups also apply to cultures of individuals. Each of us has a cultural identity.

CULTURAL IDENTITY. The interactions of many factors, including language, religion, gender, socioeconomic status, age, values, beliefs, race, and ethnicity, form a person's **cultural identity**. This identity is adapted throughout a person's life in response to his or her experiences.

The words *race, ethnicity,* and *culture* are often used interchangeably, but they do not have the same meaning. As teachers, we need to understand the meanings of the terms to better navigate the complexities of our students' lives. Although the color of our skin (race) and the country of our origin (ethnicity) may contribute strongly to our cultural identity, neither encompasses the total concept of culture. Let's consider race and ethnicity separately.

Racial Component of Culture. The word **race,** when applied to a group of people, simply categorizes them according to the physical characteristics they have at birth, such as skin color and facial features. Characterization by race is a social, political, economic, and psychological reality (Mukhopadhyay & Henze, 2003). Some researchers say there are actually as few as three races, whereas others claim there are more than 300 (Gollnick & Chinn, 2009). Not a very precise way to categorize people, is it?

The federal government uses race to categorize people in the United States. For census taking, five races are designated: white, Hispanic, black, Asian/Pacific Islander, and American Indian/Eskimo/Aleut. We still refer to races other than white as minorities. Table 3.3 lists the minority student populations by state. Note the wide range, with Maine at 4% and the District of Columbia at 96%.

Categories of race are indistinct, without consideration of family or country of origin. Beginning in 2000, the census form allowed people to check more than one race. Because race is based solely on physical characteristics, what box would a person check whose mother is Chinese and father is Cuban? Half of Asian immigrants' children marry non-Asians,

State	Total Students	Minority Students	Percentage of Minority Students	State	Total Students	Minority Students	Percentage of Minority Students
				Tennessee	936,681	269,541	29
District of Columbia	78,057	74,690	96	Rhode Island	159,375	45,475	29
Hawaii	183,609	146,540	80	Washington	1,021,349	291,137	29
New Mexico	323,066	217,243	67	Michigan	1,757,604	478,955	27
California	6,413,862	4,166,409	65	Massachusetts	980,459	249,148	25
Texas	4,331,751	2,653,701	61	Pennsylvania	1,821,146	431,511	24
Mississippi	493,540	260,269	52	Kansas	470,490	109,208	23
Louisiana	727,709	375,099	52	Missouri	905,941	201,670	22
Arizona	1,012,068	514,413	51	Oregon	551,273	126,668	23
Maryland	869,133	430,663	50	Wisconsin	880,031	186,264	21
Florida	2,587,628	1,260,936	49	Ohio	1,845,428	372,406	20
Georgia	1,552,611	729,218	47	Nebraska	285,542	58,499	20
Nevada	385,401	189,721	49	Minnesota	842,854	166,950	20
New York	2,864,775	1,321,845	46	Indiana	1,011,130	186,754	18
South Carolina	699,198	318,812	46	Utah	495,981	81,922	17
Illinois	2,100,961	895,179	43	Idaho	252,120	40,160	16
New Jersey	1,380,753	581,591	42	Montana	148,356	22,062	15
Delaware	117,668	50,252	43	South Dakota	125,537	18,899	15
North Carolina	1,360,209	567,168	42	Wyoming	87,462	12,277	14
Alaska	133,933	55,052	41	Kentucky	663,885	82,314	12
Alabama	731,220	293,015	40	North Dakota	102,233	12,271	12
Virginia	1,192,092	453,961	38	Iowa	481,226	56,885	12
Oklahoma	626,160	241,311	39	West Virginia	281,215	16,563	6
Colorado	757,693	268,351	35	New Hampshire	207,417	11,938	6
Connecticut	577,203	182,036	32	Vermont	99,103	4,090	4
Arkansas	454,523	136,647	30	Maine	202,084	8,472	4

Source: National Center for Education Statistics (2006). Common Core of Data (CCD), "Public Elementary/Secondary School Universe Survey," 2003–04, and "State Nonfiscal Survey of Public Elementary/Secondary Education," 2003–2004.

Khammany, one of our focus students at Roosevelt High School, is Laotian, while most of the Asian students at the school are Hmong or Cambodian. Cultural differences exist among Asian students that are important for teachers to understand. Watch her interview, including her mom, in the Teaching in Focus section for Chapter 3 in MyEducationLab for this course.

and 35% of Latino immigrants marry members of other races (Diversity Data, 2000). According to the 2000 census, about 7 million people indicated they were multiracial by marking more than one of the five races listed.

Ethnic Component of Culture. We will use the word **ethnicity** to mean simply an individual's country of origin (Gollnick & Chinn, 2009). Even if families are two, three, or more generations removed from their ancestral country they may still strongly identify with both the country and the people who share their ethnicity. The category of ethnicity often reveals much more about our students than race. Knowing that a student is Hispanic (race) doesn't necessarily tell us much, but knowing that the child is of Cuban, Chilean, or Mexican heritage may be much more revealing and much more personalized (Hodgkinson, 2001).

CULTURAL PLURALISM. We often hear the United States referred to as a *melting pot*, a metaphor that conjures up visions of a big caldron into which we all jump, are warmed to the melting point, and stirred with a big spoon that blends us together until we lose unique and characteristic traits. This pretty much describes **assimilation,** the process of bringing

Student Similarities and Differences

persons of all races and ethnicities into the mainstream by having them behave in ways that align with the dominant culture. Some assimilation is inevitable, and even productive, but the notion that to be successful we all must look, think, and act in similar ways is unhealthy in a nation that values individualism and human rights.

Cultural pluralism involves the recognition that our nation is populated by a rich variety of people of varying races and ethnicities, and thus cultures, all with potential to positively contribute to our common goal of a productive, free society. So what would a school that purposefully promotes cultural pluralism look like? Such a school would teach a curriculum that includes the history and contributions of a variety of cultures; encourage the expression of cultural traditions in the school setting; work toward closing achievement gaps that exist among racial, ethnic, and cultural groups; and assure that no student is excluded from participation in school activities based on race, ethnicity, or any other aspect of culture.

CULTURAL DIVERSITY: IMPLICATIONS FOR TEACHERS

Three broad concepts have implications for effective teaching and learning with regard to cultural diversity.

GLOBAL AWARENESS AND 21ST-CENTURY SKILLS. One of the themes of the Partnership for 21st Century Skills (P21) is global awareness, not just for inclusion in what we teach students but as a vital component for teachers themselves. **Global awareness** involves understanding environmental, societal, cultural, political, and economical concepts and issues that impact our world. We must know what's happening on our planet and understand, as well as respect, the fact that there are many worldviews and perspectives among people (Partnership for 21st Century Skills, 2009). Not being globally aware is a disservice to our students.

MULTICULTURAL EDUCATION. The response of many U.S. educators to the fast-paced growth of diversity is **multicultural education,** an approach that celebrates diversity and promotes equal educational opportunities. James Banks (2004), an expert in the field, tells us that multicultural education has several goals, including

- the creation of equal opportunities for students of all cultures
- the development of knowledge, attitudes, and skills needed to function successfully in a diverse society
- the promotion of communication and interaction among groups that work for the common good

Unfortunately, many teachers attempt to include multicultural education by simply observing February as Black History Month or including a social studies unit on Native Americans. Chances are these lessons have little impact on the day-to-day lives of students. Some people actually oppose any attempt to address cultural diversity, fearing that multicultural education will divert attention from more important curriculum or weaken the sense of continuity and tradition in a school. According to Banks, those who promote the inclusion of multicultural education neither approve of shallow inclusion of concepts nor intend for it to in any way weaken U.S. schools.

Sonia Nieto (2003), a leading author on the topic of multicultural education, is concerned about the simplistic ways in which multicultural education is taught in schools. She proposes that multicultural education permeate all areas of schooling. Nieto says that if we ask ourselves the following four questions and then spend our careers as educators answering them, facing the answers, and making continual corrections, we will take multicultural education where it needs to go.

- "Who's taking calculus?" (student population in challenging courses)
- "Which classes meet in the basement?" (distribution of the best resources and facilities)

Points of Reflection 3.2

What is your race? What is your ethnicity? How would you define your cultural identity?

Student Similarities and Differences

- "Who's teaching the children?" (distribution of the most effective teachers in our profession)
- "How much are the children worth?" (issue of funding—where the money for education goes and why) (pp. 8–10)

CULTURAL RESPONSIVENESS. To make multicultural education a reality in the classroom requires culturally responsive teaching. A culturally responsive teacher is sensitive to diversity and regularly asks questions such as these:

- Do I know the culture of each of my students beyond their obvious race and ethnicity?
- In what ways might I help my students see their similarities as clearly as their differences?
- How can I help validate the cultures represented in my classroom?
- How can I promote communication among all students?
- How can I assure equal opportunities for learning for all students?

LANGUAGE DIVERSITY

We have looked at race and ethnicity as major contributors to our cultural identity. These two factors are largely based on nature and can't be changed. Our language, however, is rooted in nurture and can be changed. **Language** is our primary means of communication and, through it, we transmit knowledge. Assimilation in terms of language, with all students becoming proficient in English, has benefits because most public school classrooms are conducted in English. Few would argue with the notion that communicating proficiently in English is a major factor for academic success in the United States. The dilemma, however, is how to ensure this for all students.

Not all immigrants are non-English proficient, but for most, English is not their first language. Some immigrant students arrive in the United States with strong records of academic achievement in their native languages, but most do not. Some students may have mastered conversational English in that they can speak and understand it, but they lack the ability to use English to keep up with grade-level coursework (Short & Fitzsimmons, 2007). School settings require **Standard English,** a composite of the language spoken by educated middle-class people in the United States. There are two forms of Standard English: one that's spoken in our everyday lives and a more formal version that is written and considered grammatically correct (Gollnick & Chinn, 2009).

But even within the English language there are variations. In the United States there are at least 11 regional **dialects,** or deviations from standard language rules used by identifiable groups of people. You may have been the brunt of jokes when you traveled outside your region, or you may have poked fun at someone in your college dorm who spoke with a regional dialect unlike your own. Black English, sometimes referred to as **Ebonics,** is one of the best known and most controversial dialects in the United States. In most school settings, Black English, along with Hawaiian Pidgin and Appalachian English, is associated with lower levels of both intelligence and social class (Gollnick & Chinn, 2009).

Focus students Guillermo, from Mexico, and Khammany, from Laos, are part of the rich fabric of diversity at Roosevelt High School in Fresno, California.
Sara Davis Powell

Student Similarities and Differences

ENGLISH-LANGUAGE LEARNERS. Students with **limited English proficiency (LEP)** may speak and understand some English but not enough to be successful in classes taught in English without additional assistance. Non-English speakers and students with LEP are referred to as **English-language learners (ELLs)**. So LEPs are ELLs. We serve them through TESOL, ESOL, ESL, SEI, and any number of bilingual education program configurations. Confused? If your answer is yes, you are more than justified. The dilemma faced by students who do not speak English well enough to learn at adequate levels in a timely fashion in U.S. schools is both recent and rapidly growing. Not only are we unsure about how best to serve this population, our vocabulary pertaining to this situation hasn't solidified either, with overlapping and indistinct definitions.

Whether in the mall or filling out a job application, the value of fluency in English is obvious to students who are ELLs. Children in immigrant families often believe that continuing to speak their native language will hurt them in school settings where often language is the most obvious characteristic that sets them apart. Another phrase used to refer to students whose native language is other than English, regardless of their current level of English proficiency, is **language minority students**. Figure 3.5 is a snapshot of language minority students. An interesting fact to consider is that in 1910, 97% of immigrants to the United States were from Europe or Canada. One hundred years later, only about 10% of the immigrants to the United States are from these parts of the world (Rance-Roney, 2009).

Craig Cleveland's class roll in Table 3.4 mirrors the ethnic mix at Roosevelt High School, California. Although Craig is fluent in Spanish and that's very helpful, notice that most of the designated LEP students are of Asian ethnicity. To meet this challenge head on, Craig involves all his students by

- giving them as many curricular and instructional choices as possible
- having them talk to each other in their native languages about class content
- using role-playing (read more about role playing as an instructional strategy in Chapter 4) to reinforce concepts
- reading picture books that make concepts more transparent
- using written materials in students' native languages when available

Hector Mancia, one of our Rees Elementary focus students, is fluent in English, but in his home, Spanish is the predominant language. Watch Hector's interview, including his mom, in the Teaching in Focus section for Chapter 3 in MyEducationLab for this course.

Figure 3.5 Snapshot of language minority students

There are more than 14 million language minority students in K–12 schools.

Children from immigrant families comprise most of the language minority students.

About 1 in 5 children ages 5 to 17 in the United States are from immigrant families.

The population of children in immigrant families is growing faster than any other group of children in the nation.

Almost 80% of children from immigrant families were born in the United States, making them U.S. citizens.

Immigrant families continue to be concentrated in California, Texas, New York, Florida, Illinois, and New Jersey, but many states are now experiencing sharp increases.

English-language learners in the United States speak more than 350 languages, with more than 75% speaking Spanish.

Language minority students are more likely than native-English-speaking students to come from low-income families.

Language minority students tend to be more transient than native speakers, with families trying out different housing options or moving to build closer family connections.

English-language learners with fluently bilingual and culturally responsive teachers tend to perform better in school than those without such teachers.

Source: August and Shanahan (2006); Capps, Fix, Murray, Ost, Passel, and Herwantoro (2005); Garcia and Cuellar (2006); Hernandez, Denton, and Macartney (2008); Rance-Roney (2009).

Student Similarities and Differences

TABLE 3.4 Craig Cleveland's second period class roll

Name	Gr.	Primary Lang.
1. Acevez, Miguel*	12	Spanish
2. Avelar, Margarita	11	Spanish
3. Chavez, Jennah	11	English
4. Conriquez-Reyes, Dan	11	Spanish
5. Douangsavanh, Khammany	12	Laotian
6. Esqueda, Meagan	12	English
7. Garcia, Alberto	11	Spanish
8. Garcia, Diana	11	Spanish
9. Garcia, Guadalupe	11	Spanish
10. Hurtado, Cassandra	11	Spanish
11. Lopez, Crystal	12	Spanish
12. Maldonado, Sarah	11	English
13. Martinez, Andrew Jame	11	Spanish
14. Perez, Yvonne	10	Spanish
15. Rodarte, Silvia	10	Spanish
16. Rodriguez, Antonio	11	Spanish
17. Rodriguez, Daniel	12	Spanish
18. Romero, Norma	11	Spanish
19. Sanchez, Javier*	11	Spanish
20. Sepulveda, Elizabeth	11	English
21. Toscano, Guillermo	11	English
22. Valles, Leanna Marie	10	English
23. Vang, Doug*	10	Hmong
24. Vang, Ka Yeng*	11	Hmong
25. Vang, Mong Her*	11	Hmong
26. Vang, Pa*	11	Hmong
27. Vang, Sandda*	11	Hmong
28. Vang, Xoua*	11	Hmong
29. Vang, Zoua*	11	Hmong
30. Yang, Don*	11	Hmong
31. Yang, Gloria*	10	Hmong
32. Yang, Tom*	11	Hmong

*Considered limited English proficient (LEP).

You don't have to be in an urban area to have ELLs in your classroom. One of our focus schools, Summit Primary, Ohio, has gone from a mostly white, all English-speaking school to one with the 17 languages listed in Figure 3.6.

Figure 3.6 Native languages at Summit Primary School, Ohio

English	Russian	French
Somali	Macedonian	Creole
Ohomo	Serbo-Croatian	Korean
Bosnian/Albanian	Spanish	Japanese
Sierra Leone/Creole	German	Tagalog/Filipino
Chinese/Cantonese	Croatian	

Student Similarities and Differences

SERVICES ADDRESSING ELL. The acronyms mentioned earlier indicate the variety of ways we attempt to meet the needs of English-language learners. Let's look briefly at three approaches to delivering ELL services to students: bilingual education, English as a second language (ESL), and structured English immersion (SEI).

Bilingual Education. One of the primary responses of public education to the needs of English-language learners is **bilingual education,** the delivery of instruction in two languages. Attempts are made to preserve native language abilities as students acquire skills in English. Perhaps the greatest barrier to bilingual education programs is the lack of teachers who speak both English and another language fluently. In addition to speaking two languages fluently, however, teachers in bilingual programs must also be qualified to teach math, science, social studies, reading, writing, and other subjects. Angelica Reynosa, one of our focus teachers at Roosevelt High School in Fresno, California, teaches bilingual classes. In her lesson she switches between Spanish and English as she engages her students in their own learning.

Watch Angelica's lesson in the Teaching in Focus *section for Chapter 3 in MyEducationLab for this course.*

English as a Second Language. In **English as a second language (ESL)** programs, students receive individualized assistance once or twice a week for about an hour each session. Unlike bilingual education, ESL services are delivered only in English. With ESL, little or no emphasis is placed on preserving native language or culture, and ESL teachers do not need to speak another language. ESL programs are far less expensive than bilingual programs for school districts to implement if they have limited numbers of students to serve.

Structured English Immersion. In response to observations that we may be teaching *in* English, but possibly not *teaching* English, **structured English immersion** (SEI) was developed. This approach includes significant amounts of the school day dedicated to the explicit teaching of the English language, with other content supporting instruction, but not as the primary focus (Clark, 2009). In SEI students and teachers speak, read, and write in English. Teachers treat English as a foreign language and apply instructional methods of teachers of foreign languages. Students are expected to transition out of SEI programs on a specified timetable with the skills necessary to be successful in English-only classes.

As of 2009, three states, California, Arizona, and Massachusetts, had passed laws requiring the development of SEI programs to replace many of the existing bilingual programs. SEI is perhaps the least understood of the three approaches. States and districts are creating SEI programs, given their student populations and resources available (Clark, 2009). Figure 3.7 is a schedule for students in the SEI program at George Washington Elementary School in Madera, California, which enrolls more than 500 English-language learners in grades K to 6.

Points of Reflection 3.3

Is English your primary language? If not, what is? Has language ever been a barrier to you? Do you know people who are English-language learners?

Figure 3.7 Structured English immersion sample schedule

Emphasis/Activity	Time Allotted
Pronunciation and listening skills	20 minutes
Vocabulary	30 minutes
Verb tense instruction	20 minutes
Sentence structure	20 minutes
Integrated grammar skills application	20 minutes
English reading and writing	60 minutes
Math (specially designed academic instruction in English)	40 minutes
Science, social science, P.E.	40 minutes

Source: Clark, C. (2009). The case for structured English immersion. *Educational Leadership, 66*(7), 45.

LANGUAGE DIVERSITY: IMPLICATIONS FOR TEACHERS

Language diversity presents a major challenge for educators in the United States. As we welcome increasing numbers of English-language learners to U.S. schools, both teaching and learning are affected. Here are some questions to keep in mind as you consider teaching in a language-diverse classroom:

- How can I make my classroom an academically, emotionally, and socially safe place for students who are ELLs?

- How can I include the cultures of students who are ELLs in my classroom?

- What resources will I need to communicate subject-area concepts to all students?

- How will I communicate with families who are ELLs?

- What community services might benefit students who are ELLs and their families?

Hugo Martinez, one of our Roosevelt High School focus students, is an English-language learner and his parents speak little or no English. Watch Hugo's interview, including his parents, in the Teaching in Focus section for Chapter 3 in MyEducationLab for this course.

The influx of diverse cultures with varied languages can be a source of richness for the United States rather than a phenomenon that is feared or avoided. Striking a balance between preserving native cultures while helping students adjust to life in a basically English-speaking environment is a worthy goal.

Before we turn our attention to diversity in family structure, religion, and socioeconomic status, respond to this chapter's ***Diversity Dialogue*** focusing on language diversity in an early childhood setting.

DIVERSITY DIALOGUE

Sara Davis Powell

Principal Laura Hill has detected that the teachers at one of our focus schools, Summit Primary, have become increasingly concerned about the children in their K–2 classrooms. Until about 2002 the community was rural, with farms and small businesses scattered throughout. Summit students were primarily white, living in middle to lower income homes. The change to today's student population was rapid, taking many educators by surprise. They are sensing a lack of preparation and a feeling of inadequacy. Laura called them all together to discuss what she knows is a hot topic in the teachers' lounge. Here are two teacher comments.

Brandi: "My morning kindergarten class this year consists of 12 kids whose families are long-time residents of the county. Then I have four children who speak little or no English. Two are twins from Somalia, and the other two are children of migrant farm workers from Mexico. Here we have three families where English isn't spoken in the home."

Melissa: "What good is 2 hours a week in an ESL class? It's not enough time to do any good and, besides, the kids are sometimes taken out of my class when we are doing something they actually understand how to do."

Think about what you have learned so far and respond to these items by writing one well-developed paragraph for each.

1. Melissa's concerns about ESL are understandable, but are there other options? Given what you know about Summit Primary, would bilingual education or structured English immersion be better options, or even possible? What would you recommend and why?

2. Our focus teacher Brandi and her colleague Melissa both teach kindergarten, along with seven other teachers. They each have two to four language minority students representing three different languages. How might they work together to help ELLs become proficient in English?

What Is the Impact on Students of Diversity in Family Structure, Religion, and Socioeconomic Status?

FAMILY DIVERSITY

The 1970s *Brady Bunch* television situation comedy introduced many Americans to the concept of the blended family. Today, blended families come in a variety of configurations. Many students live with people other than their biological parents. With the divorce rate over 50%, single-parent homes have increased more than 300% since 1980 (U.S. Census Bureau, 2008).

The increasing mobility of American families also adds to the instability of students' home lives. Consider, for example, the increasing influx of both documented (legal) and undocumented (illegal) immigrants and the rapidly growing migrant population. These families may move two to four times a year, with children changing schools, enrolling and withdrawing from the same school multiple times, or simply not going to school (NCES, 2004). Not only is all this mobility potentially harmful for students, but it can also wreak havoc on classroom teaching and learning.

FAMILY DIVERSITY: IMPLICATIONS FOR TEACHERS.
Knowing with whom our students live can give teachers insight into behavior and achievement patterns. Ideally, families are our partners in educating children and adolescents. If this is going to be a reality in classrooms, our tactics for gaining and maintaining family support must be sensitive and flexible. Here are some questions to consider for your classroom:

- How can I restructure volunteer opportunities to include evenings and weekends?
- Are options available for child care that might lead to greater parental participation?
- Can the school provide easily accessible transportation to boost family involvement?
- Can I be more inclusive by practicing simple tactics such as addressing correspondence with "Dear family" rather than "Dear parents"?

RELIGIOUS DIVERSITY

Religion and faith have considerable daily influence on many of our lives. Over 230 million people, or about 4 of 5 of us, affiliate with a religious group. About 96% of Americans who practice a religion align with Christianity. However, religious diversity exists in urban, suburban, and rural areas in every state, and among Americans who align with a religion, about 1.4% are Jewish and about 0.5% align with each of Islam, Hinduism, and Buddhism (Pew Forum, 2010). Freedom to practice a religion, or not, is central to our common political, social, and cultural heritage. This chapter's *Letter to the Editor* addresses both cultural and religious expression in our schools.

Letter to the Editor

This letter appeared in the Ogden, Utah, newspaper, *The Standard-Examiner*. It was written by a citizen responding to recent local controversy over an expression of cultural and religious diversity.

November 4, 2009

STUDENT AND NOSE STUD

Recently Bountiful Junior High School has been in a tizzy over little 12-year-old Suzannah Singh for wearing a tiny jeweled stud in the nub of her nose (Oct. 28, "Nose-piercing Indian girl readmitted to class").

Is it just me or is there something wrong with this picture? What's even harder to believe is that after Suzannah had worn the accessory for about two weeks (reportedly, according to the Standard's account, even admired by some of her teachers), her stud was "spotted" by none other than a reading teacher. Oh my, spies are everywhere!

(continued)

And here's the best-worst part, all of this time I was led to believe that reading was the greatest opportunity to explore and expand our horizons about religious, cultural and social mores and traditions.

While this is not meant to cast a dim light on the many good citizens of Bountiful, I wish to remind anyone who might have temporarily forgotten, there are plenty of folks in this wide world of ours who possess diverse religious and cultural persuasions, be they Sikh or Sunni, Mormon or Muslim, Episcopalian or Evangelical, Jewish or Jehovah's Witnesses, Buddhist, Baptist, or Bahai, who care for the spiritual and cultural lives of themselves and their loved ones as much as the next guy. And for that reason, I seriously question why this young girl was immediately sent to detention by the school administration and then asked to stay home until her gracious parents agreed on a compromise, of a clear, presumably inoffensive, stud.

The jeweled stud Suzannah had worn had meant something special to her. Isn't that what we wish for our young daughters and sons? A special identity?

What is wrong with this picture? It's cliché. There are much more important issues. Some of us need to learn to pick our battles. Time is too precious. Can we just enjoy it and not make mountains out of tiny nose studs?

Liz Shaner

Now it's your turn. Write a letter to the editor from the perspective of a future teacher expressing your views about this incident and any broader issues you feel it invokes. You may comment on any, or all, of the writer's expressed opinions. The following questions may help you frame your thinking, but should not limit nor determine what you write.

1. Are you surprised that a small nose stud would cause any kind of friction among community members?

2. Is it important that symbolic expressions that appear to be outside a community's comfort zone be cultural or religious to be allowed?

3. Do you think Suzannah's nose stud was disruptive to the education process?

4. Is it the school's responsibility to allow or disallow items of clothing, jewelry, and other accessories deemed disruptive?

5. Do you agree or disagree with the letter writer about the relative importance of the issue? Is there a larger issue here that needs to be addressed?

Write your letter in understandable terminology, remembering that readers of newspaper Letters to the Editor are citizens who may have limited knowledge of school practices and policies.

Private schools are often established to cater to and promote a particular religion. Public schools are open to all and are obligated to serve all. Although separation of church and state is the official stance, religion has considerable influence on what we do in schools. Most of the issues teachers face in terms of religious diversity can be dealt with positively simply through awareness.

RELIGIOUS DIVERSITY: IMPLICATIONS FOR TEACHERS. Our response to religious diversity must be within legal bounds and delivered with sensitivity. Here are some questions classroom teachers should consider concerning religious diversity:

- How do I make sure tolerance is modeled in my classroom?
- How can I guard against being offensive to students of varying faiths?
- How should holidays be observed?
- How can I best respond to the community in which I live and teach?

Points of Reflection 3.4

What do you remember about family support, or lack of it, in your own K–12 experience? How did your religious affiliation and beliefs impact you and your school experiences?

The last question will be very important to you. While singing "Jesus Loves Me" at nap time in a southern kindergarten might be not only tolerated, but encouraged, singing the same song in a kindergarten in suburban Denver might be seen as offensive and grounds for dismissal.

SOCIOECONOMIC DIVERSITY

One area of diversity that transcends differences in gender, culture, language, family, and religion, and has widespread impact on student success in school, is **socioeconomic status** (SES). The gap between the haves and the have-nots is wider in the United States than in most other industrialized nations. We might call this a **privilege gap**. Approximately 11% of the U.S. population lives below the poverty line. A family of four—two parents and two children—that earns less than about $20,000 a year is considered to be in poverty.

A family can be above the poverty line but still qualify for free or reduced-price school meals. Of all the states, New Hampshire, at 15%, has the lowest percentage of students who qualify for free or reduced-price meals, and Kentucky, at 69%, has the highest percentage (U.S. Census Bureau, 2006).

CHALLENGES OF LOW SES. The federal government acknowledges there are unique challenges in teaching students living in low-income settings. Title I funding, additional money given to public schools when more than 50% of the students qualify for free or reduced-price meals, is the government's attempt to make school experiences equitable. These funds are intended to help educators better meet the needs of students in low-income settings who often are students with histories of low achievement.

The following are some generalizations about students from low-income settings. As you read them, keep in mind that they are not true of all students from low-income settings, and they may not be true of those in your classroom. Students from low-SES settings

Points of Reflection 3.5

How has your own SES affected your school experiences? Were you aware of socioeconomic differences among your classmates? Did this affect how you viewed your own circumstances or the circumstances of other students?

- may enter first grade having been read to about 25 hours, compared to 1,000 hours in middle-class homes (Neumann, 1999)
- may have been exposed to 30 million fewer words by the age of 4 than children from high-SES settings (Neumann, 2003)
- may be disorganized, lose assignments, not do homework, have many excuses (Payne, 2005)
- may perform poorly on class and standardized tests (Payne, 2005)
- may dislike authority, talk back to adults, not monitor their own behavior, not use middle-class courtesies (Payne, 2005)
- may be physically aggressive (Payne, 2005)
- very often attend schools with inadequate facilities and less effective teachers (Payne, 2005)

SES DIVERSITY: IMPLICATIONS FOR TEACHERS. Ruby Payne (2008) tells us that teachers are in a position to support students and families in poverty by attending to their resource needs, which include

- emotional resources—the stamina to withstand difficult and uncomfortable emotional situations
- mental resources—the ability to learn; to read, write, and compute
- spiritual resources—belief that help is available through a higher power that alleviates hopelessness
- physical resources—having a healthy body
- support systems—knowing who to turn to for everyday and future needs and information
- relationships/role models—having people around who demonstrate appropriate relationships and successful living
- knowledge of unspoken rules—knowing how to get along in a particular group (pp. 17–18).

How Are Learning Differences Manifested in Schools?

The revered **intelligence quotient (IQ)** affixes a number to intelligence that, in one single freeze-frame, labels us for life. Scores on IQ tests may provide useful information, but they are no longer considered the final answer in determining a child's intellectual capacity. We have moved beyond the notion that intelligence is a fixed attribute. Researchers now believe that **intelligence,** a capacity for knowing and learning, can change and is manifested in various ways, as illustrated in Figure 3.8.

Student Similarities and Differences

Figure 3.8 How our views of intelligence have changed

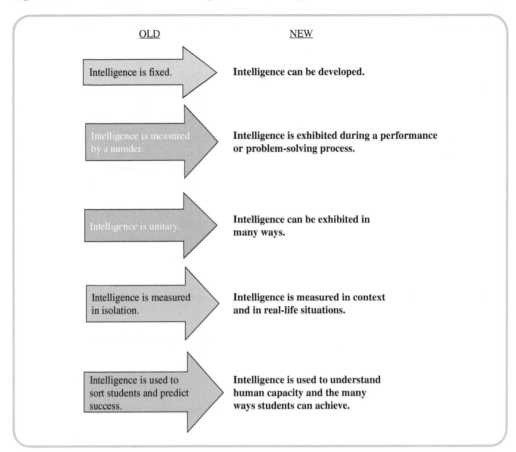

Source: Silver, H. F., Strong, R. W., & Perini, M. J. (2000). *So each may learn: Integrating learning styles and multiple intelligences.* Alexandria, VA: Association for Supervision and Curriculum Development.

MULTIPLE INTELLIGENCES THEORY

Harvard psychologist Howard Gardner added an "s" to the word *intelligence* and revolutionized how we view the concept. In 1983 he theorized that intelligence is multidimensional, that individual brains work in ways that give each of us our own personal intelligences. He called this **multiple intelligences (MI) theory**. The implication of multiple intelligences is that we learn differently.

Gardner (1999) proposed distinct intelligences that can be activated and connected in very individual ways. Table 3.5 lists the nine intelligences he proposed and suggests ways to address the intelligences when planning for instruction.

LEARNING STYLES

Whereas Gardner's theory of multiple intelligences helps explain different forms of intelligence with implications for how we learn, theories of **learning styles** give us more explicit insight into the variety of ways the learning process happens. Perhaps the simplest way to characterize learning styles is through the four commonly accepted **learning modalities,** or preferences: auditory (hearing), visual (seeing), tactile (touching), and kinesthetic (moving). We use all four in the process of learning, but each individual tends to favor one or two over the others. Traditional classrooms rely most heavily on auditory and visual modalities, such as lectures and visual supports, especially in the upper grades, while active learning techniques, such as hands-on manipulatives and

Student Similarities and Differences

TABLE 3.5 Multiple intelligences and planning for instruction

Disposition/Intelligence	Plan Lessons That Include:
Verbal-Linguistic Intelligence	Speaking, writing, listening, reading, communicating
Logical Mathematical Intelligence	Finding patterns; making calculations; formulating hypotheses; recognizing cause and effect; working with numbers and reasoning
Spatial Intelligence	Representing ideas visually; creating mental images; noticing details; drawing; working puzzles; using colors and shapes
Bodily-Kinesthetic Intelligence	Activities requiring touch, movement, strength, speed, flexibility, hand-eye coordination, balance, and physical expression
Musical Intelligence	Listening, singing, and playing an instrument; using tone, beat, tempo, melody, pitch, and sound to create music
Interpersonal Intelligence	Working with others; understanding body language, moods, and feelings
Intrapersonal Intelligence	Setting goals; assessing personal abilities; reflecting on one's own strengths and weaknesses
Naturalist Intelligence	Identifying and classifying living things and natural objects; analyzing ecological and natural situations; learning from living things; working in natural settings
Existentialist Intelligence	Considering the big picture; imagining very large or very small quantities; seeking answers to seemingly unanswerable questions

Source: Silver, H. F., Strong, R. W., & Perini, M. J. (2000). *So each may learn: Integrating learning styles and multiple intelligences.* Alexandria, VA: Association for Supervision and Curriculum Development.

group work, activate tactile and kinesthetic modalities and may engage students more effectively. Figure 3.9 helps us understand students who learn best through hearing, seeing, touching, or moving.

Figure 3.9 Learning styles and learner preferences

Auditory learners tend to. . .
    Enjoy reading and being read to.
    Be able to explain concepts and scenarios verbally.
    Like music and hum to themselves.
    Enjoy both talking and listening.

Visual learners tend to. . .
    Have good spelling, note-taking, and organizational skills.
    Notice details and prefer neatness.
    Learn more if illustrations and charts accompany reading.
    Prefer quiet, serene surroundings.

Kinesthetic learners tend to. . .
    Be demonstrative, animated, and outgoing.
    Enjoy physical movement and manipulatives.
    Be willing to try new things.
    Be messy in habits and surroundings.

Tactile learners tend to. . .
    Prefer manipulatives when being introduced to a topic.
    Literally translate events and phenomena.
    Tolerate clutter.
    Be artistic in nature.

Source: From *Introduction to Middle School* (p. 59), by S. D. Powell, 2011, Boston: Allyn & Bacon. Copyright 2011 by Allyn & Bacon.

Student Similarities and Differences

DIFFERENCES IN HOW WE LEARN: IMPLICATIONS FOR TEACHERS

Incorporating what we know about multiple intelligences and learning styles into our plans for instruction helps meet the learning needs of more students. Here are some questions to keep in mind when considering these challenges:

- Do I view the students in my classroom as a collection of individuals, each with unique ways of being smart?
- Do I continually seek to understand the ways in which my students learn best?
- Do I plan some experiences that address and incorporate each of the multiple intelligences?
- Does my awareness of my students' various learning styles change how I teach?

Acknowledging there are many ways to learn leads us to understand that some students have particular difficulties learning, while others learn more quickly and perhaps more deeply. These are students with exceptionalities.

Who Are Students with Exceptionalities and How Do We Serve Them?

Learners with abilities or disabilities that set them apart from other learners are often referred to as **students with exceptionalities**. Heward (2006) tells us that exceptional children

> differ from the norm (either below or above) to such an extent that they require an additional program of special education and related services to fully benefit from education. . . . Thus, exceptional children . . . refers to children with learning and/or behavior problems, children with physical or sensory impairments, and children who are intellectually gifted or have a special talent. (p. 10)

Some exceptionalities are the result of nature; others may be the result of injury or illness, aspects of nurture. Two factors are especially important when we consider the education of students with exceptionalities:

- Identification: Deciding who has what exceptionality and to what degree
- Intervention: Determining how best to meet their educational needs

STUDENTS WITH DISABILITIES

The categories of student exceptionalities considered disabilities, along with the percentage of all disabilities they represent, are shown in Table 3.6. Considering all the categories, about 12% of American students receive **special education services,** services provided by schools to help students function and learn in ways optimal to the individual (Goldstein, 2003).

Many disabilities, especially those that impair daily functioning, such as orthopedic disabilities and hearing, sight, and disease-related impairments, are diagnosed before children enter school. However, disabilities that are more subtle, and perhaps academic, are often officially identified through a team of educators equipped with expertise and diagnostic tools.

A designation of **learning disabled (LD),** which accounts for almost half the students receiving special education services, includes a general category of students with disorders involving problems understanding or using language that results in significant differences between learning potential and achievement (Turnbull, Turnbull, & Wehmeyer, 2010). Misdiagnosis or the absence of diagnosis is problematic. Many students develop coping strategies that mask their learning problems for years and very possibly for life. Students with LD may

- have difficulties with word recognition and text comprehension
- feel overwhelmed by the idea of getting started

Student Similarities and Differences

Disability	Percentage of Total Students Receiving Special Services
Specific learning disabilities	47.2
Speech or language impairments	18.8
Mental retardation	9.6
Emotional disturbance	8.1
Multiple disabilities	2.2
Hearing impairments	1.2
Orthopedic impairments	1.1
Other health impairments	7.5
Autism	2.3
Visual impairments	.4
Traumatic brain injury	.4
Developmental delay	1.1
Deaf-blindness	.1

Source: U.S. Department of Education. (2009). *Building the legacy: IDEA 2004.*

- struggle to organize and use the mechanics of writing
- have difficulty differentiating numbers or copying shapes
- have difficulty identifying, using, and monitoring problem-solving strategies (Turnbull et al., 2010)

Intervention for students with LD may include time each day with a special education teacher, often referred to as a **resource teacher,** who will help them develop strategies for school success.

Identification of **attention deficit hyperactivity disorder (ADHD)** may be as problematic as identification of learning disabilities. Students with ADHD demonstrate three defining characteristics: inattention, hyperactivity, and impulsivity. ADHD is defined by the American Psychological Association (APA, 2000) as the frequent existence of these three characteristics in a persistent pattern that is more severe than in others of the same age. The APA estimates that 3% to 7% of students in an average class have ADHD, which falls within the "other health impairments" category of Table 3.6. The intervention for students with ADHD may include specific strategies to help modify behavior or medication. They receive services through special education only if they qualify through impairments other than ADHD (Turnbull et al., 2010).

LEGAL SUPPORT FOR STUDENTS WITH DISABILITIES

Until recently, students with disabilities were often isolated in a room at the end of a hallway—out of sight, out of mind—unless they happened to be seen walking as a group or boarding one of those short buses designed to hold that "special" group of kids. Prior to 1975, most students with disabilities, designated as special education students, weren't even in the same facilities as other students; there were no provisions for them to attend public schools. In 1975 the landmark legislation **Public Law 94-142 (PL 94-142)** changed all that.

Today special education is viewed as a service rather than a place to send children (Jackson & Harper, 2002). The **Education for All Handicapped Children Act (PL 94-142)** opened all public schools to students with disabilities and mandated that students with disabilities be given the opportunity to benefit from special education services at no cost to families. The law established six governing principles, listed in Figure 3.10, that apply to the education of students with disabilities.

In 1990 PL 94-142 was amended and renamed the **Individuals with Disabilities Education Act (IDEA)**. Students with autism and traumatic brain injury were added to those entitled to services under PL 94-142. A change in attitude and philosophy was also evident in the law when the language changed from "disabled individuals" to "individuals

Student Similarities and Differences

Figure 3.10 Six principles governing the education of students with disabilities

1. **Zero reject:** A rule against excluding any student.
2. **Nondiscriminatory evaluation:** Requires schools to evaluate students fairly to determine if they have a disability and, if so, what kind and how extensive.
3. **Appropriate education:** Requires schools to provide individualized education programs for each student based on evaluation and augmented by related services and supplementary aids and services.
4. **Least restrictive environment:** Requires schools to educate students with disabilities alongside students without disabilities to the maximum extent appropriate for the students with disabilities.
5. **Procedural due process:** Provides safeguards for students against schools' actions, including a right to sue in court.
6. **Parental and student participation:** Requires schools to collaborate with parents and adolescent students in designing and carrying out special education programs.

Source: Turnbull, R., Turnbull, A., & Wehmeyer, M. (2010). *Exceptional lives: Special education in today's schools* (6th ed.). Upper Saddle River, NJ: Merrill/Prentice Hall.

with disabilities." The person comes first, with the disability secondary. In 2004 IDEA was reauthorized as the **Individuals with Disabilities Education Improvement Act**. This latest reauthorization is the most comprehensive yet, including all U.S. laws affecting children with disabilities in one statute (Heward, 2006).

INDIVIDUALIZED EDUCATIONAL PROGRAMS

Serving students with disabilities (ages 3 to 21), regardless of the setting or combination of settings, requires an **individualized educational program (IEP)** as prescribed by Principle 3 of PL 94-142. An IEP is developed by educators, the family, and others as appropriate and involves a detailed plan to reach specific goals. A student's IEP must be revisited annually and student progress evaluated. Although IEP formats may vary, the required elements are listed in Figure 3.11.

An important part of an IEP is the designation of where and with whom students with disabilities will spend their school time. Principle 4 of PL 94–142 explicitly states that students with disabilities will be in the **least restrictive environment (LRE)** possible. The LRE is generally a setting with students who do not have disabilities that also meets the educational needs of the students with disabilities. This is often the regular education classroom.

INCLUSION

Whether you are interested in teaching students with disabilities or not, you may be doing exactly that in a regular inclusive classroom setting if a student's IEP designates it as the LRE. **Inclusion** means that "students attend their home school with their age and grade appropriate

Figure 3.11 Components of an IEP

An IEP must include a statement of:

1. student's present level of academic achievement and functional level
2. measurable academic and functional annual goals
3. how the student's progress toward meeting the annual goals will be measured
4. special education and related services to be provided to the student
5. extent to which the student will not participate with nondisabled students and the regular classroom
6. accommodations necessary to measure the student's achievement on state assessments
7. date of beginning services
8. postsecondary goals and transition services at age 16

Source: Turnbull, R., Turnbull, A., & Wehmeyer, M. (2010). *Exceptional lives: Special education in today's schools.* Upper Saddle River, NJ: Merrill/Prentice Hall.

Student Similarities and Differences

peers, participate in extracurricular activities, and receive special education and support services, to the maximum extent possible, in the general education classroom" (Rosenberg, O'Shea, & O'Shea, 2006, p. 14). If inclusion is not appropriate, chances are a student with disabilities is served in a self-contained setting with other students with disabilities for much of the day and served by teachers with specific training to work with students with disabilities.

Inclusive classrooms provide opportunities for students with and without disabilities to learn and work together. Scott Cunningham/Merrill

Simply placing students with disabilities in a regular classroom does not mean inclusive practices are in place or that a rigorous learning environment will be maintained. Teachers still must effectively focus on individualized objectives for every student, facilitate interactions and cooperative learning among students at every learning level, and maintain collaborative relationships with students, parents, and special educators. Given this approach, inclusion can be a healthy and positive experience for students without disabilities as well (Heward, 2006). There is a growing trend toward co-teaching, involving a regular classroom teacher and a special educator in a single classroom.

Inclusion is not embraced by all. Some parents believe their students with disabilities are better served in smaller, special education classrooms where they are more likely to receive one-on-one attention from teachers specifically trained to work with them. Some regular education teachers are wary of having a student with disabilities placed in their classrooms, an understandable hesitation if they receive little or no training in meeting the emotional, social, and cognitive needs of the student. Although the **Council for Exceptional Children** (CEC), the professional organization of special education, endorses inclusion, the official stance is support of a continuum of services with inclusion as a desirable goal, but not the only appropriate option for all students with disabilities.

ASSISTIVE TECHNOLOGY

The Technology-Related Assistance to Individuals with Disabilities Act of 1988 authorized funding for **assistive technology** devices and services. These devices and services benefit students with disabilities by helping them communicate, increasing their mobility, and aiding in multiple ways that enhance their capacity to learn. The range of assistive technology includes wheelchairs, voice-activated and touch-screen word processors, sound-augmenting devices, and closed-captioned television (Turnbull et al., 2010). Technology is making it possible for students with disabilities to function and learn at levels unimaginable only a decade ago.

STUDENTS DESIGNATED AS GIFTED AND TALENTED

Characteristics of students who are **gifted and talented** include phrases such as

- evidence of high performance capabilities
- intellectual, creative, artistic, or leadership ability well beyond average
- excelling in specific academic fields

Identification of students who are gifted and talented can be objective or quite subjective, depending on the criteria accepted by a particular school district. When IQ is used for identification, the threshold number is 125 to 130, achieved by only about 2% to 3% of the general student population. However, evaluating creativity along with IQ testing allows more students to benefit from gifted and talented services.

Services for students who are gifted and talented vary significantly and include pull-out programs, with students working on projects or an accelerated curriculum. In-school options, such as grade skipping, concurrent enrollment in two levels of schooling, curriculum compacting (faster pace), and advanced placement courses (rigorous high school courses with possible college credit for completion), enhance the opportunities of students designated as gifted and talented. There are also specifically designed magnet schools for them.

Differentiated instruction is discussed in Chapter 4.

Student Similarities and Differences

Were you diagnosed with a disability while in PreK–12 school? If so, explain. Did you know students who were diagnosed with a disability while in PreK–12 school? If so, describe one.

Were you designated as gifted and talented? If so, what do you remember about being set apart from other kids?

When students who are gifted and talented are in regular classrooms, and most are, we can better meet their needs by

- being flexible
- accepting unusual ideas and encouraging alternative solutions to problems
- not being intimidated by the intellectual and creative capabilities of students who have IQs that exceed our own
- differentiating instruction often (more about this in Chapter 4)

STUDENTS WITH EXCEPTIONALITIES: IMPLICATIONS FOR TEACHERS

The most important aspect of teaching students with exceptionalities is to recognize that each student is an individual with learning potential and at least part of his or her mind "amply equipped to thrive" (Levine, 2003, p. 13). Seeing and seeking strengths before, or

GETTING TO KNOW TRISTA

Trista Kutcher is one of our focus students. She is a very special young lady. Her happy life and remarkable accomplishments are evidence of what dedicated parents and sensitive, knowledgeable education professionals can do to help children, even those with disabilities, realize their potential. Trista has Down syndrome.

Provided by the Kutcher family

Trista's mom, Rebecca, teaches eighth grade English language arts at Cario Middle School in Mount Pleasant, South Carolina, and Trista's dad, Joe, teaches math at Wando High School, where Trista is a freshman. Trista has two younger sisters, Suzanna, age 12, and Samantha, age 4. As a member of the 2003 USA Special Olympics gymnastics team, Trista won five medals at the Dublin, Ireland, games. She is a cheerleader at Wando High and is included in many regular education classes.

After reading Trista's story, watch the interview of Trista and her family and friends in the Choosing Your Teaching Path section of MyEducationLab. Click on Cario Middle School, and then on Trista.

Rebecca has written about many of her experiences as Trista's mom. Here's an abridged version of one of her pieces, entitled "We Danced."

We Danced

Joe and I had the perfect life. . . . We dated in high school and married right out of college. Life was grand! We got pregnant and things were sailing along as we **danced** through life. People would often ask, "What do you want—a boy or a girl?" I never said more than my prayer that the baby would be healthy! Joe's response was that we just wished for "10 fingers and 10 toes." Deep down, however, I really wanted a little girl with blond hair and blue eyes who would **dance** in a recital, **dance** on the beach, and **dance** into everyone's heart!

Provided by the Kutcher family

The pregnancy was perfect, as was the delivery. Joe and I held Trista Sue and cooed over her late into the night.

A few hours later the music stopped. The doctors told us our little blond-haired, blue-eyed Trista Sue had Down syndrome. Joe and I no longer felt like **dancing**.

Knowing breastfeeding was important for her in many ways, I wanted to continue her feeding schedule, even though she was still in the hospital. I would wake up during the night at 1:00 and 5:00 and travel to the hospital to nurse her. I would waltz around the room with her in my arms. How wonderful those **dances** were . . . just us, loving each other.

Provided by the Kutcher family

I decided I was going to get Trista involved in activities that every "normal" girl does. At age two I took her to Tapios School of Dance and Gymnastics. I asked the owner if Trista could enroll in her tap and ballet classes. She welcomed her with open arms and taught her to dance with grace and poise.

Around this time Trista's sister, Suzanna, was born. How proud she was to be a big sister! Oh, the mischief they could get into together. Eventually, Trista and Suzanna were in a dance recital together, Trista 6 and Suzanna 3. Suzanna was amazed at the lights and people in the audience. She completely forgot her dance. Big sister to the rescue! Trista decided this was unacceptable and took matters into her own hands. Trista marched across the stage, positioned herself behind Suzanna, and proceeded to move her arms and legs for her. The audience roared with laughter while Trista made Suzanna **dance**.

Provided by the Kutcher family

When Trista started school, we decided she should be included in the regular classroom. Speech was definitely a concern and having her with the other kids would be great modeling. Each of her accomplishments was celebrated by kids in the class and by teachers who were initially worried about how they would teach her.

Student Similarities and Differences

concurrently with, acknowledging limitations helps us embrace possibilities for each individual, whether in an inclusive classroom or in a special education setting.

Including students with exceptionalities in the classroom is beneficial to all students because instruction is delivered in a variety of ways to engage diverse learners. To do so successfully, teachers need support and time for planning, as well as an appropriate curriculum, materials, and resources. Ongoing professional development is essential.

Here are some questions teachers of inclusive classrooms need to ask:

- Do I take the time to get to know each student as an individual?
- Do I look for the strengths and abilities of all my students?
- Is cooperative learning used frequently in my classroom?
- Do I continually diagnose the progress of my students and adjust my instruction appropriately?

During your field experiences, look closely for evidence of inclusion. Ask teachers to help you understand more about students with exceptionalities.

Watch Trista Kutcher's interview, which includes her family, as well as teachers and students who know her, in the Teaching in Focus *section for Chapter 3 in* MyEducationLab *for this course.*

Through elementary and middle school Trista thrived, making friends and showing all of us what she could do, rather than what she couldn't do. In high school she eats, drinks, and sleeps cheering during the fall and, like her gymnastics, loves it dearly. The other girls could not be more accepting and supportive of her.

Poem written by Trista's sister

Trista-
Famous, idol,
Likes to run, jump, and play,
Annoys me when she says she is right when she is wrong.
She can do cartwheels—I wish I could.
She wishes she could play basketball like me.
I do not like to go to the same parties as she does
Because then I feel like I have to look after her
and I cannot have fun.
It amazes me when she does flips and is not scared.
It makes me sad when she says hi to someone
and they do not respond back to her.
I am proud to tell my friends about all the gold medals she has.
I like when she smiles and her nose crunches up . . . it is so cute.
She has Down syndrome.
She is my sister!

By Suzanna Kutcher
12 years old

Along with regular gymnastics competitions, Trista competed in Special Olympics gymnastics. She was the state champion from the age of 8. Being involved provided many opportunities for independence and pride. During the summer of 2002, she received another very important letter. It asked her to be a part of the Special Olympics team USA for the 2003 World Games. As she opened that letter she beamed from ear to ear. This adventure was one of meeting the governor and the mayor, being featured in a commercial, being on the news and in the newspaper regularly, and having an official day in Mt. Pleasant proclaimed by the mayor as Trista Kutcher Day! Everywhere we went people knew her. Suzanna began to make a joke about all of us being her entourage! Never did we think we would be **dancing in her shadow!** She was leading us on the adventure of a lifetime!

The competition in Ireland was tough but she was ready! She won five medals, two of which were gold! As she stood on the podium, she cried and told me later that she was so proud because "She did it"! After the awards ceremony, the audience flooded the gym floor, joined hands, and **danced the Irish jig**. What a celebration!

The **dance** has been wonderful. The music has played nonstop for 15 years! Our dance began with three people on the floor . . . and ended with **a whole community kicking up its heels!**

Sara Davis Powell

Sara Davis Powell

Student Similarities and Differences

CONCLUDING THOUGHTS

Now that we have looked at how students are similar and how they are different, perhaps the concept that all students can learn seems elusive to you. How, indeed, do we make "all children can learn" a reality given the circumstances that pervade some children's lives?

Understanding the uniqueness of each of us calls for an absolute commitment to individuality. Thomas Jefferson expressed the thought that there is nothing so unequal as the equal treatment of unequals. All children are equal in terms of their right to fulfill their own promise, but certainly children are unequal in the many ways we have discussed. The spirit of inclusion draws them all in; the unwavering determination to meet their needs requires attention and action based on each individual.

Yes, all children can learn. These complex questions logically follow this statement:

What can they learn?

When can they learn it?

In what ways will they learn it best?

As always, "And how are the children?" should be the center of our focus.

After reading the ***Chapter in Review***, interact with Craig Cleveland in this chapter's ***Developing Professional Competence***.

Chapter in Review

How are we similar?

- As human beings, we are more similar than dissimilar.
- Nature (genetics) influences human traits we are born with.
- Nurture (environment) influences who we are through every aspect of our lives that nature does not determine.
- Human beings share the same basic hierarchy of needs.
- We all experience physical, cognitive, emotional, social, and character development.

How are gender differences manifested?

- Anatomical differences between males and females determine sex, whereas gender is the sense of being male or female.
- Gender determines many of the choices we make and the expectations others have for us.
- Homosexuality is often the basis of discrimination.

How are cultural and language diversity manifested in schools?

- Race, although a social, political, economical, and psychological reality, is based solely on physical characteristics.
- Racism is a form of prejudice stemming from a belief that one race is superior to another.
- Ethnicity refers to a person's country of origin.

- Culture has many components and is learned, shared, and adaptive.
- Cultural identity relies on many factors, such as race, ethnicity, language, gender, religion, income level, values, and beliefs.
- Multiculturalism involves beliefs concerning the value of looking at the world through the eyes of people who are different from us.
- To be most effective, multicultural education needs to permeate all areas of schooling.
- Language is an aspect of cultural identity that can be augmented and enhanced.
- Bilingual education involves instruction delivered in two languages.
- English as a second language (ESL) is a pull-out program assisting English-language learners in English only.
- Structured English immersion (SEI) includes significant amounts of the school day dedicated to the explicit teaching of the English language, with other content secondary.

What is the impact on students of diversity in family structure, religion, and socioeconomic status?

- Blended families and family structures other than two biological parents and children are becoming more prevalent.
- The increasing mobility of American families potentially harms students and wreaks havoc on classrooms.

- Religion and faith have considerable influence on lifestyles and choices.
- The religious beliefs of families and communities influence decisions that relate to school issues.
- The gap between the haves and have-nots is wider in the United States than in most other nations.
- Low-income settings contribute to many at-risk situations and behaviors.

How are learning differences manifested in schools?

- There are many different ways to be smart and to exhibit intelligence.
- We all have learning style preferences.

Who are students with exceptionalities and how do we serve them?

- Students with exceptionalities include those with disabilities and those considered gifted and talented.
- A designation of learning disabled accounts for about half of students receiving special services.
- The concept of least restrictive environment means that students with disabilities are to be placed in the highest-functioning setting possible, usually the regular education classroom.
- Students considered gifted and talented are most likely to be included in the regular education classroom and pulled out for special classes for brief periods of time.

Developing Professional Competence

Visit the Developing Professional Competence section on Chapter 3 of the MyEducationLab for this text to answer the following questions and begin your preparation for licensure exams.

You met Craig Cleveland in **Meet the Teachers and Students**. In this chapter we learned about one of Craig's classes. Craig has a student teacher this semester. Jenny Langley grew up in the suburbs of Fresno and attends Fresno State. Jenny never attended a Title I school and her PreK–12 school experiences were ideal by most standards, complete with advanced placement classes, a stable group of friends, and extracurricular activities that rounded out her high school years. In a conversation several weeks before her student teaching semester began, Craig discovered that Jenny's peer group had little diversity, although Jenny told him she had lots of experience with diversity because she was in the International Baccalaureate program and she knew two exchange students, one from Japan and one from Russia. Craig smiled to himself as she talked about her open-minded approach with those who are different from herself, knowing she was about to begin one of the most turbulent experiences of her young life.

Think through this scenario and answer the following multiple-choice questions:

1. Guillermo, one of our focus students, is a really good-hearted young man with acceptable English skills and a desire to help other people. Before and after class,

Jenny might be able to best learn more about students with LEP by

a. asking Guillermo to help her talk more easily with students whose primary language is Spanish
b. staying close to Guillermo and listening to his casual conversations in both English and Spanish
c. talking with Guillermo about what he knows about students who are ELLs
d. watching Guillermo's easy demeanor with other students and trying to develop the same persona

2. Craig explains Khammany's situation to Jenny by telling her that Khammany, Mom, and younger brother moved into a project apartment with only two rooms and the difficulties they face since Dad died last year. Khammany, one of our focus students, has to work at least 30 hours a week to help support the family. Which of the following benefits of longer blocks of time (the four-block model) will Craig probably say is most important to Khammany?

a. During the 100-minute class, Khammany has more time to concentrate on history.
b. The longer blocks afford more time for a variety of participation activities.
c. The block allows for time to begin homework assignments with Craig available to assist.
d. Khammany can earn eight credits per year.

3. Remember Craig's class list? Which is the least important reason that longer blocks of class time benefit ELLs?
   a. They get to spend more concentrated time on one subject with one teacher.
   b. There is more time to fully develop a concept, using a variety of communication methods from the standards.
   c. There are fewer subjects to learn at a time.
   d. Fewer passing periods limit opportunities to be involved in turf issues among diverse groups of students.

4. What do you think will be the best way for Jenny to begin to acclimate to her student teaching situation?
   a. study the culture of the students she will encounter at Roosevelt
   b. spend at least 5 days simply shadowing Craig
   c. jump in and begin working with students
   d. spend the month before student teaching brushing up on her Spanish-language skills from taking 2 years of Spanish in high school

5. Jenny has started her 16-week student teaching experience with enthusiasm based on the fact that she had 2 years of Spanish in high school. Which reason most likely causes her enthusiasm to quickly dim?
   a. She can read and write in Spanish to a moderate degree, but conversational Spanish is another story.
   b. There aren't many written resources in Craig's classroom that are in Spanish.
   c. Most of the students with LEP are Hmong.
   d. Craig's class is not desigated as a bilingual class.

Now it's time for you to respond to three short essay items. In your responses, be sure to address all the dilemmas and questions posed in each item. Each response should be between one half and one double-spaced page. As you consider your responses, think about how these standards may apply.

NCATE Standard 4 on Diversity: The new professional teachers should be able to apply effective methods of teaching students that are at different developmental stages, have different learning styles, and come from diverse backgrounds.

NBPTS, Proposition 1: Accomplished teachers recognize that in a multicultural nation students bring to schools a plethora of abilities and attitudes and aptitudes that are valued differently by the community, the school, and the family.

INTASC Principle #2: The teacher understands how children learn and develop, and can provide learning opportunities that support their intellectual, social, and personal development.

INTASC Principle #3: The teacher understands how students differ in their approaches to learning and creates instructional opportunities that are adapted to diverse learners.

INTASC Principle #6: The teacher uses knowledge of effective verbal, nonverbal, and media communication techniques to foster active inquiry, collaboration, and supportive interaction in the classroom.

6. Jenny is walking into a world that is foreign to her. Explain two reasons why she may be apprehensive or even fearful.

7. As a suburbanite from a middle-income family, Jenny is now experiencing adolescents who live in poverty. What characteristics might the students display that will require Jenny to adjust her attitudes and expectations to meet their needs effectively?

8. Given what we know about the students at Roosevelt, which of the three methods for serving their language needs (bilingual education, ESL, SEI) would you recommend and why?

Where DO I Stand NOW?

In the beginning of this chapter you completed an inventory that gauged your prior knowledge of diversity among PreK–12 students. You also had the opportunity to respond to items that addressed your experiences with diversity. Now that you have read the chapter, completed exercises related to the content, engaged in class discussions, and so on, answer the following questions in your course notebook.

1. Has reading the chapter triggered memories about experiences with diversity that perhaps you had forgotten? If so, explain.

2. Explain one aspect of gender diversity you find surprising or interesting.

3. Explain one aspect of cultural and language diversity you find surprising or interesting.

4. Explain one aspect of family and religious diversity you find surprising or interesting.

5. Explain one aspect of socioeconomic diversity you find surprising or interesting.

6. Write briefly about one person you remember in your PreK–12 school experiences who received special education services. If you received services, write about your own experiences.

MyEducationLab

The MyEducationLab for this course can help you solidify your comprehension of Chapter 3 concepts.

- Explore the classrooms of the teachers and students you've met in this chapter in the Teaching in Focus section.

- Prepare for licensure exams as you deepen your understanding of chapter concepts in the Developing Professional Competence section.

- Gauge and further develop your understanding of chapter concepts by taking the quizzes and examining the enrichment materials on the Chapter 3 Study Plan.

- Visit Topic 2, Student Diversity, to watch ABC videos, explore Assignments and Activities, and practice essential teaching skills with the Building Teaching Skills and Dispositions unit.

References

American Psychological Association. (2000). *Diagnostic and statistical manual of mental disorders* (4th ed., rev.). Washington, DC: Author.

August, D., & Shanahan, T. (Eds.). (2006). *Developing literacy in second language learners: Report of the national literacy panel on language minority youth and children*. Mahwah, NJ: Erlbaum.

Bandura, A., Barbaranelli, C., Caprara, G. V., & Pastorelli, C. (2001). Self-efficacy beliefs as shapers of children's aspirations and career trajectories. *Child Development, 72*, 187–206.

Banks, J. A. (Ed.). (2004). *The handbook of research on multicultural education*. San Francisco: Jossey-Bass.

Campbell, A., Shirley, L., & Candy, J. (2004). A longitudinal study of gender-related cognition and behavior. *Developmental Science, 7*, 1–9.

Capps, R., Fix, M., Murray, J., Ost, J., Passel, J., & Herwantoro, S. (2005). *The new demography of America's schools: Immigration and the No Child Left Behind Act*. Washington, DC: Urban Institute.

Clark, K. (2009). The case for structured English immersion. *Educational Leadership, 66*(7), 42–46.

Delgado-Gaitan, C., & Trueba, H. (1991). *Crossing cultural borders: Education for immigrant families in America*. New York: Falmer.

Diversity Data. (2000). *Principal Magazine, 79*(5), 18.

Feldman, R. S. (2008). *Development across the life span* (5th ed.). Upper Saddle River, NJ: Prentice Hall.

Gallahue, D. L., & Ozmun, J. C. (2006). *Understanding motor development: Infants, children, adolescents, adults*. Boston: McGraw-Hill.

Garcia, E., & Cuellar, D. (2006). Who are these linguistically and culturally diverse students? *Teachers College Record, 108*(11), 2220–2246.

Gardner, H. (1999). *The disciplined mind: What all students should understand*. New York: Simon & Schuster.

Gathercoal, P., & Crowell, R. (2000). Judicious discipline. *Kappa Delta Pi Record, 36*(4), 173–177.

Gay, G. (2000). *Culturally responsive teaching*. New York: Teachers College Press.

Glazer, S. (2005). Gender and learning. *Congressional Quarterly Researcher, 15*(19), 445–468.

Gober, D. A., & Mewborn, D. S. (2001). Promoting equity in mathematics classrooms. *Middle School Journal, 32*(3), 31–35.

Goldstein, L. (2003, April 16). Special education growth spurs cap plan in pending IDEA. *Education Week, 22*(31), 1–17.

Goleman, D. (1995). *Emotional intelligence.* New York: Bantam Books.

Gollnick, D. M., & Chinn, P. C. (2009). *Multicultural education in a pluralistic society* (8th ed.). Upper Saddle River, NJ: Merrill/Prentice Hall.

Hernandez, D. J., Denton, N. A., & Macartney, S. E. (2008). Children in immigrant families: Looking to America's future. *Social Policy Report, 22*(3), 3–22.

Heward, W. L. (2006). *Exceptional children: An introduction to special education* (8th ed.). Upper Saddle River, NJ: Merrill/Prentice Hall.

Hodgkinson, H. (2001). Educational demographics: What teachers should know. *Educational Leadership, 58*(4), 6–11.

Jackson, R., & Harper, K. (2002). *Teacher planning and the universal design for learning.* Wakefield, MA: National Center on Accessing the General Curriculum.

Kohlberg, L. (1984). *The psychology of moral development: Essays on moral development* (Vol. 2). San Francisco: Harper & Row.

Levine, M. (2003). Celebrating diverse minds. *Educational Leadership, 61*(2), 12–18.

Maslow, A. H. (1999). *Toward a psychology of being* (3rd ed.). New York: Wiley.

McDevitt, T. M., & Ormrod, J. E. (2010). *Child development and education* (4th ed.). Upper Saddle River, NJ: Merrill/Prentice Hall/Pearson.

Mukhopadhyay, C., & Henze, R. C. (2003). How real is race? Using anthropology to make sense of human diversity. *Phi Delta Kappan, 84*(9), 669–678.

National Association for Single-Sex Public Education [NASSPE]. (2010). Single-sex schools/schools with single-sex classrooms/what's the difference? Retrieved January 3, 2010, from http://www.singlesexschools.org/home-introduction.htm

Neuman, S. B. (1999). Books make a difference: A study of access to literacy. *Reading Research Quarterly, 34*(3), 286–311.

Neuman, S. B. (2003). From rhetoric to reality: The case for high-quality compensatory prekindergarten programs. *Phi Delta Kappan, 84*(4), 286–291.

Nieto, S. M. (2003). Profoundly multicultural questions. *Educational Leadership, 60*(4), 6–10.

Partnership for 21st Century Skills. (2009). Global awareness. Retrieved August 1, 2010, from http://www.p21.org/index.php?option=com_content&task=view&id=256&Itemid=120

Payne, R. (2008). Nine powerful practices. *Educational Leadership, 65*(7), 48–52.

Pew Forum. (2010). *U.S. religious landscape survey.* Retrieved August 1, 2010, from http://religions.pewforum.org/reports/

Powell, S. D. (2011). *Introduction to middle school* (2nd ed.). Boston: Allyn & Bacon.

Rance-Roney, J. (2009). Best practices for adolescent ELLs. *Educational Leadership, 66*(7), 32–37.

Richardson, R. C., & Norman, K. I. (2000). Intrinsic goodness: Facilitating character development. *Kappa Delta Pi Record, 36*(4), 168–172.

Rosenberg, M. S., O'Shea, L. J., & O'Shea, D. J. (2006). *Student teacher to master teacher: A practical guide for educating students with special needs.* Upper Saddle River, NJ: Merrill/Prentice Hall.

Scherer, M. (2009). In the neighborhood. *Educational Leadership, 66*(7), 7.

Short, D. J., & Fitzsimmons, S. (2007). *Double the work: Challenges and solutions to acquiring language and academic literacy for adolescent English language learners—A report to the Carnegie Corporation of New York.* Washington, DC: Alliance for Excellent Education.

Silver, H. F., Strong, R. W., & Perini, M. J. (2000). *So each may learn: Integrating learning styles and multiple intelligences.* Alexandria, VA: Association for Supervision and Curriculum Development.

Sternberg R. J. (2007). Who are the bright children? The cultural context of being and acting intelligent. *Educational Researcher, 36*(3), 148–155.

Turnbull, R., Turnbull, A., & Wehmeyer, M. (2010). *Exceptional lives: Special education in today's schools* (6th ed.). Upper Saddle River, NJ: Merrill/Prentice Hall.

Underwood, M. (2003). *Social aggression among girls.* New York: Guilford.

U.S. Census Bureau with U.S. Department of Education. (2006). *Income, poverty, and health insurance coverage in the United States: 2005.* Retrieved April 6, 2006, from http://www.census.gov/prod/2006pubs/p60-231.pdf

U.S. Census Bureau. (2008). U.S. population projections. Retrieved August 1, 2010, from http://census.gov/population/www/projections/summarytables.html

U.S. Department of Education. (2009). *Building the legacy: IDEA 2004.* Retrieved August 1, 2010, from http://idea.ed.gov/explore/home

Vermeer, H. J., Boekaerts, M., & Seeger, G. (2000). Motivational and gender differences: Sixth-grade students' mathematical problem-solving behavior. *Journal of Educational Psychology, 92,* 308–315.

Assessment **and** Accountability

Sara Davis Powell

Effectively determining what students know and are able to do involves *assessment.* Considering who bears the responsibility for student learning involves *accountability.* Here are some of the questions we consider:

✦ What is involved in classroom assessment?

✦ How do teachers evaluate student learning and assign grades?

✦ What are standardized tests, and how are their results used?

✦ Who is accountable for student learning?

Before we discuss assessment and accountability, explore your own views in this chapter's *Where Do I Stand?*

Shutterstock

From Chapter 5 of *Your Introduction to Education: Explorations in Teaching*, 2/e. Sara Davis Powell.

Where DO I Stand?

This inventory addresses your general perceptions of classroom and standard-ized assessment in K–12 school. It also gauges your preference with regard to two broad categories of test formats. After reading an item, indicate your level of agreement by choosing a number 0 to 4 and placing it in the blank before the statement. Following the inventory are directions for how to organize your responses and what they may indicate in terms of where you stand.

4   I strongly agree
3   I agree
2   I don't have an opinion
1   I disagree
0   I strongly disagree

_____ **1.** My experiences with assessment had a kind of "gotcha" feel to me.

_____ **2.** Standardized tests made me uncomfortably nervous.

_____ **3.** My teachers only monitored my learning through tests.

_____ **4.** I preferred tests that asked me to choose the right answer.

_____ **5.** I enjoyed projects more than tests to show what I knew and could do.

_____ **6.** Being compared with other students on stan-dardized tests seemed unfair to me.

_____ **7.** The grades I received were not an accurate representation of my knowledge and skills.

_____ **8.** My end-of-course grades did not show how much I really learned.

_____ **9.** Oral reports allowed me to shine as I showed what I knew and could do.

_____ **10.** Too much emphasis was placed on standard-ized tests and their results.

_____ **11.** My teachers didn't reteach material that stu-dents didn't seem to get on a test.

_____ **12.** My teachers rarely gave feedback on assess-ments that helped me learn from my mistakes.

_____ **13.** I had trouble understanding assignments and following directions.

_____ **14.** I preferred essay tests over other forms of as-sessment with single right answers.

_____ **15.** Multiple-choice tests gave me a chance to ac-curately show what I knew.

_____ **16.** I had a hard time understanding how teachers arrived at my grades.

_____ **17.** When I had a test, I felt more nervous and anxious than most of my friends.

_____ **18.** I preferred true-false tests and did well on them.

_____ **19.** I experienced obvious test preparation tactics that seemed to detract from real learning.

_____ **20.** If I had one or two bad days, my overall grade suffered.

_____ **21.** Results of standardized tests didn't show how much I knew.

_____ **22.** I liked opportunities to be creative in how I demonstrated what I knew.

_____ **23.** I liked multiple-choice tests.

Record your responses to the following items, then divide by 15 to get an average (round to nearest tenth).

ITEM	RESPONSE
1	
2	
3	
6	
7	
8	
10	
11	
12	
13	
16	
17	
19	
20	
21	
Sum A	
Average A (divide by 15)	

Now plot Average A on this number line. The closer to zero, the more positive your experiences were with classroom and standardized assessment in K–12 school.

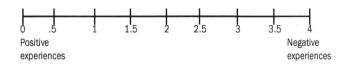

0   .5   1   1.5   2   2.5   3   3.5   4

Positive experiences   Negative experiences

You will learn in this chapter about forced-choice assessment with only one possible answer on a paper-and-pencil test. Assessment that may have a variety of answers or may be experiential is considered open ended and/or performance based. Your responses to the designated items will indicate your preference when you find average responses to the items as indicated by dividing Sum B by 4 and Sum C by 4.

ITEM	RESPONSE	ITEM	RESPONSE
4		5	
15		9	
18		14	
23		22	
Sum B		Sum C	
Average B		Average C	

Now plot your averages and compare your preference for forced-choice assessment and open-ended, performance-based assessment.

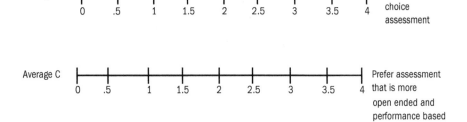

Average B

0   .5   1   1.5   2   2.5   3   3.5   4   Prefer forced-choice assessment

Average C

0   .5   1   1.5   2   2.5   3   3.5   4   Prefer assessment that is more open ended and performance based

Teaching in Focus

Renee Ayers believes that ongoing assessment is vital to her teaching. The progress her second graders are making at Summit Primary, Ohio, is recorded and analyzed in multiple ways. She even finds ways for her students to view their own progress.

One of Renee's favorite uses of student self-assessment involves writing. She asks her second graders to write their best about any topic they choose during the first week of school. She then tucks these little masterpieces away until the last week of second grade when the students again choose a topic and write about it. Renee surprises her students by giving them their first week's writing to compare. She says it's one of the most joyous celebrations a 7- or 8-year-old can experience. The looks on their faces and their obvious pride in recognizing their progress are priceless!

Renee keeps anecdotal records on her students in two distinct and user-friendly ways. One method involves a clipboard and note cards. She tapes the first card to the board so the bottom of the card and the bottom of the clipboard are even. She writes a student's name on the bottom of the card. Then she tapes another card so that its lower edge lines up just above the name on the first card and writes another student's name on the bottom of that card.

She continues this process, taping cards up the board to the clip. She carries this board around as she talks with students about their reading or math or a project they may be working on. In doing so she is practicing teacher observation with the added benefit of recorded notes.

Renee uses another clipboard to hold pages of sticky-back labels. She writes students' names, the date, and her observations about student learning on the labels. Later she simply puts the labels in a notebook on pages designated for each student. This is a quick way to record informal assessments all day and then easily organize them.

Of course Renee also does more formal assessments similar to what most early childhood teachers do. But she feels that her informal assessments help her develop the kind of rapport with her students she values and give her clear insights concerning their learning.

Renee models both attitudes and techniques that promote the use of assessment as an integral part of classroom practice. She takes seriously her responsibility to understand her students' strengths and weaknesses, to know their learning profiles, and to monitor their continual progress. Her innovative approach contains ideas you can adapt to your own classrooms.

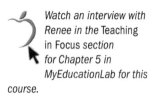

Watch an interview with Renee in the Teaching in Focus section for Chapter 5 in MyEducationLab for this course.

What Is Involved in Classroom Assessment?

Classroom assessment encompasses all the possible ways teachers determine what students know and can do measured against standards or other learning goals. The assessments developed and used by individual teachers are **criterion referenced,** meaning that student results indicate levels of mastery of a subject and do not depend on how other students score. In its many forms, classroom assessment serves multiple purposes that are appropriate for the variety of curricula and instructional strategies used in U.S. schools.

PURPOSES OF CLASSROOM ASSESSMENT

Determining student achievement and reporting grades are the most commonly understood reasons for classroom assessment, but these are not the only purposes. The National Council of Teachers of Mathematics (NCTM) broadened our view of the purposes of assessment. Figure 5.1 illustrates NCTM's four purposes of assessment.

MONITORING STUDENT PROGRESS. Ongoing assessment allows teachers to be continuously aware of where students are in the learning process. Assessing student knowledge and skill levels before beginning a unit of study is called **diagnostic assessment** or, more commonly, **pretesting**. Diagnostic assessment is only possible when desired results have been identified and a plan for collecting evidence has been made, the first two stages of backward design. For instance, a teacher may plan a unit of study based on the Industrial Revolution. The teacher decides on the major concepts (content) and skills the students should understand and be able to do. The teacher then decides how to determine when the students have mastered the major concepts and skills. A diagnostic assessment is then formulated that will diagnose what the students may already know about the topic.

Assessment and Accountability

Figure 5.1 NCTM's four purposes of assessment

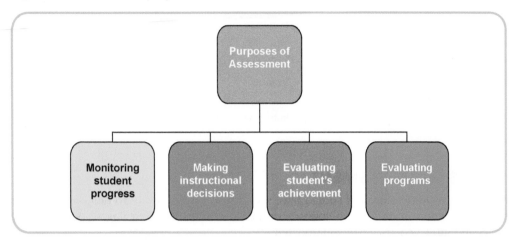

Source: National Council of Teachers of Mathematics. (1995). *Assessment standards for school mathematics.* Reston, VA: Author.

The results of diagnostic assessment should be used to plan the daily lessons of the unit, including multiple **formative assessments** in a variety of formats that gauge student progress toward learning objectives. Feedback is the key to making formative assessment effective. Feedback needs to be timely and specific enough to make students aware of not only where they are in the learning process but also what they need to do to move forward.

MAKING INSTRUCTIONAL DECISIONS. Assessment can be a waste of time and effort if it does not influence the content, the instructional strategies, and the pacing or sequencing of classroom experiences. Effective monitoring of student progress provides the information and insight to make instructional decisions that promote student growth. These decisions may involve reteaching or teaching differently to help more students master the unit content and skills.

A teacher's instructional decisions should be guided by the results of ongoing monitoring of student progress through formative assessment and not by what materials are available, how last year's class responded, or the fact that a favorite topic already has complete detailed lesson plans.

EVALUATING STUDENT ACHIEVEMENT. Assessment allows teachers to measure if, and how much, students learn. Formative assessments and their results may have a part in the measurement, but **summative assessment** is most often used to evaluate student achievement. A summative assessment is typically more formal than a formative assessment and involves judging the success of a process or product. Summative assessments most often occur at the end of a unit of study. Paper-and-pencil tests are traditional summative assessments, but they need not be the only format used. Students should be given opportunities to demonstrate what they know and are able to do in a variety of ways, such as completion of a project or performance of an authentic task. When students succeed, teachers can and should recognize accomplishments.

Look closely at Figure 5.2. Notice the flow from diagnostic to formative to summative assessment. The double arrows between formative assessment and instruction indicate that formative assessment helps teachers make decisions about instruction. There is fluidity between ongoing formative assessment and what is planned in the classroom. Summative assessment occurs at the end of the formative assessment/instruction ebb and flow.

EVALUATING PROGRAMS. The fourth purpose of assessment may extend beyond the classroom. Instructional materials and formalized programs such as Scholastic 180, the literacy program used by Deirdre at Cario Middle School, South Carolina, are purchased by schools and districts. The components of these programs are monitored for effectiveness, and decisions are made regarding their value based on results of various forms of assessments.

Assessment and Accountability

Figure 5.2 Diagnostic, formative, and summative assessment in the classroom

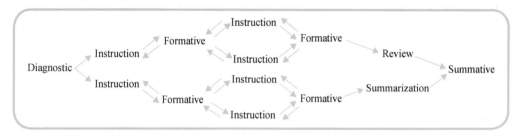

FORMS OF ASSESSMENT

Students learn differently and should have a variety of opportunities to demonstrate what they know and can do. Varying assessment format ensures that differing student learning styles and intelligences are accommodated.

Robert Marzano (2000), a researcher with Mid-continent Research for Education and Learning (McREL), formulated the seven basic forms of classroom assessment listed in Table 5.1. Read about each and think about if and how it might serve a diagnostic, formative, and/or summative function.

One of the forms of assessment, teacher observation, is a given. We watch, we listen, and we make mental or written notes about student progress. One of our focus students

TABLE 5.1 Seven forms of assessment	
Form of Assessment	**Characteristics**
1. Forced choice	• Multiple choice, matching, true/false, fill-in-the-blank • Can be scored objectively • Most common form of assessment • Choose from among alternatives given
2. Essay	• Good for assessing thinking, reasoning, and expression skills • Opportunity to demonstrate knowledge of relationships • Gives information on how students process knowledge • Scoring can be subjective
3. Short written responses	• Mini-essays • Brief explanations of information or processes • Scoring more objective than for essays
4. Oral reports	• Assess student speaking ability • Similar to essay but more impromptu • Require acute listening skills to score
5. Teacher observation	• Informal • Best for process-oriented and nonachievement factors • Good when linked to interview • Teacher notes used to record observation results
6. Student self-assessment	• Most underused form of assessment • Helps develop higher-order metacognitive skills • Assessment conference allows student to clarify own level of learning
7. Performance tasks	• Require student to construct responses, apply knowledge • Require more than recall of information • Can assess a variety of forms of knowledge and skills • Scoring dependent on task

Source: Marzano, R. J. (2000). *Transforming classroom grading.* Alexandria, VA: Association for Supervision and Curriculum Development.

Assessment and Accountability

at Summit Primary School in Ohio is repeating kindergarten, not so much for academic reasons as for social ones. Dylan Todd was a young 5-year-old when he started kindergarten. A bright little boy living in a comfortable socioeconomic status (SES) home with adoring parents, Dylan experienced expected academic growth in his first year at Summit Primary. But, as his teacher observed, he was still quite immature at the end of his initial year in kindergarten. Teacher observation, as we see in Table 5.1, is particularly effective when assessing nonachievement factors. In consultation with Mom and Dad, the decision was made to have Dylan repeat kindergarten, this time in the enrichment class. In this group designed for children who have mastered a set of basic skills, Dylan is thriving.

PERFORMANCE ASSESSMENT. The last of Marzano's seven forms of assessment involves performance. This simply means that students actually show what they know and can do in ways that do not solely involve paper-and-pencil tests. **Performance assessment** may be a project, a demonstration, a creation, or anything that requires the application of knowledge and skills. You may hear the terms *alternative assessment* and *authentic assessment* used interchangeably with performance assessment. **Alternative assessment** is assessment that doesn't fall within Marzano's first three categories. **Authentic assessment** means that students show what they know and can do in a real-life setting or situation. Performance assessment is alternative assessment and may also be authentic.

Forced choice, essay, and short written responses continue to dominate classroom assessment.
Sara Davis Powell

PORTFOLIO ASSESSMENT. One way to put a variety of assessments together to reflect student learning is to use portfolios. To create a **portfolio,** students or teachers, or both, assemble a cohesive package of representative evidence of student learning. A portfolio may serve as

Watch a video featuring Dylan, his teacher Brandi Wade, and his mom and dad in the Teaching in Focus *section for Chapter 5 in MyEducationLab for this course.*

- A compilation of all the work a student does over a period of time. The student may feel a greater sense of accomplishment from reviewing a portfolio than from seeing individual assessments that are quickly discarded.
- A selected collection of work intended to show growth over time.
- A display tool for work samples that showcase the student's best work.

You are likely creating a portfolio, or will be soon, of products related to your education coursework. Your portfolio will show your professional growth. At some point your instructors will evaluate your portfolio and assign a grade that indicates your achievement.

ASSESSMENT OF 21ST-CENTURY KNOWLEDGE AND SKILLS

The Partnership for 21st Century Skills (2009) defines goals for assessment that reflect their philosophy and practical advice you have read about in each of the preceding chapters. They endorse assessment that

- Promotes balance, including both standardized assessment and classroom formative and summative assessment.
- Emphasizes the role of feedback as part of learning.
- Uses technology and measures student mastery of 21st-century skills.
- Includes development of portfolios.

Assessment and Accountability

Teaching in Focus

Sara Davis Powell

Brenda Beyal, Grades 3–5 Multiage Classroom, Rees Elementary School, Utah. *In her own words....*

What a wonderful, scary, exhilarating, confusing, demanding profession you have chosen. Wonderful because you spend it with children. Scary because you have to teach them to become literate, capable human beings. Exhilarating because your creative juices have a place to flourish. Confusing when students come with baggage and with very little room for instruction, practice, and evaluation. And, finally, demanding because it takes hard work, perseverance, and commitment. To help with your journey, I offer the following five bits of advice.

1. Be present in your classroom. Be intellectually, emotionally, and socially present in your room. Pay attention to the students, what they are saying and doing. Keep yourself present.

2. Search out colleagues who will nourish you and your profession. Find the teachers who aren't protective and territorial over their teaching. Search out the ones who share, don't compete, and have a philosophy similar to yours.

3. Continue learning, read education journals, subscribe to a professional publication, and read for pleasure.

4. Focus on student learning and not on your teaching. Teach to see students grasp ideas and come up with their own ideas. You may have delivered a lesson that was outstanding, uses all the bells and whistles and the correct language you have been taught, and still not reach a child. Focus on student learning.

5. Live a rich life. Children need teachers who experience, explore, and discover. Take vacations, learn to knit, do it.

Given all the possible ways to assess what students know and can do, it is important to create a balanced assessment plan for the classroom. Each assessment method has appropriate uses and each has limitations. Paying close attention to which assessment is appropriate and when will help ensure assessments align with curriculum, instructional strategies, and the needs of students. In *Teaching in Focus,* Brenda Beyal, one of our three focus teachers at Rees Elementary School in Utah, gives valuable advice about balance in teaching and the merits of focusing on student learning.

Points of Reflection 5.1

What forms of assessment do you remember from your K–12 experiences? Did you have preferences? If so, what aspects of the different assessments did you prefer? Why?

How Do Teachers Evaluate Student Learning and Assign Grades?

Now that we have discussed the purposes and forms of assessment, let's look at how we use assessment to evaluate student learning and, ultimately, assign grades. Recall that evaluating student achievement is one of the four purposes of assessment.

EVALUATION

The words *evaluation* and *assessment* are often used interchangeably, but they are not the same. Assessment is gathering evidence of student learning. **Evaluation** makes judgments about, and assigns values to, the results of assessments. For example, a student writes an essay about the effects of rail travel on the gold rush of the 1800s. The teacher uses the essay as an assessment of what the student learned in a unit on the events leading to the statehood of California. The assessment provides the evidence to evaluate the quality of student learning.

It is not necessary, or advisable, to evaluate all evidence of student learning. In our previous example, the teacher may assess the note-taking skills of the student by checking on the completeness of note cards the student filled out during research in the library (first formative assessment). This assessment and teacher feedback help the student make corrections in the research process and move forward with the project. The teacher may simply record a check in the grade book to indicate that student progress was assessed through an examination of note cards. There's no need to make an evaluation at this point. When the student submits an outline for approval, a second formative assessment occurs. Later the teacher may read through the essay rough draft and give feedback on it (third formative assessment), yet still not record an evaluation. In this scenario there are three formative assessments without evaluation. When the student turns in the completed essay, the teacher will use a rubric to do a summative assessment of this student's alternative performance, and then record an evaluation.

RUBRICS

One of the most productive innovations in assessment is the **rubric,** an assessment tool that makes explicit what is being assessed, lists characteristics of degrees of quality, and provides a rating scale to differentiate among these degrees. Rubrics add consistency to subjective evaluation and serve several distinct, yet related, purposes:

- Rubrics provide clear expectations for assignments. Therefore, they are instructional tools as well as assessment tools.
- Rubrics allow teachers to differentiate consistently among performance levels.
- Rubrics provide guidelines for student improvement.
- Rubrics make grading more transparent and consistent.

There are two basic types of rubrics. A **holistic rubric** uses one scale for an entire project. In Table 5.2 you can see that a student may receive a score of 0 to 5 according to the descriptor that most closely matches the work being assessed.

An **analytic rubric** specifies separate parts of an assessment task, product, or performance and the characteristics of various levels of success for each. An analytic rubric gives much more information than a holistic rubric. The sample analytic rubric in Table 5.3 could be used to evaluate a demonstration lesson you may create and deliver in a teacher preparation class.

Along with numbers for scoring, most rubrics include descriptors of what the numbers mean. For instance, on a 0 to 5 scale, the numbers may be interpreted as follows:

5 – Advanced		5 – Highly accomplished
4 – Proficient		4 – Developed
3 – Adequate	or	3 – Developing
2 – Basic		2 – Emerging
1 – Below basic		1 – Preparing to begin
0 – Not attempted		0 – Not attempted

TABLE 5.2 Sample holistic rubric

Score	Descriptor
5	Student clearly understands the assessment task and the product fulfills all the requirements accurately and completely.
4	Student understands most of the assessment task and the product fulfills the requirements.
3	Student understands just enough of the assessment task to fulfill most of the requirements.
2	Student has little understanding of the assessment task and fulfills a minimum of the requirements.
1	Student does not understand the assessment task and fulfills none of the requirements.
0	Student does not attempt the assessment task.

Assessment and Accountability

TABLE 5.3 Sample analytic rubric

Criterion	4	3	2	1	0
Topic choice	Relevant, interesting	Appropriate	Shallow, lacks interest	Very limited	Not appropriate
Planned assessment	Creative, matches instruction	Adequate and appropriate	Only addresses part of topic content/skills	Does not address topic	Not included
Standard(s) objective(s)	Appropriate, well written	Appropriate	Improperly written	Not appropriate	Not included
Lesson procedures	Clear, detailed, could be easily implemented by others	Clear and adequately detailed	Not detailed enough to be implemented by others	Unclear	Not included
Handout for class	Professional, detailed, few mechanical errors	Adequate detail, useful, few mechanical errors	Not enough detail, distracting mechanical errors	Not useful	Not included

Many Internet sites provide templates for the creation of rubrics for multiple content areas and performance tasks. To take advantage of all the benefits of using rubrics to evaluate classroom assessment tasks, products, and performances, teachers should

1. create rubrics for as many tasks as appropriate

2. explicitly teach students how to read and use rubrics

3. distribute rubrics when the task is explained or assigned

4. refer to the rubric when giving directions, answering questions, guiding students, and so on

5. provide samples of work (sometimes called anchors or **exemplars**) that fit the various criteria for scoring so that students actually see what a product that earns a particular number looks like

6. inform families about the use and benefits of rubrics as assessment tools so they will understand the evaluation criteria and know how to help guide their students

ASSIGNING GRADES

A **grade** is a judgment of assessment quality, or an evaluation, with a number attached to it. A student may receive a grade on an individual assignment, assessed using a rubric, as well as a grade at the end of what is sometimes called a grading period, for instance, a 9-week or semester time frame.

The wisdom of assigning grades has been questioned for decades by many who have viewed grades as harmful to student self-esteem and detrimental to progress (Powell, 2011). Even so, Marzano (2000) states that "Americans have a basic trust in the message that grades convey—so much so that grades have gone without challenge and are, in fact, highly resistant to challenge" (p. 1).

REASONS FOR GRADES. Perhaps the most compelling reason for grades is that they are expected by students, families, administrators, and the public in general. In *How to Grade for Learning*, O'Connor (2002) summarizes reasons for grading as follows:

1. Instructional uses: Clarify learning goals, pinpoint strengths and weaknesses, motivate

2. Communication uses: Inform students and parents about achievement

Assessment and Accountability

3. Administrative uses: Promotion, graduation, honors, eligibility
4. Guidance uses: Help students and parents make educational and vocational plans

GUIDELINES FOR GRADING. There are guidelines that assist teachers in making grades fair and accurate depictions of student learning, including:

1. Relate grading procedures to learning goals.
2. Relate grades to an individual's achievement on learning goals, not an individual's relative achievement to other students.
3. Grade individual achievement only.
4. Include a sampling of student work, not all work, in a student grade.
5. Update grades to reflect how much learning occurs by the end of the grading period, not a compilation of scores when topics were new.
6. Carefully arrive at a final grade by considering the method of averaging to be used and the significance of zeros.
7. Base all grades on quality assessments.
8. Involve students in the grading process whenever possible and appropriate. (O'Connor, 2002, pp. 243–244)

As you consider implementing classroom assessment, remember this mantra: "Teach what you test; test what you teach." Return often to the four purposes of assessment discussed earlier in this chapter.

What Are Standardized Tests, and How Are Their Results Used?

A **standardized test** is one that is given to multiple groups of students, designed for specific grade levels, and typically repeated annually. These tests are administered and scored under controlled conditions, and their exact content is unknown to everyone except the test makers before they are administered.

Let's begin by comparing standardized tests and standards-based tests. A **standards-based test** is one that is devised according to the content of a specific set of standards. For instance, state standardized tests are also standards based because state content standards are addressed in the writing of the test items. But to say a test is standardized doesn't necessarily mean it's standards based. The content may be derived from textbooks or various curriculum guides but not necessarily from a specific set of standards.

In the previous section we discussed ongoing classroom assessment in varied formats that provides a broad view of learning over time. In contrast, standardized tests and their results tend to be more isolated snapshots of learning. These are often termed **high-stakes tests**—standardized tests that have far-reaching consequences, sometimes referred to as high-stakes consequences. A single test administered in one format once a year is very different from ongoing classroom assessment.

STANDARDIZED TESTS IN THE UNITED STATES

Standardized tests are given in some form in every public school in the United States. Let's explore four broad categories.

TRENDS IN INTERNATIONAL MATHEMATICS AND SCIENCE STUDY. As the only international test that compares students worldwide, the **Trends in International**

Mathematics and Science Study (TIMSS) has been administered every 4 years since 1995. In general, the TIMSS test

- provides achievement data to show trends in performance over time
- fosters public accountability
- allows achievement comparisons among countries

In 2007, 36 countries administered the TIMSS test to sample populations of fourth graders and 48 countries administered the TIMSS test to sample populations of eighth graders. Note that the conditions under which the TIMSS exams are given are not tightly regulated. Some nations do not follow the appropriate guidelines for randomly selecting students. Here are some highlights from the most recent administration of the test.

- The average mathematics score of U.S. fourth graders was higher than those in 23 of the 35 other countries.
- The average mathematics score of U.S. eighth graders was higher than those in 37 of the 47 other countries.
- The average U.S. fourth grade science score was higher than those in 25 of the 35 other countries.
- The average U.S. eighth grade science score was higher than those in 35 of the 47 other countries.
- Both U.S. fourth and eighth graders improved in mathematics in 2007 compared to 1995.
- Neither U.S. fourth nor eighth graders showed any detectable change in science achievement in 2007 compared to 1995.
- All of the countries scoring higher than U.S. students in both fourth and eighth grade were Asian or European. (National Center for Education Statistics [NCES], 2010)

NATIONAL ASSESSMENT OF EDUCATIONAL PROGRESS. Often called the nation's report card, the **National Assessment of Educational Progress (NAEP)** is the only standardized test systematically administered to a sampling of students across the United States. The NAEP is administered to fourth, eighth, and twelfth graders in math, reading, writing, science, history, economics, geography, civics, foreign language, and a variety of the arts. The grade levels and subjects are rotated so that not every subject is assessed in every grade each year. The results are not reported by student, school, or district but only by race, grade level, and state. The NAEP

- allows for the achievement tracking of students at specific grade levels over time, both nationally and by individual states
- provides a basis for state-to-state comparisons
- allows for results tracking for a particular subject area and for comparisons among subject areas

Scores on the NAEP are divided into three categories: basic (partial mastery), proficient (solid performance on grade-level content/skills), and advanced (superior). Unfortunately, many students do not even achieve at the basic level. With a few exceptions, scores on the NAEP have remained about the same over the years. One exception occurred in 2005, when fourth and eighth grade math scores were the highest since NAEP testing began in 1969. However, in all subject areas except reading, the percentage of twelfth graders at the proficient and advanced levels is consistently lower than the corresponding percentage for fourth and eighth graders. Over the years, scores at all grade levels in social science subjects such as history, civics, and geography have been lower than the scores in other areas. In all subjects, significant gaps remain between the scores of white students and those of African American, Hispanic, and Native American students (NCES, 2006).

GENERAL STANDARDIZED TESTS. Mandatory testing of students using standardized tests has existed for decades. The most frequently administered general standardized tests include the California Achievement Test (CAT), the Comprehensive Test of Basic Skills (CTBS), the Iowa Test of Basic Skills (ITBS), the Metropolitan Achievement Test (MAT), and the Stanford Achievement Test (SAT). Chances are, you've taken one or more of these tests multiple times.

Many nationally published standardized tests provide detailed score reports for individual students that serve diagnostic purposes when studied by teachers. If given annually, it's possible to track a student's progress in a variety of content and skill areas within a subject.

A major thrust of national standardized tests involves comparing students, both individually and in groups. Comparison is possible because the tests are **norm referenced,** meaning that they are administered to a group of students selected because they represent a cross section of students. The scores of these representative students become the norm against which all other students are compared. Students receive percentile rankings. For instance, if Enrique's reading comprehension performance on the MAT is 78%, this means that 78% of students in his grade-level norm group scored lower than he did, and 22% scored higher.

Two important concepts of standardized assessment are validity and reliability. **Validity** means that an assessment measures what it is intended to measure. Think about how backward design has the potential to increase validity. If desired learning results are known by the test makers, the assessment will likely measure what it's supposed to measure. **Reliability** means that an assessment yields a pattern of results that is repeated and consistent over time. Makers of standardized tests expend much effort to ensure validity and reliability and to assure the users of the tests that both of these critical components are in place.

STATE STANDARDS-BASED STANDARDIZED TESTS. The newest category of standardized tests in the United States is the standards-based test, with items based on state standards. All 50 states now have their own tests based on specific state standards and usually administered at a minimum to students in third through eighth grade. This widespread use of standards-based tests resulted from the No Child Left Behind Act of 2001, a reauthorization of the Elementary and Secondary Education Act. In the first decade of the 21st century, NCLB dramatically changed the public education landscape in the United States in a number of ways, notably in the area of assessment.

Test results in some states are not reported in ways that are useful to teachers as they make instructional decisions. For instance, many state tests simply place students in one of four categories, such as below basic, basic, proficient, and advanced. These types of results do not provide information about performance within a particular subject area. In science, for example, the tests do not reveal whether students lack understanding in earth science, biological science, or both. In other words, the results are evaluative and summative, not educative. "Educative feedback is immediate, relevant, and useful, and it promotes student learning" (Reeves, 2004, p. 9). Teachers and other educators have expressed disappointment that many state standards-based tests do not provide educative feedback.

State standards-based assessments are high-stakes tests because there may be drastic consequences associated with inadequate results. For instance, the results are used to make decisions about funding and human resources, which students are promoted or held back, and who graduates and who doesn't (Stiggins, 2001). States threaten (and sometimes follow through) to close schools, dismiss principals and teachers, and then reopen schools with new staffing and perhaps new programs. This chapter's *In the News* examines the high-stakes consequences in Florida, where large numbers of children and adolescents are repeating grade levels or not graduating from high school because of low scores on the Florida Comprehensive Assessment Test (FCAT).

This chapter's *Letter to the Editor* revolves around the CSAP, the Colorado Student Assessment Program. The principal of a middle school made the decision to have two assemblies before the test was administered, one for eighth graders and one for sixth and seventh graders. Not so unusual, except that all the students in the assemblies were African American. The African American students of Morey Middle School make up about 25% of the total population. An article addressing the assemblies appeared in the *Denver Post* and is shown in Figure 5.3. Read the article carefully before reading the Letter to the Editor. Then respond with your own letter, using the questions to help guide your writing.

Assessment and Accountability

In the News

The Test

High-stakes testing has become a way of life for students in U.S. schools. The state of Florida, during the governorship of Jeb Bush, has taken the consequences of this testing to extremes, as explained in this ABC video. Large numbers of students are being required to repeat grade levels or do not graduate from high school based on the results of a snapshot of their learning taken through the lens of the Florida Comprehensive Assessment Test, the FCAT. We hear proponents of the strict use of test results acknowledge that the test won't fix the ills in the schools but will clarify how bad the problems actually are.

To view this video, go to the In the News section of Chapter 5 on MyEducationLab for this text and watch the clip *The Test*. Think about our discussion of standardized testing, and then respond to these questions.

1. We hear a parent say of students that the FCAT and subsequent use of the results "takes the wind out of their sails." And then we hear a counselor say that the tests are "deflating." What do they mean by these statements?

2. In the Little Havana section of Miami, 98% of the children are on free or reduced lunch. Most live in homes where English is not the primary language spoken. How might these facts skew the percentages of students who are not promoted based on FCAT results?

3. We hear Marie talk about the fact that she works hard in school to earn a 2.8 grade point average and yet cannot graduate because of her FCAT scores. What is your opinion of this situation?

4. Stephanie asks a pertinent question in the video. She wants to know whether the large number of students failing the FCAT might indicate there is something wrong with the schools and the curriculum, not just a lack of student achievement. How would you answer Stephanie's question?

5. Governor Bush says there are some positive results of this stricter use of test results and that students who couldn't read before are now doing so. The state is providing multiple opportunities for students to get extra help and retake the tests. What suggestions do you have for how to turn what appears to be primarily a negative issue into one with promise and hope for success?

Figure 5.3 Article in the *Denver Post*

Pep talk for black students raises eyebrows

By Allison Sherry
Denver Post Staff Writer
March 20, 2007

Before students at Morey Middle School took CSAP tests this year, school administrators pulled all the African-American students into two assemblies and told them that, as a whole, they were not performing as well as their peers at the school. The sixth-, seventh- and eighth-graders were told that the school's principal and assistant principal care about them and that they wanted to hear from them about what they could do to help.

This has sparked controversy at the Denver middle school, where some parents say the achievement gap is so dramatic that drastic conversations such as this must take place. Others, though, decry the assemblies as inappropriate and insensitive because they unfairly single out students by their skin color. "The students were made to feel like they were worse than the white kids," said Stacey DeKraker, whose daughter was at the assembly. "If even one of the students got that message, was it worth it?"

Morey principal Dori Claunch, who has spoken with DeKraker about her concerns, said she decided to call the assembly after winter break because she noticed that black students were lagging behind other ethnic groups at the school.

College fair also broached

Fifty-three percent of African-American sixth-graders at the school are proficient readers. Among white sixth-graders, that number is 89 percent. "The idea of the assembly wasn't just to talk about how African-American kids aren't performing well," Claunch said. "We wanted to talk to our

Assessment and Accountability

African-American students to let them know we care about them and to let them know they have the best opportunity at Morey." She said she also talked to the eighth-graders about attending a college fair.

Of the roughly 773 students at the school, 24 percent are African-American, and 51 percent are white. Twenty percent of the students are Latino.

"I think it's necessary"

Claunch said several Morey children—in all ethnic groups—are not meeting the school's student-achievement expectations and that the school has interventions for these students. These include "DPS Success," a tutoring program offered before the Colorado Student Assessment Program tests, as well as giving students who are below grade level in reading and math a double dose of those core subjects during the school day.

Claunch, and her assistant principal, Gwen Victor, didn't pull out students from other ethnic groups for an assembly. And that is fine, said Tracey Peters, who has two children at Morey. "I think it's necessary. I'm sorry if our students are being targeted, but when a large group of our students fails to achieve, then drastic measures must be taken," said Peters, who is a member of the school's African-American parent-advisory council. "We can't ignore the problem because it makes us feel uncomfortable."

Must be explained well

Lawrence Borom, head of Denver Public Schools' Black Education Advisory Council, said pulling students out based on race isn't wrong, but it must be explained well. "If you don't let people know what you're doing, if you don't explain it to people, it can be misinterpreted," Borom said. "You have to make sure parents know what's going on, and the message is correct."

DeKraker said she wished she would have known about the assemblies in advance because she would have pulled her daughter out of school that day. "She struggles in school," DeKraker said. "Does she need to be reminded of that in an assembly?"

Source: Reprinted with permission of the *Denver Post.*

Letter to the Editor

This letter appeared in the *Denver Post.* It was written by Dr. Thomas D. Russell, a professor of law at the University of Denver. He is responding to the article reprinted in Figure 5.3 about the assemblies for African American students at Morey Middle School in Denver.

PRINCIPAL'S CSAP PEP TALK FOR BLACK STUDENTS

Re: "Pep talk for black students raises eyebrows," March 20 news story.

However well-intentioned Morey Middle School principal Dori Claunch may have been, her decision to segregate her African-American students in order to deliver a CSAP pep talk may have had an effect exactly opposite to what she intended.

Some years ago, Stanford psychologist Claude Steele discovered that when subjected to racial stereotyping, students perform less well on standardized tests. In one experiment, Professor Steele separated white *male Stanford undergraduates into two groups. He told one group that the exam would compare their math skills to Asian students. He said no such thing to the other group. After testing, those white students who had been subjected to the racial stereotype in advance of testing scored lower than the other group. He found the same results with other racial groups including African-Americans.*

The performance gap between students of different races, ethnicities or genders is not attributable solely to such stereotyping, of course. Nonetheless, my prediction would be that Ms. Claunch's pep talk had the unintended effect of lowering the CSAP scores of Morey's African-American students.

Thomas D. Russell, Denver

Now it's your turn. The information about the assemblies and the various perspectives expressed in the *Denver Post* article provide the context for Dr. Russell's letter. Consider this information along with these questions as you formulate your own letter.

(continued)

1. Dr. Russell talks about research that he feels applies to this incident. Does his conclusion make sense to you? Why or why not?

2. The principal knew the history of the performance of many African American students on the CSAP test. She wanted the students to know that she and the staff cared about them and their success. Do you think this justifies the assemblies? Why or why not?

3. The article does not reveal that both assemblies were actually led by African Americans, one by a teacher and one by the assistant principal. What, if any, influence does this fact have on your opinion of the assemblies? Do you think this knowledge might have influenced the letter writer's stance?

Your letter to the editor should be in response to the *Denver Post* letter—supporting it, adding information, or refuting it. Write your letter in understandable terminology, remembering that readers of newspaper letters to the editor are citizens who may have limited knowledge of school practices and policies.

THE GOOD, THE BAD, AND THE UGLY OF STANDARDIZED TESTING

Many educators, parents, concerned citizens, and others loudly criticize standardized testing, particularly state standards-based standardized testing practices. Among the most well-known critics are James Popham, Susan Ohanion, Alfie Kohn, Anne Lewis, Richard Stiggins, and David Sadker. Critics of current standardized testing practices are not against assessments that are well-constructed tools for improving instruction. Their criticisms are directed at certain current practices. We hear them say, in essence, "You can't fatten cattle by weighing them," meaning that testing alone won't result in more learning. Alfie Kohn's (2000) criticism is graphically portrayed when he likens standardized testing to a horror movie monster that swells and mutates and threatens to swallow schools whole (p. 60).

In a series of focus groups in 2003, Public Agenda, an education watchdog organization, asked questions about accountability issues. The groups of teachers, parents, students, employers, and professors all overwhelmingly responded that using one test to judge what and how much is learned has questionable merit. They agreed that basing high-stakes consequences on the results of a single test is not appropriate (Johnson & Duffet, 2003). High-stakes consequences for those accountable for learning are attached to the results of most standardized tests, even while the tests are considered by many to be narrow measures of learning.

There's an adage that says, "What we measure, we do." This means that assessment often drives progress—and the curriculum. With test-based accountability and high-stakes consequences, this is probably inevitable. As long as assessments address a solid standards-based curriculum, it may be acceptable for testing to drive the curriculum. However, this approach has some problems. Often what gets tested gets taught, and little else. For instance, announcements of which subjects will be tested at which grade levels influence how teachers allocate time, often leading them to exclude valuable curricular components for the sake of test preparation. In elementary schools in states where only math and language arts are tested, social studies and science are often relegated to 30 minutes or less in late afternoon. This practice leaves obvious holes in the curriculum to which students are exposed. The consequences of ignoring standards that are not tested show up in later grades when students lack prior knowledge upon which the curriculum may depend. What *isn't* taught can have far-reaching consequences.

Figure 5.4 contains statements about the good and the bad of standardized testing. Of course, the statements don't apply to all tests, just as the statements don't paint a complete picture. The issues are much too complex to be examined adequately in a chart. For our purposes, however, Figure 5.4 serves as an overview.

Assessment and Accountability

Figure 5.4 Pros and cons of standardized testing

Standardized testing is a *positive* component of public education in the United States because

- many tests align with acknowledged learning goals (standards) and measure progress toward those goals
- administering the same test to large numbers of students allows for comparisons to be made and resources to be allotted where they are most needed
- standardized tests are cost effective because they are administered and scored uniformly
- without testing on a grand scale there is no way to make sure schools and teachers are doing the jobs they are assigned

Standardized testing is a *negative* component of public education in the United States because

- the results are often misused, with consequences that are out of line with the relative importance or meaningfulness of the scores
- the tests are often poorly constructed, with items that are not grade-level or subject-area appropriate
- standardized testing often reduces the curriculum by requiring teachers to concentrate on what is tested and eliminate what is not
- inadequate evidence is available to show a correlation between raising scores on state standardized tests and learning as reflected on the NAEP, ACT, SAT, or other nationally published standardized tests
- test-taking skills have an undetermined effect on raising scores, making increased learning a questionable result of better scores
- low-income, mostly minority, students predictably score below students with higher socioeconomic status, validating the opinion that the tests may actually test what's learned, or not, outside school
- teachers generally support standards, but undue pressure from high-stakes standardized tests can undermine productivity
- standardized tests don't measure important concepts such as cooperation, creativity, and flexibility

The purpose of considering the good and bad, or the pros and cons, of standardized testing is to develop a sense of balance. Standardized tests serve several positive purposes, as we have seen. Do they serve these purposes adequately? Maybe not. Can we "fatten cattle simply by weighing them"? No. But used reasonably and as one of several indicators, standardized tests can inform us about instruction that is successful, as well as where improvement is needed. Once again, balance is the best approach.

Now that we've looked at the good and the bad, let's briefly touch on some of the ugly aspects of standardized testing. This will give you perspective on the fact that, as with any widespread program, abuses can occur unless management at all levels is both vigilant and consistent. Susan Ohanion, an often published outspoken critic of standardized testing, refers to the following examples as "weirder and more vicious" than anything she could make up (2003, p. 739).

- Tenth graders in one state take a math exam required for high school graduation that consists of items too tough for graduate engineering students.
- In one state, a third grade teacher complained about how difficult certain items were for her students, and then she discovered the items were subsequently moved to the seventh grade test.
- Parents in one state were told that only 6 of 90,000 students tested received top marks in writing. Is it possible that the other 89,994 students somehow missed out on writing instruction that would lead them to achieve high scores on an appropriately leveled test?
- In one school, teachers were pulled out of their regular classroom to drill low-scoring students full time while the other students were left with aides, deprived of their teachers.

Points of Reflection 5.2

Did you approach standardized tests in grades K–12 with confidence? Or did you feel anxious and intimidated on test days? Recalling your own reactions to high-stakes testing will help you approach this fact of life with understanding in your own classroom.

Assessment and Accountability

- In one state where tests are given in October, teachers stay with their students from the previous year until tests are completed, rather than beginning a new school year in August with a new group of students.
- Some states find ways to actually push students out of school on their 16th birthday if they perform poorly on tests so they won't adversely affect school scores.

Standardized testing is not going away. Recognizing that reality, and making classrooms positive places in spite of testing pressures, is the challenge facing us in this age of accountability. Classroom teachers can take the reality of standardized testing and use it in beneficial ways by

- modeling mature and reasoned responses to the assessments
- encouraging positive attitudes in colleagues and students
- teaching students that life is full of challenges we may not like or agree with, but that we must meet head on with our best efforts

TEST-TAKING PREPARATION

"Teaching to the test" is a phrase almost always viewed negatively. Stop and think for a moment. If the test is a good one that aligns with standards and contains reasonable questions, then teaching to it is a positive thing. "Teaching to the test" means emphasizing particular content and format. There's nothing inherently wrong with this if the practice doesn't limit the curriculum more narrowly than the standards or inhibit the implementation of a variety of engaging instructional practices. However, these are big ifs and may constitute pitfalls in the name of accountability.

Test preparation is an expectation. However, "many teachers... experience a disconnect between their vision of a challenging and rewarding career and the day-to-day grind of test preparation" (Renzulli, Gentry, & Reis, 2004). It doesn't have to be this way. Creative teachers are able to weave test-preparation strategies throughout a rich curriculum and engaging instruction in ways that benefit students and expand their learning. Here are some examples of appropriate strategies.

- Practicing the format of a standardized test increases students' chances of success. If students are familiar with the way the test looks and the way answer choices are arranged on the answer sheet, the possibility of non-content-related errors is reduced, and the test itself becomes a more accurate assessment of student knowledge and skills. For instance, if students are accustomed to listening to directions and working in silence, test day will not seem quite so extraordinary.
- If an anticipated test is in multiple-choice format, it's a good idea to occasionally provide classroom assessments in multiple-choice format.
- If short written response items are anticipated, teaching students to compose succinct, logical answers to prompts should be part of a teacher's instructional strategies.
- Almost every state provides practice materials that supposedly align with their state tests. Districts and individual schools often purchase commercially produced materials designed to prepare students for standardized tests and make them available to teachers, or even mandate that they be used. If used on a limited basis, this practice is acceptable.

Focus teacher Deirdre McGrew has difficulty accepting the impact of standardized testing on students in the Cario Middle School CARE program. Read about her dilemma in ***Diversity Dialogue***.

You met Deirdre Huger-McGrew in *Meet the Focus Teachers and Students*. She teaches language arts and social studies for 3 hours a day to a special

Sara Davis Powell

Watch an interview with Deirdre in the Teaching in Focus section for Chapter 5 in MyEducationLab for this course.

group of students who generally work below grade level. As one of two teachers in the Cario Middle School Academic Recovery and Enrichment program (CARE) in Mt. Pleasant, South Carolina, Deirdre has some major concerns about how standardized assessment impacts her students in the CARE program. Deirdre's students have not experienced academic success in school. Most have at some point been diagnosed with a learning disability or have been designated as low achievers. These are the kids on the low end of the academic diversity spectrum. In Deirdre's interview she tells us that her goal is for her students to work at grade level.

Deirdre believes her students are capable of much more than annual standardized tests reveal. When she works one on one with them she sees understanding and conceptual knowledge that multiple-choice questions don't adequately measure. But the students must take the annual state standardized tests just the same. Almost without exception they score in the below basic category in all subjects. Deirdre knows that part of her job is to prepare the CARE students for the annual tests. She doesn't believe in constant drill and practice but knows the students need to be exposed to as much of the content of the standards as possible.

Respond to these items by writing one well-developed paragraph for each.

1. Why is it especially important for Deirdre to know the standards inside and out? With what you know about planning for instruction, how might she link language arts and social studies in meaningful ways for her students?

2. What test preparation strategies do you recommend for the students in the CARE program? Explain your choices.

3. What role might Deirdre's belief in the abilities of the CARE students play in their level of success on standardized assessment?

Who Is Accountable for Student Learning?

When *A Nation at Risk* was published in 1983 by the National Commission on Excellence in Education (a commission appointed by President Reagan), America's public schools were painted as inadequate. Too many students were dropping out or graduating without basic literacy and math skills. People began asking who should be held responsible for student learning or the lack of it. Who should ask, "And how are the children? Are they all well?" and accept responsibility for the answer?

Students have the choice of listening, participating, behaving, and learning—or not. Given the finest and most equitable opportunities and full support from home, students should be held **accountable** for their own learning. And they are. Teachers grade them, and much of their future success rests on their school accomplishments. But students have very different starting positions when it comes to learning. Some have built-in family and community support and advantages, but others do not.

Parents and families bear a share of the accountability burden. If students are not supported in terms of adequate shelter and food, encouragement to value education, and physical and emotional surroundings conducive to studying, then families are not doing their part to promote student learning.

The adults who spend the most time with students outside the home are their teachers. Few teachers would ever deny that they are accountable, but most will be quick to add they are not alone in their accountability. They expect their principals to support their efforts in every way possible, as well as the other adults in the lives of students. Teacher evaluations often include their students' score reports from year to year. The days of assuming a teacher is effective based on pleasant personality or self-declaration of competency are over. It has become absolutely necessary for teachers to follow a curriculum that is standards based. If student scores on state standards-based standardized tests are not acceptable, or at least improving, then teachers do not meet expectations.

Local school districts and school boards are also accountable for student learning because they make financial, programmatic, and personnel decisions that affect schools and classrooms.

Communities are accountable for student learning. If financial support of schools and a fundamental respect for education are not present, then communities are failing to accept their portion of accountability. Elected representatives of communities—legislators, members of city councils, mayors, governors—all play roles in accountability because they are responsible for policies that either promote or thwart student learning.

State and federal governments share in accountability for student learning. Both levels of government pass laws and deliver mandates that directly affect schools.

So we see that "Who's accountable?" may be answered, "All of us." In other words, "And how are the children? Are they all well?" should be asked and answered over and over by everyone in the United States.

Points of Reflection 5.3

Who bears the heaviest load of accountability for student learning? If you do not believe only one group is totally responsible, explain your view of balance with regard to accountability.

CONCLUDING THOUGHTS

In today's educational and political environment, accountability for student learning falls most heavily on teachers and schools. Whether student learning occurs, and to what degree, may be gauged by classroom tests. For the sake of coordination of state and national goals, a standardized system is necessary. Both classroom and standardized assessment results should guide the decisions teachers make every day in terms of curriculum and instruction. It is important to see the big picture of teaching and learning that involves the interconnectedness of assessment, curriculum, and instruction. Given that, a great deal of work is required to create a fair and equitable system that does not stifle imaginative teaching and learning and that yields results teachers can use to make the very best instructional decisions.

To hear about and see Renee's classroom organizational scheme, go to her room tour in Teaching in Focus *for Chapter 5 in MyEducationLab for this course.*

We began this chapter by looking at assessment through the practices of Renee Ayers at Summit Primary School in Ohio. Now as the chapter comes to an end we join Renee as she decides to use portfolio assessment in her second grade class. Read through *Chapter in Review* to help refresh your memory of what we have discussed, and then interact with Renee as she plans for portfolio assessment in *Developing Professional Competence*.

Chapter in Review

What is involved in classroom assessment?

- The four major purposes of classroom assessment are to monitor student progress, make instructional decisions, evaluate student achievement, and evaluate programs.
- The three major kinds of assessment are diagnostic, formative, and summative.
- The seven basic forms of assessment are forced choice, essays, short written responses, oral reports, performance tasks, teacher observation, and student self-assessment.

- Both performance and portfolio assessment provide information on what students know and can do.
- 21st-century assessment promotes balance, includes feedback, uses technology, and encourages portfolio development.

How do teachers evaluate student learning and assign grades?

- To evaluate is to make judgments about quality and quantity.

- Rubrics are instructional and assessment tools that make expectations explicit.
- A grade is an evaluation with a number attached to it.

What are standardized tests, and how are their results used?

- Most standardized tests are high-stakes tests.
- The Trends in International Mathematics and Science Study compares student achievement among countries.
- The National Assessment of Educational Progress is called the nation's report card because it allows comparisons to be made among states.

- State standardized tests are also standards based.
- There are both benefits and drawbacks to standardized testing.
- There are appropriate ways to prepare students for standardized tests in addition to providing a rigorous and standards-based curriculum.

Who is accountable for student learning?

- Teachers, principals, and schools bear much of the burden of accountability.
- Families, the government, and local and state administration are often viewed as less accountable for student learning.

Developing Professional Competence

Visit the Developing Professional Competence section in Chapter 5 of the MyEducationLab for this text to answer the following questions and begin your preparation for licensure exams.

In the Teaching in Focus opening segment of this chapter you read about Renee Ayers's focus on using assessment as an avenue for growth for her second grade students. She understands the value of keeping track of growth over time. In her classroom, Renee has a filing system that allows her to conference conveniently with parents about their child's progress. With all these measures in place, Renee is ready to employ portfolio assessment in more formal ways with her students at Summit Primary School in Ohio.

Think through this scenario and answer the following multiple-choice questions:

1. Renee is most likely planning to use portfolios to
   a. Display each student's best products
   b. Substitute for traditional report card grades
   c. Primarily teach students how to be organized
   d. Show student growth over time

2. Knowing Renee as we do leads us to predict that compiling work will be done by
   a. Students alone to teach organizational skills
   b. Renee and students working together
   c. Renee alone because she knows which pieces best accomplish the purposes of portfolio assessment
   d. Renee, in conjunction with Principal Laura Hill

3. Given what you know about Summit Primary School, how will Principal Laura Hill get the word out to all the other second grade teachers in the district if Renee's experiment with portfolio assessment is successful?
   a. Ask Renee to explain what she experienced and her perceptions of results in a faculty meeting
   b. Report Renee's success in a district principal's meeting
   c. Invite all the district second grade teachers to a special portfolio showcase event at Summit Primary
   d. Ask Renee to write about her experiences for the district educator newsletter

Now it's time for you to respond to two short essay items involving Renee and portfolio assessment. Your responses should each be between one half and one double-spaced page.

4. Given what you know about Renee and her classroom practices, why is portfolio assessment the next logical step for her?

5. Consider the NBPTS Core Proposition 3, which says "Accomplished teachers . . . employ multiple methods for measuring student growth and understanding and can clearly explain student performance to parents." Explain how Renee's plan addresses this standard.

Assessment and Accountability

Where
DO I Stand *NOW*?

In the beginning of this chapter you completed an inventory that gauged where you stood concerning assessment. Now that you have read the chapter, completed exercises related to the content, engaged in class discussions, and so on, answer the following questions in your course notebook.

1. What have you learned that will make assessment in your future classroom more fair and accurate than what you experienced in K–12 school? Briefly explain.

2. How will you establish assessment balance in your classroom? What assessment strategies appeal to you most? Which of these strategies did you experience in K–12 school?

MyEducationLab

The MyEducationLab for this course can help you solidify your comprehension of Chapter 5 concepts.

- Explore the classrooms of the teachers and students you've met in this chapter in the Teaching in Focus section.

- Prepare for licensure exams as you deepen your understanding of chapter concepts in the Developing Professional Competence section.

- Gauge and further develop your understanding of chapter concepts by taking the quizzes and examining the enrichment materials on the Chapter 5 Study Plan.

- Visit Topic 8, "Assessment, Standards and Accountability," to watch ABC videos, explore Assignments and Activities, and practice essential teaching skills with the Building Teaching Skills and Dispositions unit.

References

Johnson, J., & Duffett, A. (2003). *Where we are now: 12 things you need to know about public opinion and public schools.* New York: Public Agenda. Retrieved April 11, 2007, from http://www.publicagenda.org/research/PDFs/where_we_are_now.pdf

Kohn, A. (2000, September 27). Standardized testing and its victims. *Education Week,* pp. 60, 46–47.

Marzano, R. J. (2000). *Transforming classroom grading.* Alexandria, VA: Association for Supervision and Curriculum Development.

National Center for Education Statistics [NCES]. (2006). *The nation's report card.* Retrieved April 10, 2007, from http://nces.ed.gov/nationsreportcard/

National Center for Education Statistics [NCES]. (2010). *TIMSS 2007 results.* Retrieved August 2, 2010, from http://nces.ed.gov/pubsearch/pubsinfo.asp?pubid=2009001

National Council of Teachers of Mathematics. (1995). *Assessment standards for school mathematics.* Reston, VA: Author.

O'Connor, K. (2002). *How to grade for learning.* Arlington Heights, IL: Skylight Professional Development, Pearson Education.

Ohanion, S. (2003). Capitalism, calculus, and conscience. *Phi Delta Kappan, 84*(10), 736–747.

Partnership for 21st Century Skills. (2009). About us. Retrieved November 17, 2009, from http://www .21stcenturyskills.org/index.php? option=com_ content&task=view&id=42&Itemid=69

Powell, S. D. (2011). *Introduction to middle school* (2nd ed.). Boston: Allyn & Bacon.

Reeves, D. B. (2004). *Accountability for learning: How teachers and school leaders can take charge.* Alexandria, VA: Association for Supervision and Curriculum Development.

Renzulli, J. S., Gentry, M., & Reis, S. M. (2004). A time and place for authentic learning. *Educational Leadership, 62*(1), 73–77.

Stiggins, R. J. (2001). Building a productive assessment future. *National Association of Secondary School Principals, 85*(621), 2–4.

Creating and
Maintaining a Positive and Productive Learning Environment

Provided by the author

It's not too soon to begin thinking about the learning environment you want to create in your future classroom as you continue your journey toward becoming a teacher. In this chapter we explore answers to these questions:

✦ How do teachers create a positive learning environment?

✦ What routines contribute to maintaining a productive classroom environment?

✦ How do teachers establish expectations, incentives, and consequences?

✦ How can I develop a classroom management plan?

Before beginning our discussion, explore your experiences with the learning environment and your opinions about creating and maintaining a positive and productive classroom by completing the inventory *Where Do I Stand?*

Shutterstock

From Chapter 6 of *Your Introduction to Education: Explorations in Teaching*, 2/e. Sara Davis Powell.

Where DO I Stand?

This inventory will help you think about your own experiences in K–12 school regarding the learning environment. As you consider each item, you may have memories from most of your years in grades K to 12 that align with the statement or you may have never experienced what is described, and various shades in between. Use the 0 to 4 scale to indicate the frequency of your experiences. There are no wrong answers, just differing experiences. Following the inventory are directions for how to organize your responses and what they may indicate in terms of where you stand.

> 4 Most or all of my experiences
> 3 Many of my experiences
> 2 Maybe half of my experiences
> 1 Only a few of my experiences
> 0 I don't recall this as part of my experiences

_____ 1. My classrooms were pleasant environments.

_____ 2. My teachers attempted to decorate my classrooms in appealing ways.

_____ 3. I remember classrooms with couches or chairs that students were allowed to use for reading or working together.

_____ 4. My teachers had plants and/or small animals in my classrooms.

_____ 5. Seating arrangements were flexible and changed to match what was planned in the classroom.

_____ 6. There were interesting things displayed in my classrooms.

_____ 7. There were colorful and appealing posters and displays.

_____ 8. Student work was displayed in the classroom.

_____ 9. It was obvious that teachers were caring individuals.

_____ 10. My teachers made a point to develop relationships with students.

_____ 11. Teachers talked informally with students before, during, and after class.

_____ 12. Teachers knew and used student names.

_____ 13. I felt a sense of trust among teachers and students.

_____ 14. Teachers appeared glad to see students.

_____ 15. Teachers accepted students for who they were rather than what they did.

_____ 16. Teachers seemed to have "eyes in the back of their heads" in the classroom.

_____ 17. Teachers used time wisely in classes.

_____ 18. Classroom routines were in place.

_____ 19. Materials were readily available in classrooms.

_____ 20. Transitions between classes were relatively orderly.

_____ 21. Rest room and water passes worked smoothly.

_____ 22. I understood behavior guidelines in my classrooms.

_____ 23. My teachers kept off-task behaviors from interrupting learning.

_____ 24. My teachers were able to prevent cheating.

_____ **25.** Fighting and violence among students was minimal and not disruptive.

_____ **26.** Students and teachers treated each other with respect.

_____ **27.** My classrooms were places where order ruled.

_____ **28.** Teachers were the authorities in my classrooms.

_____ **29.** My teachers used praise wisely to motivate students.

_____ **30.** My teachers provided appropriate incentives for students to behave.

_____ **31.** My teachers gave incentives that led to productive behavior.

_____ **32.** My teachers were fair as they accomplished classroom management.

_____ **33.** Teachers handled discipline problems without administrative intervention.

_____ **34.** School property was treated respectfully.

_____ **35.** My teachers were consistent and impartial when dealing with behavior problems.

_____ **36.** My teachers followed through with discipline procedures rather than just making idle threats.

Now add all your responses and divide by 36 to get an average.

_____ sum

_____ sum divided by 36

If your average is **between 3 and 4**, your K–12 experiences with the learning environment were positive and productive.

If your average is **2.5 to 3**, your K–12 experiences with the learning environment were mostly positive.

If your average is **1.5 to 2.5**, your K–12 experiences with the learning environment were less than positive overall.

If your average is **less than 1.5**, you have very little experience with a positive, productive learning environment.

What memories did this inventory bring back to you? Look at the items you marked with 2, 1, or 0. Do you see a pattern of teacher actions or circumstances that did not promote positive and productive classrooms? Explain.

Teaching in Focus

When Jeff walked into Tim Mendenhall's multiage classroom at Rees Elementary School, Utah, in late September, he had one of those "I don't want to be here" looks. His entrance was more of a shuffle than a walk, and his demeanor was obvious to other students as well as to Mr. Mendenhall. Jeff had just moved to Spanish Fork from Los Angeles. He was 12 and entering fifth grade for the second time. Tim sensed that Jeff would prove to be quite a challenge. When it was time for the third, fourth, and fifth graders in Tim's multiage class to go out for recess, Tim asked Jeff to spend the time with him so they could get to know each other. Jeff's first words were "Why do I have to be in here with all these babies?"

Fortunately for Jeff he had come to a school and a homeroom with structure, and a teacher with a classroom management philosophy that responds to students as individuals. Tim applies a theory that might be called game therapy. He believes in playing with kids—on the field and in the classroom. He tells us, "If you earn the kids' respect by being respectful, consistent, and fun, there are few problems. If you make learning enjoyable and meaningful, then students stay on task and want to be with you. Wanting to learn, wanting to be with you, and wanting to do whatever you have planned is motivation enough to behave."

Tim had his work cut out for him. Jeff had no intention of joining in. The first week or so he sat silently and sullenly. He resisted any kind of group work and refused to take part in classroom and outside games until Tim tossed a basketball his way. He threw it back. Tim shot at the basket and missed. Jeff picked up the ball, made the basket, and grinned. That's all Tim needed to plan his strategy. Back in the classroom he placed a three-ring binder filled with basketball player cards on Jeff's table.

Jeff had the potential to be very disruptive to the classroom community Tim had so carefully built. By being sensitive and purposeful, Tim was able to avoid power struggles and give Jeff a behavioral comfort level. Although behavior didn't become a problem, Jeff continues to struggle academically. That's the challenge Tim faces daily. However, Tim has cleared a major hurdle because he has won Jeff's respect and Jeff wants to be with him.

Watch an interview with Tim Mendenhall and a lesson in his classroom in the Teaching in Focus section for Chapter 6 in MyEducationLab for this course.

How Do Teachers Create a Positive Learning Environment?

Creating and maintaining a positive and productive learning environment is complex and compelling—complex because there are multiple variables to consider, and compelling because without a positive and productive learning environment, teaching has little effect. New and experienced teachers alike are often puzzled by the whole process. They sometimes think of the learning environment in narrow terms of student cooperation and student misbehavior. But the learning environment is so much more. When teachers expand their view to include the elements discussed in this chapter, it becomes clear that creating and maintaining a positive and productive learning environment is indeed a puzzle, one with many interlocking pieces that depend on one another to form a complete, stable picture. Some of the most important pieces of the puzzle are shown in Figure 6.1. A positive and productive learning environment that includes these vital components doesn't just happen. It takes planning, continuous effort, and a watchful eye.

PHYSICAL SPACE

A welcoming, well-organized, student-friendly environment goes a long way toward helping accomplish both learning and affective goals. John Dewey's wisdom concerning the physical surroundings of learning includes his statement that "any environment is a chance environment so far as its educative influence is concerned unless it has been deliberately regulated with reference to its educative effect" (1944, p. 19). This statement tells us that our classrooms themselves matter. The learning environment can actually enhance teaching and learning when we deliberately and thoughtfully arrange and decorate with student well-being in mind.

Teachers seldom have much to say about which classroom they are assigned or the general condition of the school building. You may have gone to school in well kept, relatively modern buildings; in older stately surroundings; or in dilapidated structures beset with never-ending maintenance problems. Your teachers may have had clean, comfortable spaces

Creating and Maintaining a Positive and Productive Learning Environment

Figure 6.1 A positive and productive learning environment

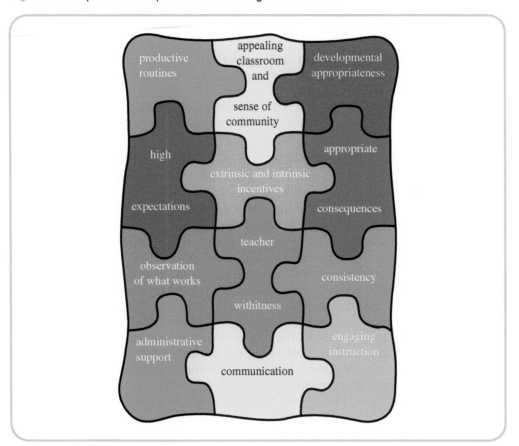

to decorate, or they may have fought off bugs and fungus in a dingy, poorly lit room plagued with a leaky roof. Teachers are responsible for making the most of room assignments. Even under dismal circumstances, designing a classroom can be both challenging and fun. Do it for your students, and do it for yourself. The classroom truly is "home away from home."

Watch Deirdre Huger-McGrew's room tour in the Teaching in Focus *section for Chapter 6 in MyEducationLab for this course.*

HOME AWAY FROM HOME. As a teacher you will spend 8 to 9 hours a day for almost 200 days every year in your classroom. Early childhood and elementary students will spend almost all of their days in the classroom with you, whereas middle and high school students will generally spend about a sixth of their school time in any one classroom. The classroom atmosphere is important for all students, but it is particularly influential for students who may, through circumstances beyond their control, find that school and their classrooms are the cleanest, most welcoming environments in their lives.

If space allows, adding a comfortable couch, chairs, lamps, rugs, plants, curtains, and other homey items does wonders for inviting students in to learn. Focus teacher Deirdre Huger-McGrew of Cario Middle School, South Carolina, created a reading center in her classroom with a couch, chairs, tables, and lamps, as you can see in her room tour.

Deirdre's classroom at Cario Middle School takes on a home-like appearance with the addition of furniture other than desks.
Sara Davis Powell

SEATING ARRANGEMENT. The arrangement of desks and tables in a classroom depends on a number of variables, including the level of the school, the subject(s) taught, and available floor space and furniture. Traditional rows of desks are fine for whole group

Creating and Maintaining a Positive and Productive Learning Environment

instruction, whereas clusters of desks or students sitting together at tables work well for group work. Ideally, the arrangement will be flexible so seating can accommodate various instructional strategies.

PROXIMITY. Whatever the seating arrangement, one vital element to keep in mind is **proximity,** the accessibility of teacher to students. The teacher needs to be able to approach each student quickly and easily, without having to negotiate narrow pathways that could lead to stumbling or a complex maze that makes it difficult to work one-on-one with students. Students also need to have visual access to boards and screens.

Tour the classrooms of Brenda Beyal, Angelica Reynosa, Chris Roberts, and Derek Boucher in the Teaching in Focus section for Chapter 6 in MyEducationLab for this course.

WALL SPACE AND INTEREST CENTERS. Creative teachers often find ways to entice students to come into the classroom and browse. Walls and tables offer tremendous opportunities to create spaces that students will want to explore just to see what's up. Brenda Beyal (Rees Elementary, Utah) uses part of her classroom to display artifacts from her Native American culture; Angelica Reynosa (Roosevelt High School, California) displays Hispanic cultural items; Chris Roberts at Rees Elementary displays objects from his worldwide travels, along with inspirational pieces that are meaningful to him; and Derek Boucher at Roosevelt High School has an extensive classroom library.

A simple yet potentially powerful use of wall space is the organized display of student work. Preprinted posters may be appropriate on classroom walls, but they should not be used to the exclusion of regularly updated student work. Displaying student work fosters student ownership of the classroom. Some teachers only display exemplary work, such as tests that received As or perfectly colored maps. This practice stops short of being optimally effective if half or more of the students never see their work displayed because their achievement on traditional assignments never rises to the top of the class. Ingenious teachers who know students well incorporate creative assignments that give average and even below-average achievers opportunities to excel. It is well worth the time to arrange physical classroom space thoughtfully, which in many ways shapes the interactions of the people who inhabit the classroom and contributes to building classroom community.

Points of Reflection 6.1

Think about the classrooms in your PreK–12 experiences. Were they inviting and conducive to learning? Why or why not? How do you envision your future classroom's appearance?

BUILDING COMMUNITY

A **classroom community** is not just a place but also a way of actively learning together. Dewey (1944) expands on this thought by telling us that people in a community are "like-minded," that they have common beliefs, understandings, and aims (p. 4). Maintaining what Dewey calls like-mindedness can be thought of as maintaining **classroom climate,** the everyday environment in which teachers and students work together.

Let's look at four ways teachers can maintain a classroom climate that builds community among themselves and their students:

1. Demonstrate care
2. Develop trust
3. Teach unconditionally
4. Embrace social media

DEMONSTRATE CARE. A teacher must care about curriculum, instruction, assessment, society, the past, the present, the future, and, most of all, about students. Nel Noddings, noted educator and author, believes strongly that care is the vital foundation for building community. She tells us, "Caring is the very bedrock of all successful education" (1992, p. 27). As Angela Lumpkin writes, "When students know that their teachers genuinely care, they respond by exerting greater effort to reach their potential" (2007, p. 158).

A caring classroom centers on relationships—between teacher and students and among the students themselves. Taking a personal interest in students is the first step in developing caring relationships. Linda Darling-Hammond (1997) states, "Environments that attend to students as individuals also help heighten the probability that school relationships

Creating and Maintaining a Positive and Productive Learning Environment

Figure 6.2 Ways to develop student-teacher relationships

- talking informally with students before, during, and after class about their interests
- greeting students outside of school, such as at extracurricular events or at stores
- singling out a few students each day in the lunchroom, and talking to them
- being aware of and commenting on important events in students' lives, such as participation in sports, drama, or other extracurricular activities
- complimenting students on important achievements in and outside of school
- including students in the process of planning classroom activities, soliciting their ideas and considering their interests
- meeting students at the door as they come into class and saying hello to each child, making sure to use each student's name

Source: Marzano, R. J. (2003). *What works in schools: Translating research into action* (pp. 100–101). Alexandria, VA: Association for Supervision and Curriculum Development.

will be characterized by respect and caring rather than by demeaning interactions, threats, and sanctions" (p. 137).

So how do we get to know individual students? Early childhood and elementary classrooms of 15 to 30 students allow teachers to know students and their families well. The numbers are manageable, and teachers have most of the day, every day, to develop relationships. Middle and high school teachers are challenged by both numbers and time because they may have 60 to 120 students a year in their classes for only a small portion of each school day. Marzano (2003b) suggests a number of ways teachers can get to know students, shown in Figure 6.2.

DEVELOP TRUST. For a classroom community of learners to function optimally, trust is an absolute necessity: trust between teacher and students, and among students. A safe environment—academically, emotionally, and physically—is necessary. Maslow's hierarchy of needs indicates that physiological needs, safety, love, and belongingness form the basis for meeting higher-order needs. All of these needs must be met by a classroom characterized by trust.

In a trust-filled classroom, students are more comfortable with the environment and willing to take risks that lead to learning. They know that if they attempt a task and don't succeed, they will be encouraged to try again and given tools that increase the likelihood of success. They are more willing to answer questions and to pose them as well, knowing they won't be ridiculed or demeaned in any way. Trust fosters learning. In ***Teaching in Focus***, Craig Cleveland at Roosevelt High School, California, tells us that teacher-student relationships characterized by trust and respect encourage students to take more risks that lead to learning.

Teaching in Focus

Sara Davis Powell

Craig Cleveland, history, Roosevelt High School, Fresno, California. *In his own words....*

Educators first teach who they are. Their dispositions, views of life, and how they perceive their students is picked up on and learned by the students before the first quiz. The opportunity for excellent student performance in the classroom is directly related to how the teacher interacts with the students. I believe that teachers must be fair, have no favorites, and be liberal in providing needed help. Kindness is the fundamental rule for communication between student and teacher. Kindness is hopeful, encourages students to do better, and shows respect for others. Both Guillermo and Khamanny [*two of our focus students*] come from supportive families where they are loved. They thrive in a classroom environment where their ideas are listened to and respected. I believe that students are more willing to take risks in class when they know that their contribution will be appreciated.

Creating and Maintaining a Positive and Productive Learning Environment

TEACH UNCONDITIONALLY. When we practice **unconditional teaching** we accept students for who they are, not for what they do. It's an attitude that conveys clearly to students that they matter to us, no matter how many times they may fail to achieve or misbehave. Unconditional teaching requires that we allow students to begin fresh, that we don't take their misbehavior or lack of effort personally. We are adults who do what we can to help students grow. Alfie Kohn (2005) tells us that unconditional teaching involves

- showing students we are glad to see them
- showing students we trust and respect them
- displaying an appealing informality
- spending time with students even when we don't have to
- asking about students' lives outside school and remembering their answers
- finding something appealing about each student

EMBRACE SOCIAL MEDIA. It has been estimated that in approximately 1 minute, 42,000 people will update their Facebook status, 36,000 tweets will be sent, and 15 hours of video will be uploaded to YouTube (Ray, 2010). Social media are part of our lives, whether we choose to recognize it or not. In addition to Facebook, Twitter, and YouTube, outside of school social media tools such as Ning communities, Google Groups, EtherPad, Wordle, and VoiceThread, to name a few, are connecting both adults and students.

So what does all of this have to do with the learning environment? Plenty, says Marc Prensky, author and founder of Games2train. Prensky (2010) tells us that when we think that virtual relationships, or those that exist online, are somehow less real or important than face-to-face ones, we are barriers to our students' progress by limiting their relationships and harming the learning community. Computers, to be of optimal value, must be personalized so they become extensions of the students' personal self and brain, customized to be tools of expression—communication tools.

Checking technology tools at the door of the school or telling students to keep cell phones turned off while in the school building is not going to stop texting and other technology-enhanced communications from happening. Cell phone communication is the new form of note passing. Try as we might, for the last two and a half centuries of American public education, note passing persists, just in ever-changing formats. To fight it is to lose.

School-provided technology, typically classroom computers, have filters in place with the purpose of protecting students from admittedly dangerous situations. But once students leave school, the filters are gone and they face the perils alone. Steve Johnson (in Ray, 2010) advises teachers to teach students about the devastating possibilities of **cyberbullying,** for instance, by teaching them **cybercitizenship**. Using an abstinence stance when it comes to social media cheats our students of wisdom we could convey.

Johnson (in Ray, 2010) urges us to stop ignoring and blocking and to start embracing and amplifying social media. He tells us to be open and willing to learn as we explore possibilities. The use of social media can help build community in creative and ever-expanding ways.

KOUNIN'S PHILOSOPHY

As a result of observation and analysis, Jacob Kounin (1970) described what effective classroom managers do. To create and maintain a positive and productive learning environment, teachers must practice **withitness**. This term refers to a teacher's awareness of what's going on in the whole classroom, which enables the teacher to step in when needed to keep the environment positive. Teacher withitness often surprises students because they perceive the teacher must have eyes in the back of his or her head. Withitness allows teachers to do what Kounin calls **overlapping,** which means multitasking, or taking care of several things at once. A teacher who has withitness and the ability to overlap can help a small group with an assignment, see a student pestering another student, and give a "cut-it-out" look while answering a question and checking the clock to see how much time remains in the class period.

In addition, Kounin says effective classroom managers understand the **ripple effect,** an effect that occurs when one action directly affects another. He tells us that the cut-it-out look given to one student may help deter another student from the same off-task behavior. This is a positive ripple effect. Similarly, but with negative results, if the teacher interrupts the whole class, loudly saying, "Jeremy, stop that right now. You do nothing but continually disturb," other students may perceive that the teacher overreacted and begin to display the same pestering behaviors (Lemlech, 2010).

Kounin's research has yielded the commonsense view that teachers who know what's going on, who can switch from one activity to another smoothly, and who can maintain positive momentum will be successful in maintaining a productive classroom environment. As you continue reading this chapter, keep withitness, overlapping, and the ripple effect in mind.

Points of Reflection 6.2

Do you recall teachers who appeared to have withitness? Describe one of these teachers and why you believe withitness was part of his or her style.

USING TIME WISELY

One constant in schools is time; how we spend that time is variable. Although some communities have increased the length of the school day, and even the number of days in a school year, most have 180 school days a year, and about 7 hours a day, for impacting students. This 180/7 configuration is based on tradition and not necessarily on what we know about teaching and learning. The length of the school year and the hours in a school day are often political pawns and are not likely to change before you enter your first classroom as a teacher.

Our challenge is to maximize the time we have with students. Early childhood and elementary teachers may have 7 hours a day with students, but that doesn't mean they have 7 hours of **instructional time,** the time available for teaching and learning. Middle and high school teachers may have 65 minutes in each class period, but that doesn't mean they have 65 minutes in which to actually implement instruction. If we are not careful, too much time is spent in nonproductive ways or at least in ways that do not promote academic learning. Given administrative demands such as collecting lunch money, taking attendance, responding to interruptions, getting students where they need to be throughout the day, we often sense that the amount of time available for instruction is limited. Recess, transitions from class to class, lunch, and so on—all legitimate uses of time—further limit instructional time.

One study yields some fairly shocking results concerning the breakdown of the time allotted for the school day. The minimum school day in most elementary schools consists of 6 hours, or 360 minutes. After subtracting time for recess, lunch, and transitions, the time left for academics is about 4.5 hours, or 270 minutes. In the schools studied, researchers found that teachers actually used about 3 hours, or 180 minutes, for actual instruction. Of these 180 minutes, only about 120 resulted in productive learning time, or **time on task** (Weinstein, Romano, & Mignano, 2011). What this amounts to is about 2 hours a day, out of 6, spent on meaningful application of the formal curriculum. This is not acceptable. But before we view this finding too negatively, keep in mind that the informal curriculum is also very important. Interaction time between a teacher and students has positive effects on student learning in terms of relationship building and motivation, two concepts we know make a positive difference in student learning. However, a teacher's goal must be to spend more than a third of a school day in meaningful teaching and learning. Be very conscious of our responsibility to maximize the valuable commodity of time in the classroom.

What Routines Contribute to Maintaining a Productive Classroom Environment?

A **routine,** sometimes referred to as a procedure, is an expected action that occurs in a given circumstance to accomplish a task efficiently. When routines are in place in the classroom, teachers have more time to teach, and students have more time to learn.

PRACTICING ROUTINES

It is important to practice routines in the first weeks of school. In this way, the routines become habits. Three important reasons for routines that help preserve instructional time are getting student attention, responding to interruptions, and transitioning from one activity to another.

STUDENT ATTENTION. When students are engaged in class activities, and the teacher wants to make an announcement, give directions, or remind students of the time, an attention getter is necessary. Some teachers turn the classroom lights off and on or simply speak loudly enough to be heard. An excellent method for getting attention involves the teacher raising a hand and students doing likewise. Students know to stop talking as their hands go up. Once there is silence, the teacher talks while students listen. If rehearsed repeatedly during the first weeks of school, this method (and a variety of others you'll observe in field experiences) will become automatic. Having one method, practicing it, and consistently using it will return big dividends.

RESPONDING TO INTERRUPTIONS. Class interruptions constitute a real frustration for teachers. The most frequent culprit is often the public address (PA) system. The routine of students instantly "freezing" will allow the announcement to be heard and any necessary action to be taken quickly.

At all levels students have legitimate reasons for leaving a particular class to go somewhere else in the building. Perhaps it's a resource class, a special counseling group, a remedial reading class, or a gifted and talented program. The students involved need to practice the routine of watching the clock and leaving when it is time or watching the doorway for someone who may arrive to escort them. These comings and goings should not be allowed to interrupt the whole class. Students occasionally need to go to the restroom or get a drink of water during class time. Teachers should establish routines for these occasions as well.

When a visitor (an administrator, teacher, student, or parent) enters the classroom, the routine of students noticing and working more quietly will allow the teacher to respond without interference. This routine will not come naturally for students; it must be practiced.

TRANSITIONS. When students change activities or locations they are in **transition,** the time when most classroom disruptions happen (Boynton & Boynton, 2005). In early childhood and elementary schools children may transition between learning activities three or four times before going to recess or a special area class such as music or physical education. Then it's back to the classroom until lunch, perhaps followed by another recess, then back to class. Teachers typically have routines for all these transitions.

In middle and high schools the transitions between classes provide opportunities for misbehavior. Students may be in crowded, rushed circumstances, where social dilemmas can easily surface. A routine for *teachers* that can decrease the likelihood of misbehavior involves merely standing outside their classroom doors during transitions.

ROUTINES IN THE FOUR LEVELS OF SCHOOL

The nature and number of classroom routines vary depending on the school level. Early childhood and elementary classrooms have many more elements to which routines apply than middle school classrooms, and high school classrooms have even fewer. But there are some elements at all four levels that call for routines. For instance, attendance must be taken one or more times daily. Distribution of materials and entering and leaving the classroom also occur daily. Let's take a look at some of the routines of our focus teachers.

EARLY CHILDHOOD. Brandi Wade and Renee Ayers, teachers at Summit Primary, Ohio, implement routines in their classrooms for activities such as

- paying attention
- gathering supplies

- moving about the room
- working in groups
- playing with, and putting away, games and toys
- reacting to interruptions
- going to the rest room
- lining up and moving through the building
- sharpening pencils
- keeping desks in order
- filing and retrieving folders

Brandi and Renee provide a personal routine for each student in the form of classroom jobs that help develop responsibility. These routines/jobs make life in the classroom run more smoothly and increase instructional time. Some of the jobs include board eraser, floor patrol (uses small broom and dust pan), computer helper (turns off computers at the end of the day), and gardener (waters plants).

Renee tells us that her classroom space is limited and she needs to use every inch of it in optimal ways. Routines and classroom jobs for her students maximize efficiency. Each morning Renee follows a routine that organizes her students. She uses a pocket chart (plastic hanging chart with clear pockets) to display her daily classroom schedule in terms second graders can read. She changes the activities as needed so the students know ahead of time what to expect. A sample of the contents of Renee's pocket chart is shown in Figure 6.3.

Tour Renee's classroom in the Teaching in Focus *section for Chapter 6 in MyEducationLab for this course.*

ELEMENTARY. Many elementary teachers deal with classroom elements that require routines similar to those found in early childhood classrooms. Students in grades 3 through 5, however, are developmentally able to adhere to more complicated routines and to do them without direct prompting from the teacher. Chris Roberts, Tim Mendenhall, and Brenda Beyal work as a team at Rees Elementary, Utah. They have established similar routines because they share students throughout the day. Chris, Tim, and Brenda expect their students to come and go between classrooms and throughout the school responsibly. Within each classroom the routines vary, but basically, they deal with these activities:

Watch Tim Mendenhall's room tour in the Teaching in Focus *section for Chapter 6 in MyEducationLab for this course.*

- gathering/using materials
- turning in homework assignments
- borrowing library books
- dismissal procedures for walkers, bus riders, and car riders

Figure 6.3 Second grade pocket chart schedule

9:30 Welcome/Morning Work
Calendar/Morning Message
Self-Selected Reading
Working with Words
Rest Room Break/Snack
Writing
11:55 Music
12:35 Lunch
1:05 Recess
Guided Reading
Rest Room Break
Math
Science/Social Studies
4:00 Dismissal

Source: From Renee Ayer's classroom at Summit Primary School in Ohio.

Early childhood and elementary classrooms should be cheerful and organized for learning. This one includes clusters of desks and supplies for group work, a cubby and coat hook for each student, plants to care for, a word wall, and more.
Sara Davis Powell

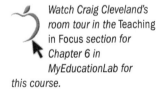

Watch Traci Peters's room tour in the Teaching in Focus *section for Chapter 6 in MyEducationLab for this course.*

Tim has a schedule on a bulletin board in his classroom. He tells us his students look at it every day and, if he doesn't keep it current, they readily remind him. Tim not only thinks a schedule is important but also organization of the classroom. He makes it easy for routines to be followed by providing resources and everyday supplies in bins that are clearly labeled. His students know where to go to get what they need, and how to do so in an orderly way.

MIDDLE SCHOOL. Because Deirdre Huger-McGrew at Cario Middle School, South Carolina, has one small group of students half a day and another small group for the other half, she finds it relatively easy to get the students to follow routines that make the classroom run smoothly. These routines revolve around the following activities:

- computer use
- gathering and returning materials
- rest room and water breaks

Traci Peters, seventh grade math teacher at Cario, believes in the value of structure. The routines she establishes include

- passing in and handing back papers
- borrowing supplies from the bins in the room
- obtaining rest room passes, used only during the first and last 5 minutes of class

Traci is extremely organized. Each desk has a number; each critical math resource has a number. A student in Traci's class knows that his seat number must match his calculator, protractor, and ruler number. There is a chart on Traci's wall assigning students to write a summary of the day on a "What did I miss?" board to which absent students go when they return. These routines save valuable instructional time in Traci's classroom.

HIGH SCHOOL. Students in high school can be expected to understand routines. There are generally fewer to deal with, but they are no less important than in the earlier grades. Craig Cleveland, Derek Boucher, and Angelica Reynosa, teachers at Roosevelt High School, California, have routines addressing these activities:

- entering and leaving class
- paying attention
- working in groups
- checking out and returning materials
- responding to class interruptions, such as announcements, hand-delivered messages, and visitors

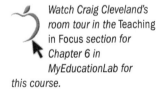

Watch Craig Cleveland's room tour in the Teaching in Focus *section for Chapter 6 in MyEducationLab for this course.*

Craig's classroom routines revolve around group work and his classroom library. Students practice working together in the beginning of the school year, learning to collaborate and cooperate. Craig teaches them. Then for the rest of the school year the students know the routine and follow it. They also know where to go in Craig's classroom to get the reading material that interests them or that is assigned. There are books on every wall in the classroom. Craig uses house gutters mounted on the wall to serve as book shelves, making book and magazine covers visible to attract students.

Creating and Maintaining a Positive and Productive Learning Environment

Establishing developmentally appropriate routines, teaching and practicing them, increases the effectiveness and efficiency of the classroom. Also necessary for classroom effectiveness and efficiency are developmentally appropriate expectations, incentives, and consequences.

How Do Teachers Establish Expectations, Incentives, and Consequences?

When you read the title of this chapter you may have thought it was just a fancy way to refer to a chapter on **classroom management,** the establishment and enforcement of rules and disciplinary actions. You should now see that creating and maintaining a positive, productive learning environment encompasses much more than the traditional notion of classroom management. There is no single recipe for effective classroom management that works all the time in every classroom. Teachers have always struggled with this part of their work.

Expectations, a word with positive connotations, will be used in place of *rules*, a word with negative connotations. **Incentives** will be used in place of the overused and value-laden word *rewards*. **Consequences** imply more natural ramifications for wrong-doing than does the word *punishment,* which can be arbitrary. The three concepts of expectations, incentives, and consequences are interdependent. However, for the sake of organization and clarity, they are addressed separately here.

Before discussing expectations, incentives, and consequences, think about the concepts of prevention and intervention. When it comes to student misbehavior, teachers have only two options: *They can prevent it, or they will need to intervene.* Obviously, prevention is more desirable. Remember that the best way to prevent behavior problems in the classroom is through engaging instruction.

EXPECTATIONS

Teacher expectations impact students in significant ways as they affect students' academic performance and behavior. Teacher expectations may become self-fulfilling prophesies for some students. Therefore, it is vital to set and communicate high expectations.

ESTABLISHING BEHAVIORAL EXPECTATIONS.
How do teachers establish expectations that are foundational, including physical norms for preserving the health and safety of students, moral norms pertaining to respect for others, and societal norms for politeness and individual responsibility? The answer, in large measure, depends on the developmental stages of the students. With young children, most expectations have to be made very explicit, for example, "Don't bother classmates," "Share materials," "Don't tease one another." For older children and adolescents, many expectations can be summed up with statements such as "Treat one another with respect."

Establishing behavioral expectations is generally a teacher task. However, proponents of what is sometimes called a **democratic classroom,** one that promotes choice, community, authentic learning, and relevant, creative curriculum (Wolk, 2003), encourage student participation in the establishment of behavioral expectations. Other influences affect the task, including expectations previously established by the school district and those held by the grade level or the whole school staff. There are few circumstances in which an individual teacher should set expectations less

This teacher should establish behavioral expectations to help maintain productive routines such as class transitions. Sara Davis Powell

stringent than grade-level, team, or whole-school expectations. However, teachers can certainly add to, or make more stringent, their own classroom expectations. For instance, if school expectations include a "no gum" rule, then a teacher cannot allow gum chewing in the classroom. But if there is no school-wide rule against gum chewing, a teacher may nonetheless establish the expectation that students will not chew gum in a particular classroom.

Here are some examples of behavior, some mild, some moderate, and some severe, that fall short of most teachers' behavioral expectations:

- talking or moving around the classroom at inappropriate times
- disturbing others (of course, there are thousands of ways students might do this!)
- tardiness and excessive absences
- off-task behaviors (missing materials, working on an assignment that is not the current task, daydreaming, sleeping)
- leaving the classroom without permission
- cheating, lying
- using obscene or vulgar language
- defacing property
- verbal or physical noncompliance (refusing to do what is asked)
- theft and vandalism
- fighting or inflicting violence
- being under the influence of illegal substances

Points of Reflection 6.3

What classroom expectations, or rules, do you remember in your K–12 experiences? Were they clear and rational, or were they ambiguous and nonsensical? On what do you base your opinion? What is the most important expectation for your future classroom?

SAMPLE EXPECTATIONS. Some teachers choose to keep their lists of expectations short and general, as illustrated in Figure 6.4. Notice that none of the sample lists of expectations mentions cheating, lying, vulgar language, vandalism, theft, substance abuse, or violence. As stated earlier, most teachers lump all of these negative actions under the word *respect*, assuming that if students show respect, they won't engage in any of these behaviors.

In this chapter's *Diversity Dialogue*, we read about experiences of focus teacher Derek Boucher at Roosevelt High School in California concerning behavioral expectations.

Why would students choose to live up to classroom expectations? Many do so because they are accustomed to living up to expectations at home or in other settings. Some students require specific incentives to comply with expectations. Most students fall somewhere in between.

Figure 6.4 Sample lists of classroom expectations

1. Pay attention.
2. Listen when others talk.
3. Treat each other with courtesy.

1. Work all class period.
2. Complete all assignments.
3. Stay in the area you are assigned.
4. Show respect at all times.

1. Respect each other and the teacher at all times.
2. Talk quietly so as not to disturb others.
3. Ask for help by raising your hand.
4. Follow all classroom procedures.

1. Arrive on time for class every day.
2. Have all materials needed to participate fully.
3. Maintain a respectful attitude.

1. Respect yourself.
2. Respect others.
3. Respect property.

Creating and Maintaining a Positive and Productive Learning Environment

DIVERSITY DIALOGUE

Focus teacher Derek Boucher at Roosevelt High School in Fresno, California, understands the value of shared expectations and routines. He agrees with the general rules and regulations published in the handbook by the Roosevelt administrators. Teachers are reasonably free to set their own classroom guidelines, and Derek has done so in two morning classes, American History and Language Arts/Reading. Each class is 90 minutes long and he has the same 9th and 10th grade students

Sara Davis Powell

in both. This is a purposeful configuration that Principal Maria Romero approved. The students are all Hispanic, some first generation in the United States and others second or third. In all cases, Spanish is the primary language spoken at home, and all the students have a history of low academic achievement with at least one incident of being retained in a grade level. They began the year as poor readers and most had little interest in reading. Derek sees potential and hope for all the students and values his 3-hour morning with them.

Derek involved his students in setting the behavioral expectations for this group. He has received criticism from a couple of the teachers in his area because he has not followed some of the traditional guidelines. For instance, he does not stick with the passing period guidelines because he has the students for 3 hours in class and a 10-minute transition between the two classes. Rather than his students milling around for 10 minutes between bells, they all agreed that they could have bathroom and water breaks at times that fit their instructional schedule, not the bell schedule. This means his students may individually or in small groups be in the halls at random times. Derek also allows students to bring food and drinks into class as long as it's not disruptive. Although there are no school-wide rules against this, most teachers do not allow it.

In terms of electronic items, Derek actually encourages this group of students to share using text messaging, and he makes use of student-created podcasts for history projects. Students use streaming video in their presentations and download pictures they take with their cell phones. The rule at Roosevelt is that cell phones and iPods may be carried but must be off during instructional time. However, when the kids hit the door of Derek's classroom, all electronics come to life. He sees social media as a way to reach these students.

Think about what you have learned about Derek Boucher and his style at Roosevelt High School. Respond to these items by writing one well-developed paragraph each.

1. What about Derek's morning group constitutes diversity? Compared to the general population of Roosevelt High, why would Derek want to set special behavioral expectations for them?

2. The teachers at Roosevelt respect Derek's passion for students and, in particular, his training to teach reading to high school students. They tend to give him leeway in some areas because they have faith in his judgment. However, when their students see Derek's students in the hall, often carrying a can of soda or texting, they understandably question these privileges. What might Derek do to prevent other teachers from resenting the behavioral expectations he and his students use? How might he explain the rationale for how students interact in his class?

INCENTIVES

An incentive is a reason for doing something. For instance, a first grade student may stay in line while walking to music class (expectation) because the teacher told the class if everyone stayed in line, the music teacher would be pleased (incentive). Keep in mind that incentives that motivate one individual may have little effect on another. If the first grade student doesn't like music or the music teacher, pleasing that teacher would not serve as an incentive. Teachers are responsible for understanding their students well enough to provide the bases for incentives that will motivate students in terms of behavior, academics, and personal growth.

The two basic kinds of incentives are extrinsic and intrinsic. **Extrinsic incentives** are those that are imposed or that originate outside the individual. **Intrinsic incentives** are those that come from within and result from students' natural drives.

Creating and Maintaining a Positive and Productive Learning Environment

EXTRINSIC INCENTIVES. Most theorists (and indeed probably most of your professors) downplay the value of extrinsic incentives in the classroom. And they are right. Extrinsic incentives are less desirable than intrinsic incentives. Extrinsic incentives depend on people other than the student. For instance, if a fourth grade teacher offers a popcorn party on Friday if the class has fewer than five names recorded for misbehavior during the week, then students depend on one another to behave and on the teacher to keep his or her word. They apply peer pressure, again external, to achieve the Friday incentive. Do you think the students will be just as motivated to behave acceptably the next week without the promise of a popcorn party? Probably not. When extrinsic incentives are taken away, positive results are less likely to be reinforced. When teachers employ extrinsic motivation, they are taking on the full responsibility for motivating their students (Erwin, 2003). Even so, extrinsic incentives are common in all levels of school.

In early childhood and elementary classrooms extrinsic incentives may include

- extended time for recess
- a movie at the end of the day or week
- special food treats
- free time for students to explore classroom centers on their own
- music to accompany an activity
- more time to engage in a favorite activity
- stickers, certificates

At some point in your field experiences you will likely encounter extrinsic incentives in the form of a **token economy,** a system of distributing symbolic rewards (tokens) for appropriate behavior and withholding or taking away rewards for inappropriate behavior. At a designated time, students can exchange their tokens for something they value. Principal Susan McCloud at T.C. Cherry Elementary School in Bowling Green, Kentucky, reports that the culture of Cherry changed remarkably when her teachers began concentrating on positive behavior and incentives rather than negative behaviors and punishment. One major aspect of the change was the establishment of a token economy, in which students accumulated Cherry Pit Points that they could later "spend" at the Cherry Pit Store. Principal McCloud says this token system gives the students a sense of power and control when they think, "'Hey, I can behave and if I do, I get things that I want'" (2005, p. 49).

A primary influence for young adolescents revolves around friends. Many middle-level teachers capitalize on this developmental trait by promising socializing time at the end of a class period or at the end of a week in exchange for appropriate behavior. High school teachers take advantage of adolescent tendencies in the same way. In middle and high school, extrinsic incentives tend to be less tangible and more social in nature, such as the use of praise as a motivator.

Praise. Praise may be a powerful extrinsic motivator for some students. It is extrinsic because it depends on someone else, the praiser. There are important guidelines for optimizing the value of praise. Specific praise is more effective than general praise. For instance, saying to a student, "Your participation in today's activity helped your whole group stay on task. Thanks, Marcus," is more valuable than simply saying, "Nice work" as Marcus's group leaves the classroom. Using the student's name is important. Whether to praise in private or in public depends in large measure on the developmental level of the students. Most early childhood and elementary students enjoy being praised in front of their classmates. Young adolescents and high school students are often embarrassed by public praise. A compliment in private is generally more motivational and increases the likelihood of the desired behavior being repeated.

Logic of Extrinsic Incentives. In a perfect world, extrinsic incentives would not be necessary. We would all behave appropriately because it's the right thing to do. We would all work hard to reach our potential and to benefit others. Real teachers in real school settings understand the theories that reject extrinsic incentives; they also understand that much of society runs as smoothly as it does because of extrinsic motivation. Ask how many people who work in service industries (fast-food restaurants, dry cleaners, etc.) actually get out of bed and go to work because they are internally motivated to do their jobs. How they do their jobs—their attitude, attention to quality, drive to be successful—may indeed be intrinsically motivated. But chances are, most go to work to earn money.

Ideally, students complete assignments and behave appropriately because they want to (intrinsic motivation). But there are tasks (drill and practice, assignments with no readily apparent value) and behaviors (walking in a straight line, being quiet when a visitor enters) that simply may not be internally motivating for some students in some settings. When it comes to extrinsic and intrinsic incentives, most teachers use a mixture to meet the real needs in their real classrooms.

INTRINSIC INCENTIVES. For lasting results, intrinsic incentives, such as the satisfaction of completing an assignment that is challenging or behaving appropriately in an assembly, have the most value. Helping students understand why a particular behavior is desirable builds an internal "want to" that is motivating. When an individual behaves appropriately because of intrinsic motivation, chances are the desired behavior not only lasts but spreads to other aspects of life with positive results.

The best classroom management involves **student self-monitoring**. This is the ultimate in intrinsic incentives because when students assume control of their own behavior, they develop a sense of ownership. Sounds good, doesn't it? We all want this for our students and our classrooms. However, helping students move toward this ideal when they may be used to being told what to do, when to do it, and how to do it, with the promise of rewards for compliance, is a difficult task. Teaching for obedience is much easier than teaching for responsibility. Methods of accomplishing student self-monitoring are beyond the scope of this text, but this discussion may plant the seed that will give you the intrinsic motivation to think about, read about, and plan for a classroom full of self-monitoring students.

Akin to intrinsic motivation is the concept that when student needs are met, misbehavior is less of an issue. When student needs are met, students behave appropriately because (1) they want to, and (2) there's little need to do otherwise. Glasser's *Choice Theory* (1998) says that five basic needs constitute the source of all intrinsic motivation: survival, love and belonging, power, freedom, and fun. Glasser contends that giving students what they need will get teachers what they want: student responsibility and more appropriate behavior. Erwin (2003) tells us that when teachers understand these needs, it is possible to "transform your classroom into a place where students . . . behave in respectful, responsible ways" (p. 21). Figure 6.5 includes ways in which teachers can address Glasser's five basic needs.

As with other aspects of teaching, teachers must remember that their classrooms are likely to include diverse groups of students. What is valued and what is motivating may be quite different classroom to classroom, and student to student. Knowing students well— their cultures, their home settings, their disabilities, and more—is vital in understanding how to help them behave in respectful and responsible ways. We'll look more closely at this issue later in the chapter.

Now let's turn our attention to what takes place when students do not respond favorably to incentives.

CONSEQUENCES

Proactive prevention strategies, coupled with a system of incentives that helps students self-monitor their behavior, is the best approach to classroom management. But when expectations are not met, and prevention isn't enough, teachers must intervene. Intervention usually involves consequences. There are two guidelines teachers should follow to help ensure that consequences are reasonable, fairly applied, and not overly reactive, punitive, or exclusionary. First, *consequences should match the inappropriate behavior.* Second, *consequences should focus on the behavior, not on the person*, thus preserving both the student's dignity and the teacher-student relationship.

Figure 6.5 Addressing Glasser's five basic needs

Survival
• provide opportunities to get food, water, fresh air
• maintain behavior guidelines that promote safety and respect
• develop routines that add a sense of order and security

Love and Belonging
• learn names and personal information quickly
• greet students as they enter the classroom
• let students know you personally
• teach cooperation
• engage students in ways that show them they are valued

Power
• give students a voice in the classroom
• be conscious of a variety of learning styles
• teach personal responsibility
• allow for second and third chances to demonstrate learning

Freedom
• give choices
• use a variety of instructional strategies

Fun
• use games in instruction
• engage students in brain teaser activities

Source: Erwin, J. C. (2003). Giving students what they need. *Educational Leadership, 61*(1), 21–23.

Points of Reflection 6.4

What do you remember about consequences in your K-12 experiences? Which appeared to be effective and why? What kinds of consequences make sense to you?

What Mr. White expects of you:

I expect you to....

1. Take responsibility for your work and grade.

2. Respect your teachers, peers, and surroundings.

3. Follow ALL directions.

4. Raise hand before speaking.

5. Come in quietly and ready to learn.

What you can expect from Mr. White:

(Positive Consequence)

You can expect....
1.) a smile.
2.) verbal praise.
3.) a positive call home.
4.) tangible rewards (candy, pencils, etc).

OR

(Negative Consequence)

You can expect....
1.) a warning.
2.) a minor referral for lunch or after school detention
3.) a negative call home.
4.) a major referral.

Setting expectations and consequences, and then making them public and explicit, helps bring order and civility to the classroom.

MATCHING CONSEQUENCES TO MISBEHAVIOR. Consequences should match misbehavior both in appropriateness and in severity. Although it would be impossible to design a distinct consequence for every type of misbehavior, teachers should attempt to match consequences whenever possible. For instance, if a student writes on desks or lockers, an appropriate consequence would involve cleaning during a school-required detention. If a student wastes class time, spending free time making up class work would

be appropriate. If teasing and hurt feelings are involved, perhaps an apology and reading a short story about how hurtful teasing can be may be effective. Most schools have a standard list of consequences ranging from mild to severe. As with expectations, these consequences need to be applied in the classroom. Teachers can go beyond school-wide agreed-upon consequences by developing and implementing consequences tailored to the misbehavior of their own students.

Unobtrusive Interventions. The variability of both students and misbehavior dictates a wide range of consequences, beginning with consequences that do not disrupt instruction. There are nonverbal and verbal ways to address relatively minor behavior problems such as student inattention; minor off-task behaviors like daydreaming, doing something other than what is expected, and not using proper materials; leaving a designated area; pestering another student; and many others.

Nonverbal interventions include moving closer (proximity) to the offending student, giving a disapproving look, stopping mid-sentence for a moment to gain student attention, and making an established gesture. To be effective, nonverbal interventions take thought

Creating and Maintaining a Positive and Productive Learning Environment

and proactive behavior on the part of the teacher. The best way to learn about nonverbal interventions is to watch experienced teachers make them work. You'll have opportunities to do this during field experiences in your teacher preparation program. Watch and listen carefully to learn from experienced teachers.

Verbal interventions can resolve minor problems if delivered quickly, calmly, and in ways that match the offense. From saying, "Everyone needs to listen," to using the offending student's name in a classroom scenario, to a class discussion about why a particular behavior is inappropriate, teachers' words can make a difference. Whatever is said should purposefully lead students back to focus on instruction or learning activities.

Simply asking a student to move to another part of the classroom temporarily, or permanently, may solve some minor misbehavior problems. Withdrawing privileges is another tactic some teachers use successfully.

Teacher-Prescribed Consequences. Teachers must move beyond unobtrusive nonverbal and verbal intervention when misbehavior warrants. The timing of this escalation depends on a number of variables, including school level, student needs, and assessment of possible damage or danger involved with the behavior.

Time-out is a consequence often used in early childhood and elementary classrooms. Students are isolated, usually within the classroom, and not allowed to participate in whatever is going on. Time-out works well as a consequence if not overused and if classroom instruction and activities are engaging, making isolation undesirable.

Detention is a consequence often used at all grade levels. It is most effective when it involves isolation and requires the student to give up time he or she would rather spend elsewhere. Some teachers, teams of teachers, and whole schools find that lunch detention works well. Students assigned to lunch detention are separated from others and required to eat lunch alone in silence. After-school detention is typically used for completion of assignments or for school-related chores such as cleaning or helping in some way. Weekend detention, sometimes called Saturday school, is generally reserved for more serious or repeated offenses.

Boynton and Boynton (2005) describe the concept of sending a student out of the classroom with the purpose of reflection and planning for better choices as **processing**. Students may be sent to another classroom, the hallway, the library, or a designated room, sometimes called a behavior improvement room (BIR). An important part of processing is what Marzano (2003a) refers to as "written self-analysis" (p. 84). He recommends that students analyze what part they played in the misbehavior, how others contributed, how it should be resolved, and what might prevent it from happening again. Processing is appropriate for minor misbehavior that occurs repeatedly or student disruptions that aren't resolved through unobtrusive nonverbal or verbal interventions.

Serious Consequences. Some misbehavior calls for consequences beyond what an individual teacher may assign. Misbehavior involving physical violence, loud or threatening verbal abuse, vandalism, theft, and possession of illegal substances or weapons dictates the involvement of building-level administrators who may elect to involve law enforcement. Such serious misbehavior often results in suspension, either in school or out of school, or expulsion. Classroom teachers should not attempt to handle such misbehavior alone. A supportive and decisive administrator can be one of the most valuable assets to teachers and the classroom management process.

Chances are most in America would be surprised to know that **corporal,** or physical, **punishment** is still practiced in 22 states today (Farrell, 2010). Interestingly, the perceived need for such punishment dates back to the early days of the United States. Figure 6.6 provides a portion of a teacher's journal dated 1776 that describes a "bad boy" and the philosophy of the day about "curing" the student. Most teachers will recognize at least some of the traits described by Master Lovell in at least a few of the students they have known. Considering the history of educational practices provides a perspective showing the struggles that teachers face in today's classrooms are not necessarily new.

The first state to ban corporal punishment was New Jersey in 1867. Many large cities in the Northeast banned corporal punishment before their states. Notably, New York City

Figure 6.6 Master Lovell's journal

A Bad Boy is undutiful to his father and mother, disobedient and stubborn to his master, and ill natured to all his playmates. He hates his books and takes no pleasure in improving himself. . . .

He is always in mischief, and when he has done a wrong, will tell twenty lies to clear himself. He hates to have anyone give him good advice, and when they are out of sight, will laugh at them. He swears and wrangles and quarrels with his companions, and is always in some dispute or other. . . .

He is frequently out of humor, and sullen and obstinate, so that he will neither do what he is asked, nor answer any question put to him. In short, he neglects everything that he should learn, and minds nothing but play and mischief. He grows up a confirmed blockhead, incapable of anything but wickedness and folly. . . . [T]o make a bad boy into a good one, he should be thrashed daily for some reason or other, and locked securely in a closet. There he can meditate upon his sins and thus avoid his fate.

Source: Loeper, J. L. (1973). *Going to school in 1776.* New York: Macmillan.

banned the practice in 1870, whereas the state of New York did not ban it until 1985. Educators may use paddling, the most common form of corporal punishment, in all the southern states, plus others. The last state to ban the practice was Ohio in 2009. Of the remaining states, paddling takes place most often in Texas, Mississippi, Tennessee, Arkansas, and Alabama. The total number of incidents has decreased sharply from about 3% of the student population experiencing some form of corporal punishment in 1976 to only 0.5% of students in 2003 (Farrell, 2010). Even though the use of corporal punishment is steadily declining, the writer of this chapter's *Letter to the Editor* is in favor of the practice.

Letter to the Editor

This letter was posted by a local teacher in *The Community Voice,* the online version of the Nashville newspaper, *The Tennessean.*

JUNE 11, 2005

As a Metro public school teacher, I deplore the elimination of corporal punishment in the elementary schools. The past three years have resulted in an increase in bullying, intimidation, and threats not only to other children but to staff itself. My school (K–4) has had teachers assaulted by 5 year olds this year! The fear of not having good ADA—average daily attendance—has paralyzed administration into ignoring repeat offenses until they often turn into zero tolerance issues. If teachers aren't given tools to keep order in class, this already bad situation will worsen. . . . We have a new generation of parents who have no respect for schools, teachers, the law or anybody. And their children are entering school now! Sugarcoat it all you want; I see it every day. Teachers spend more time keeping order than actually teaching. Visit your child's school and get involved! Demand discipline and good order! It's worse now than you think.

Now it's your turn. This chapter has given you information about possible consequences for misbehavior as well as insight into the controversial nature of corporal punishment. These questions will help you formulate your own letter.

1. Do you think there are ever instances that justify corporal punishment? If not, why not? If so, what might those instances be?
2. If you support the writer, what justification do you propose? If you do not support the writer, what would you say to an experienced teacher who believes in administering corporal punishment?
3. If you do not agree with corporal punishment, what alternative can you suggest? If you do agree with corporal punishment, how would you explain the need for it in a public forum?

Your letter to the editor should be in response to the *Community Voice* of the *Tennessean* letter—supporting it, adding information, or refuting it. Write your letter in understandable terminology, remembering that readers of newspaper letters to the editor are citizens who may have limited knowledge of school practices and policies.

Creating and Maintaining a Positive and Productive Learning Environment

School districts that practice corporal punishment must follow guidelines governing its use that have resulted from court cases. These guidelines include giving specific warnings that a behavior may result in physical punishment, having more than one adult present, and ensuring that the punishment is reasonable and humane (Dunklee & Shoop, 2002). Although corporal punishment has vocal critics and its practice has fallen out of favor with most districts and educators, some people still believe it is warranted.

FOCUS ON THE BEHAVIOR, NOT THE PERSON. Children and adolescents are developing and growing. Their misbehavior often results from fleeting moods, spontaneous impulses, and poor decision making linked to immaturity.

Constructive Correcting. Assigning consequences in ways that serve as student learning experiences is both productive and constructive—productive in that students sense that they are viewed as individuals, and constructive in that students may use the experience to build their understanding of why certain behaviors are unacceptable. Correcting students in constructive ways can turn something negative into a growth experience. For instance, a consequence for using the word *retard* in a joking manner may be viewing a video about children with Down syndrome that explains their mental retardation and the coping strategies they are taught. The disrespect shown by using *retard* as a slang word will hopefully be corrected with increased understanding.

Boynton and Boynton (2005) tell us that the goal of correcting students should be to have them reflect on their actions, be sorry for their misbehavior, and determine to make better choices next time. How teachers correct students makes a difference. If done constructively, the chances of a student walking away hating the teacher and planning to misbehave again, but not get caught, are diminished. Steps to use when correcting a student and assigning a consequence are listed in Figure 6.7.

Starting Fresh. When focus is placed on the misbehavior, not on the student, it is possible for the student to see beyond the incident and consequence to the possibility of a fresh start. Chris Stevenson (2002), noted expert on middle-level education, advises us to have an attitude that says to students, "Redemption is always close, not closed" (p. 219). In other words, when a student misbehaves and a consequence is assigned, the student deserves to be given a fresh start. This helps students build **resilience,** the ability to bounce back and meet life's challenges.

Family Communication. When communicating with the family of a student who misbehaves, it is vital to focus on the misbehavior, not the person. In essence, if a student is maligned rather than the misbehavior, then the family is maligned, with a negative effect on the family-school relationship. A wise teacher emphasizes the positive and the potential before discussing the misbehavior.

If a teacher has already had a positive family communication, such as a complimentary note sent home or a pleasant meeting at Back-to-School Night, then a phone call about a behavior problem may work wonders. For some students, just the threat of a call is enough.

Figure 6.7 Steps to use when correcting students

1. Review what happened.
2. Identify and accept student's feelings.
3. Review alternative actions.
4. Explain the building policy as it applies to the situation.
5. Let the student know that all students are treated the same.
6. Invoke an immediate and meaningful consequence.
7. Let the student know you are disappointed that you have to invoke a consequence to his or her action.
8. Communicate an expectation that the student will do better in the future.

Source: Boynton, M., & Boynton, C. (2005). *The educator's guide to preventing and solving discipline problems.* Alexandria, VA: Association for Supervision and Curriculum Development.

Creating and Maintaining a Positive and Productive Learning Environment

Points of Reflection 6.5

Were you ever involved in a teacher-initiated family conference because of behavior issues? If so, how did you feel about it? Did your behavior improve? If so, in what ways? Do you have friends or siblings who were involved in such a conference? Do you remember their reactions?

For other students, a call home is meaningless. For instance, parents may not be available for a call (and students know this) or parents may have received many such calls and may not care or may feel helpless to remedy the situation.

Parent or family conferences can be effective if they are handled professionally and result in an agreed-upon, enforceable plan to correct the problem.

Now that we have considered ways to create a positive learning environment, how routines contribute to a productive learning environment, and some of the basics of expectations, incentives, and consequences, we are ready to explore developing a classroom management plan.

How Can I Develop a Classroom Management Plan?

Considering elements that contribute to a successful classroom management plan will create an awareness of what to look for in field experiences throughout your teacher preparation program as you observe teachers dealing daily with learning environment issues.

This section looks briefly at what selected theorists and researchers have to say about classroom management; the necessity of considering students' special needs, societal context, and developmental stages; and some general guidelines for planning and implementing classroom management.

PROMINENT THEORIES OF CLASSROOM MANAGEMENT

If you presented a classroom management scenario to a room full of teachers and asked them how they would respond, you'd no doubt hear as many solutions as there were teachers. A foolproof recipe for classroom management doesn't exist. Many new teachers are dismayed to hear this because a recipe or formula would make life much easier. But take heart! Teachers can take advantage of what experienced theorists like those in Table 6.1 have to say, as well as research-based strategies, to garner ideas to consider in developing personalized classroom management plans.

CONSIDER THE STUDENTS

We have already discussed the importance of considering all aspects of students' lives when planning for curriculum, instruction, and assessment. This outlook is equally important in planning for the learning environment.

An important part of a classroom management plan involves teaching students to follow directions. Sara Davis Powell

TABLE 6.1 Overview of selected theories of classroom management

Theorist	Model	Basic Beliefs
Skinner	Behavior modification	Teachers use positive and negative reinforcements or rewards and punishments to modify or shape students' behavior.
Glasser	Choice therapy and quality schools	Schools help satisfy students' psychological needs and add quality to their lives. Teachers teach, manage, provide caring environments, and conduct class meetings in a way that adds quality to students' lives.
Gordon	Teacher effectiveness training	Teachers teach self-discipline, demonstrate active listening, send "I-messages" rather than "you-messages," and teach a six-step conflict resolution program.
Canter	Assertive discipline	Teachers and students have rights in the classroom. Teachers insist upon responsible behavior and use a hierarchical list of consequences to manage behavior.
Kounin	Instructional management	Teachers use effective instructional behaviors (teaching techniques, movement management, and group focus) to influence student behaviors.
Curwin and Mendler	Discipline with dignity	Teachers protect the dignity of students. Teachers are fair and consider individual situations (as opposed to rigid rules), list rules that make sense to students, and model appropriate behaviors.
Gathercoal	Judicious discipline	Teachers provide behavioral guidelines for property loss and damage, threats to health and safety, and serious disruptions of the educational process. They also demonstrate professional ethics and build a democratic classroom.

Source: Manning, M. L., & Bucher, K. T. (2007). *Classroom management: Models, applications, and cases* (pp. 12–14). Upper Saddle River, NJ: Merrill/Prentice Hall.

SPECIAL NEEDS. Students with special needs, those requiring unique services to optimize their learning potential, usually also require specific guidelines for classroom management. The best way to find out what the guidelines are for a student with special needs is to talk with the person in your school who has oversight responsibility for the student's education, most often one of the special educators in your building. You will be referred to the student's Individualized Education Program, which will contain information about any variances from what are considered normal, reasonable incentive-and-consequence systems necessitated by the student's disability. The Individuals with Disabilities Education Act (IDEA) includes provisions for the development of a management plan through a team of educators using a process known as **functional behavioral assessment (FBA)**. FBA looks for events and actions that may lead to misbehavior and devises strategies to help students abide by classroom expectations.

SOCIETAL CONTEXT. Students don't leave their home lives on the schoolhouse steps at 8 A.M., to be picked up again at 3:30 P.M. as they leave the classroom. The societal context in which they are growing up colors their attitudes, aptitudes, and reactions. You name it, they bring it with them into the classroom. The answer to the familiar questions, "And how are the children? Are they all well?" should guide the development and implementation of a classroom management plan.

What motivates one child to follow routines and expectations may be meaningless to another. Student perceptions, regardless of whether the source may be culturally or socioeconomically based, influence their reactions to expectations, incentives, and consequences.

Creating and Maintaining a Positive and Productive Learning Environment

Some of the everyday areas about which perceptions may differ include eye contact, physical closeness to others, competition, and receiving attention (Manning & Bucher, 2007).

To understand this issue of differing perspectives, examine what experienced educators and sociologists have to say about sensitivity and insightful management options. Some of the best sources of information, including Ruby Payne, Lisa Delpit, Alfie Kohn, and Jonathan Kozol, remind us that diversity exists within specific groups, as well as among groups. This diversity and resulting issues may impact the day-to-day functioning of classrooms as teachers strive to match their classroom management systems to students' developmental levels.

DEVELOPMENTAL APPROPRIATENESS. Understanding human development is absolutely essential when writing and implementing a classroom management plan. Let's take a look at how some of our 10 focus teachers maintain learning environments through classroom management plans that match their personal styles and respond to the developmental stages of their students.

Early Childhood. Brandi Wade at Summit Primary, Ohio, works to create a safe, loving, consistent environment for kindergartners. She attempts to match misbehavior with logical consequences. For instance, if during group time on the classroom carpet a child is disruptive, the child must go back to his or her desk, continuing to listen, but not sitting with the rest of the children.

Brandi uses a system that is theme related, and her expectations for behavior increase as the year progresses. For instance, her expectation in September may be for students not to argue as they form lines to leave the room. If students "earn" 15 apples in their class apple basket for meeting this expectation, they may enjoy an apple-tasting party.

Elementary. Chris Roberts, multiage teacher at Rees Elementary School, Utah, has a classroom management/learning environment philosophy best related in his own words.

> Maintaining a positive environment really boils down to a quote I follow by Ron Miller, "Our work is not about curriculum or a teaching method. It is about nurturing the human spirit with love." I do my best to have unconditional love for my students. I think my students feel that and do their best to work hard and learn all they can. We don't have "rules," but we do have "agreements." I believe that language change is important. Kids are smothered in rules. We meet together a lot in the beginning of the year and do experiential activities to build teamwork. We talk about how we want our village to be. We write down our discussions and sign an agreement that we will do our best to show respect for ourselves, others, and property. We continually assess how we are doing all year long. I write a lot of letters to my students telling them I appreciate the positive things they are doing. (From e-mail communication with Chris Roberts, November 11, 2005)

In the opening scenario of this chapter you read about Tim Mendenhall and a new student who came into his classroom with a history of misbehavior and poor academic performance. Tim applied his classroom management plan to help Jeff acclimate to Rees Elementary and make behavioral progress, a necessary step toward academic success. The general guidelines of Tim's management plan are presented in Figure 6.8.

Figure 6.8 Tim Mendenhall's guidelines for classroom management

1. Build trust from the moment students walk through the door.
2. Protect trust all year long.
3. Play with students on the field and in the classroom (sports, checkers, educational games, etc.).
4. Don't send students away to be disciplined unless absolutely necessary. If you do, you give away their respect for you and your role.
5. Don't ever be degrading. This ruins your relationship with students.
6. Set up clear expectations with consequences that apply when students make bad choices.
7. Make students take responsibility. Keep their problems, their problems.
8. Be sympathetic but firm, fair, and consistent.

Source: From e-mail communication with Tim Mendenhall, November 12, 2005.

Creating and Maintaining a Positive and Productive Learning Environment

Figure 6.9 Cario Middle School student expectations

1. Conduct yourself in an orderly manner.
2. Be on task.
3. Respect yourself and others.
4. Take care of all property.
5. Promote safety in everything you do.

Middle School. Focus teacher Traci Peters at Cario Middle School, South Carolina, invests a lot of time in getting to know her students and attending school events to support their participation. Building relationships is foundational to Traci's classroom management plan.

Traci and her students abide by the five basic behavior guidelines agreed on by the entire staff of Cario Middle School and listed in Figure 6.9. The Charleston County School District requires teachers to give conduct grades for each student in every 9-week grading period. Employing a system commonly found in many schools, Traci gives demerits for misbehavior. She has a system for converting demerits into letter grades. She also uses a "three strikes, you're out" policy, meaning that after three demerits in her classroom in a quarter, a student goes outside her classroom management plan and talks with a building-level administrator. Traci says, "Basically, I give kids a chance to be kids, but at the same time I expect them to respect me and those around them." She tells us that parent communication is a major help in managing a middle school classroom.

High School. A high school administrative team and staff with expectations for respect and consistent consequences can generally run a positive and productive campus. Most high school students understand behavioral expectations and the rationale behind them. If adolescents ages 15 through 19 are disruptive in the classroom, they know exactly what they're doing and, in some cases, do it because they know they can get away with it or perhaps because they want to be suspended. Students who are disruptive in high school are often sent out of the classroom, instructed to see an administrator, and may be given **suspension,** or sent off school grounds, for a specified length of time. This severe consequence should be reserved for extreme cases.

Roosevelt High School, California, publishes school rules as well as its Student Code of Conduct in a student handbook. The school rules on which Roosevelt teachers build their classroom expectations are shown in Figure 6.10. The Code of Conduct covers expectations for a safe environment, closed-campus rules and exceptions, the necessity of ID tags, absences, the use of electronics, and a sexual harassment policy. In addition, the Fresno Unified School District maintains a zero-tolerance policy for possession of firearms, weapons of any kind, explosives, controlled substances, and attempted or actual harm to another person. Immediate suspension occurs for violations, many times resulting in **expulsion,** or permanent removal from school.

Our three focus teachers at Roosevelt High, Craig Cleveland, Derek Boucher, and Angelica Reynosa, seldom have misbehavior in their classrooms that a certain look or a private word won't remedy. They are instead often faced with the dilemma of students not engaging in learning. So rather than overt misbehavior, a lack of desire or enthusiasm for the whole educative process often challenges them. This can be an even more perplexing problem than dealing with students who are disruptive.

INCORPORATE 21ST-CENTURY SKILLS

We have discussed the Partnership for 21st Century Skills (P21) in the context of curriculum, instruction, and assessment while addressing the first three 21st-century outcome categories: core subjects; learning and innovation skills; and information, media, and

Points of Reflection 6.6

Do the behavior and classroom management dilemmas of early childhood sound like something you might find intriguing? If so, in what ways?

Can you envision yourself managing an elementary classroom? If so, what appeals to you about this age group?

Does managing a classroom of unpredictable, yet wonderful young adolescents appeal to you? If so, why?

Do you have the desire to establish caring relationships with maturing adolescents who wish to be treated as adults but who may not have the self-control or self-motivation to match? If so, explain.

When planning for classroom management, always consider your students and their developmental needs.
Barbara Hairfield

Creating and Maintaining a Positive and Productive Learning Environment

Figure 6.10 Roosevelt High School behavior guidelines

Roosevelt High School students are required to conduct themselves in an appropriate, acceptable manner at all times when present in school, in classrooms and hallways, on school grounds, and at school-sponsored events. Students are to:

1. Treat others with consideration and dignity.
2. Respect the property of others.
3. Be punctual and prepared for class.
4. Follow the direction of all staff.

Figure 6.11 21st-century life skills

- Flexibility and adaptability
- Initiative and self-direction
- Social and cross-cultural skills
- Productivity and accountability
- Leadership and responsibility

technology skills. P21's philosophy is that mastering the first three outcome categories is not enough to be successful in life. The fourth outcome category is *Life and Career Skills.* The five major components of Life and Career Skills are listed in Figure 6.11. Let's briefly examine each component.

FLEXIBILITY AND ADAPTABILITY. Being flexible and adaptable doesn't mean passively going with the flow. P21 suggests that we teach students to respond to change in ways that make growth a priority and to use feedback constructively. This means that students need to develop resilience that helps them deal with both praise and criticism. Teaching students to be adaptable involves giving them experiences in different roles, responsibilities, and schedules.

Although we can control many elements in the classroom, it is inevitable that something will interrupt the flow of teaching and learning. For instance, in an elementary classroom a teacher may purposefully orchestrate a disruption in an event students helped plan, like an afternoon outdoors looking for plant samples. The teacher might lead the students to plan the event on a day when she knows the field is scheduled to be mowed. When she tells the students about the mowing the morning of their planned outing, they will be disappointed. She can have the students get into small groups and brainstorm how they might be flexible and adaptable and still accomplish their goals. Then students should share and discuss their possible alternatives. This is a life skill that is very much a part of a productive classroom environment.

INITIATIVE AND SELF-DIRECTION. The components addressed in these life and career skills include managing goals and time, working independently, and being self-directed learners. All of these components play major roles in maintaining a positive and productive learning environment. Independent, self-directed learners will be able to manage time as they accomplish their goals. Helping students become this ultimate vision of who we want them to be isn't necessarily something that becomes part of daily lesson plans. It is a teacher attitude that weaves in and out of every formal and informal encounter we have with students. For instance, a high school civics teacher may plan for students to complete a semester-long project. Many steps are built into the project, beginning with a whole-class activity of brainstorming, followed by small group work for those with similar interests. Then the individual student, armed with skills from working with two different size groups, sets off independently to work through the assignment step by step at his or her own pace. The teacher is deliberately creating experiences that lead to independence and self-direction.

SOCIAL AND CROSS-CULTURAL SKILLS. This area is all about relationships and communication, two vital aspects of a classroom community. Showing respect in a variety of circumstances and with a broad spectrum of people, based on age, gender, ethnicity, abilities, political persuasions, religion, and all the ways we may differ, is key. Every day in the classroom teachers have the responsibility to model acceptance and respectful communication. They model when to speak and when to listen, when to be open minded, and then when to stand on reasoned ground.

One way to foster social and cross-cultural skills is purposefully grouping and regrouping students in ways that expose them to all the diversity a particular setting can offer. Some demographics are rich in diversity; others are not. Even where race and socioeconomic circumstances are similar, students display diversity in learning styles, abilities, motivation, and achievement. Teachers need to look beyond the obvious and into the subtle, and then group students, teaching them how to communicate and work together in positive and productive ways.

PRODUCTIVITY AND ACCOUNTABILITY. Producing results and fulfilling responsibilities, or being accountable, are vital attributes of success. When students experience success through being productive and accountable, success will likely lead to more success. It's a cycle we often have to orchestrate the first or second time around until students experience what it's like to actually be productive. We certainly have to be close guides for younger students to first succeed, and then recognize success in the form of productivity so they understand the cycle and will want to replicate it. But adolescents often need this close guidance as well. Our hovering will have to take different forms to be effective, but that's part of understanding the development of our students. If adolescents have little experience with productivity and accountability, we have to make the elements obvious, actually *plan* for them to succeed, and then help them reflect on the big picture of the relationship between hard work and success.

LEADERSHIP AND RESPONSIBILITY. There's a reason why social studies standards begin with the study of self and family in kindergarten, neighborhoods and community in first grade, and then progress to an overview of local, state, and national dimensions before concentrating on U.S. History in fifth grade. From there, a broad view of history is tackled, followed by in-depth study of how our world works regarding people, geography, politics, and so on. Children and adolescents develop from a narrow perspective on life and their world, to an understanding of interdependence, built in large measure through the guidance of their teachers.

Integrity and ethical behavior, two attributes we hope will be part of all aspects of leadership, don't necessarily happen naturally. Pointing out moral dilemmas and then prompting students to make choices and act in responsible ways is a positive and healthy part of the informal curriculum. For instance, when a dispute arises on the playground, and it most certainly will, rather than assigning a consequence based on what appears to be a rule infraction or just a child being mean, a teacher might plan a class debriefing of the situation with students asking questions of the kids involved in the dispute, attempting to get at the cause of the problem. In this way, students begin to think through situations, look at possible causes and solutions, recognize volatile circumstances, and learn to take responsibility and lead others in that direction as well. Although this all sounds quite straightforward and simple, it takes incident after incident, solution seeking over and over again, to internalize the lessons. As adults this is a lifelong learning task, and for children we can't start too soon to help them develop leadership and responsibility skills.

GENERAL GUIDELINES FOR DEVELOPING A CLASSROOM MANAGEMENT PLAN

We have discussed some of the most important elements of developing and implementing a classroom management plan. Figure 6.12 presents Boynton and Boynton's (2005) concise version of the crucial components of an effective system.

Figure 6.12 Components of an effective classroom management system

Five components that, when implemented correctly, are crucial for establishing an effective classroom discipline system include

1. Positive teacher-student relationships
2. Strong content instruction
3. Clearly defined parameters of acceptable student behaviors
4. Use of effective monitoring skills
5. Appropriate consequences

Source: Boynton, M., & Boynton, C. (2005). *The educator's guide to preventing and solving discipline problems* (p. v). Alexandria, VA: Association for Supervision and Curriculum Development.

Certain guidelines are nonnegotiable when establishing a classroom management plan. Although it is impossible to address all of them within the scope of this book, here are several important ones:

- *Always stay within school and district policies and guidelines.*

- *Use positive rather than negative statements when establishing expectations.* Students need to know what they *should* do, not just what they *shouldn't* do. For instance, the expectation "We will show respect for others when working together or apart" is more likely to gain compliance than "We will not be disrespectful of others when working together or apart." Plant positive thoughts in students' minds to promote productive habits of appropriate behavior.

- *Consistently apply expectations and consequences.* Some teachers set an expectation and have different consequences based on the number of times a student's behavior is outside the expectation. This sort of consequence layering in no way undermines the consistency of consequences.

- *Explore conflict resolution and peer mediation.* This approach involves students trained as go-betweens to help other students work through their differences and agree to disagree amicably. Look for such programs as you observe and interact in schools.

- *Communicate and document.* Once established, a teacher's classroom management plan should be explicitly taught to students, the building administrators should receive a written plan, and parents and families should be informed of it. An aspect of communication often neglected by teachers is documentation, or record keeping. When a consequence is applied, document it.

- *Ask for help.* There are some behavior issues that classroom teachers should not handle alone. Physical violence, overt bullying, and verbal abuse of students or adults cannot be tolerated in a classroom setting. Episodes of this nature must be dealt with immediately by administrators.

DON'T BE PART OF THE PROBLEM

Think back to your days in prekindergarten through 12th grade. Can you remember a classroom behavior problem actually getting worse because of something a teacher did or didn't do? Were you ever in a class when student misbehavior escalated so that it was almost out of control even as the teacher yelled for attention? How about out-of-control behavior in the presence of a teacher who repeatedly used "shhhh" to ask for silence? Neither approach works.

Purposefully embarrassing students should never be a teacher tactic. The result may be serious psychological damage to the student. Another likely result is the student's loss of respect for the teacher who has displayed his or her own version of misbehavior.

Avoid making threats without following through. This practice can have disastrous results in a classroom. A teacher repeatedly saying, "If you don't stop that I'll . . ." may cause

Creating and Maintaining a Positive and Productive Learning Environment

the immediate misbehavior to escalate, and it guarantees future problems because students won't believe the teacher will follow through.

Teachers should never allow a classroom confrontation to escalate into a power struggle. When a student loses control of his or her temper and directs remarks at a teacher, and the teacher reacts in kind, the opportunity to be a mature, reasonable role model is lost. No one wins. Giving a student time to calm down and gracefully save face will provide a chance for student and teacher to talk about the situation. In some exaggerated cases, avoiding a power struggle prevents physical violence and gives time for administrators to get involved in a resolution.

CONCLUDING THOUGHTS

Students learn much more than academic subjects in our classrooms. They learn how to exist in society. They learn limits of what they can and can't do in terms of behavior. A positive and productive learning environment is safe—physically, emotionally, and academically. When students feel safe they are more likely to participate, learn, and grow.

Creating and maintaining a positive and productive learning environment is hard work. Teachers can learn how to cultivate appropriate relationships with students, how to establish routines that foster productivity, and how to thoughtfully develop classroom management plans that are effective. With diligence and consistent monitoring, a positive and productive learning environment can be maintained.

Well-managed classrooms are marked by civility. Some students come to school without a clear idea of what civility looks like because they don't live in the midst of it. Teachers must model civility, orchestrate an environment that fosters it, and then expect nothing less of students.

After reading the *Chapter in Review,* interact with Tim Mendenhall as he struggles to mentor a new teacher in this chapter's *Developing Professional Competence.*

Chapter in Review

How do teachers create a positive learning environment?

- The physical layout, appearance, usefulness, and overall appeal of the classroom either enhance the learning environment or detract from it.
- Care and trust help teachers and students build a sense of community.
- Teacher awareness, ability to multitask, and recognition that one action directly affects another are valuable assets in creating a positive learning environment.
- Time is a constant in schools that should be used wisely to promote learning.

What routines contribute to maintaining a productive classroom environment?

- The types of routines needed vary by school level, but their importance at all levels cannot be overemphasized.
- Students need to practice routines so they become productive habits.

How do teachers establish expectations, incentives, and consequences?

- Successful classroom management is a prerequisite for successful teaching and learning.
- The best prevention of behavioral problems is engaging instruction.
- Many issues and situations require teachers to establish behavioral expectations, incentives for achieving these expectations, and consequences for not fulfilling them.

How can I develop a classroom management plan?

- Prominent theories and classroom observations provide background and strategies for new teachers to use to formulate management plans.
- Teachers should consider student needs and development when formulating a plan.
- Classroom management plans are most effective when expectations are stated positively, when expectations, incentives, and consequences are applied consistently, and when teachers model appropriate behavior.

Developing Professional Competence

Visit the Developing Professional Competence section in Chapter 6 of the MyEducationLab for this text to answer the following questions and begin your preparation for licensure exams.

You met Tim Mendenhall in the beginning of this text when all the focus teachers, students, and schools were introduced. Then as this chapter began we learned about Tim and his relationship with a new student. We also read about his classroom expectations. He is an experienced teacher who values relationships with students and has confidence in his classroom management procedures.

Tim was asked by Principal Mike Larsen to mentor a new teacher. She came to Rees with a very strong academic record that included graduating with a 4.0 GPA and a master's degree in teaching reading. Mr. Larsen was very excited to give her an opportunity to teach a self-contained fourth grade class as her first teaching assignment. Tim was happy to be her mentor, but when Elizabeth arrived at Rees she wasn't keen on the idea of someone actually assigned to help her be successful, and she let others know it.

Tim was friendly and offered to help her set up her room and to go through the fourth grade curriculum and materials she would use. She politely listened but showed little interest. For classroom management she posted preprinted posters with rules and warnings. Tim explained that Rees has basic expectations that involve respect and that she may want to meet with her students to talk about what respect might look like in the classrooms and allow the kids to have some input. To that she said no, and told Tim that her training was as a Skinnerian behaviorist.

One afternoon in October, after hearing repeatedly from students that Elizabeth's kids were not happy and several parents had complained to Mr. Larsen, Tim overheard a conversation in the hallway. Elizabeth told Marcus that she was at the limit of her patience, that he was nothing but trouble, that she now knew how to treat him for the rest of the year, and that his parents would be very disappointed in him. Tim knew it was time to talk with Elizabeth even though she had resisted his attempts before.

Think through this scenario and answer the following multiple-choice questions:

1. Which guideline for developing positive teacher-student relationships do you think Elizabeth most likely violated in her encounter with Marcus?
   a. strong content instruction
   b. clearly defined parameters of acceptable student behaviors

   c. use of effective monitoring skills
   d. appropriate consequences

2. Elizabeth told Tim that she is a Skinnerian behaviorist. This means that
   a. She must have studied Skinner and believes that children will behave if they understand what's right.
   b. In her study of Skinner she learned that rewards and punishment will shape student behavior.
   c. In graduate school she learned that B. F. Skinner believed in verbally reprimanding students and humiliating them to gain obedience.
   d. She is a trained specialist in behavior management.

3. Based on what he heard in the hall, Tim is afraid that Elizabeth's style of classroom management will possibly destroy which quality he believes in building?
   a. Resilience
   b. Self-determination
   c. Students' love of learning
   d. A healthy sense of competition among students

Now it's time for you to respond to three short essay items involving the scenario. In your responses, be sure to address all the dilemmas and questions posed in each item. Your responses should each be between one half and one double-spaced page.

4. Refer to Tim's guidelines for classroom management in Figure 6.8. Name two guidelines for which it is likely too late for Elizabeth and this year's fourth graders. Name two guidelines that Elizabeth may have in place, given what you know from this scenario. Explain why you selected each of the four guidelines.

5. What problems does Elizabeth invite for the rest of the year by telling Marcus that she knows how she will treat him? Explain.

6. How might Tim use INTASC Knowledge Principle 5 as he tries to explain to Elizabeth the responsibilities he sees she is missing when it comes to the learning environment? How does this standard differ from her proclaimed Skinnerian approach?

INTASC Knowledge Principle 5
The teacher uses an understanding of individual and group motivation and behavior to create a learning environment that encourages positive social interaction, active engagement in learning, and self-motivation.

Where
DO I Stand NOW?

In the beginning of this chapter you completed an inventory that gauged your experiences with the learning environment in K–12 school. Now that you have read the chapter, completed exercises related to the content, and engaged in class discussions and so on, answer the following questions in your course notebook.

1. Reading this chapter has likely triggered memories of at least a few aspects of your K–12 learning environment that were not positive. What is an example of a less-than-positive experience, and what do you now see that your teacher could have done to improve the situation?

2. Has your view of what constitutes a positive, productive learning environment changed as a result of reading this chapter? If so, in what way(s)?

3. Considering your own experiences and what you have learned, what aspect of the learning environment do you predict will be most challenging for you to manage: the physical environment, relationships with students, setting expectations, matching consequences to infractions, another aspect? Explain.

MyEducationLab

The MyEducationLab for this course can help you solidify your comprehension of Chapter 6 concepts.

- Explore the classrooms of the teachers and students you've met in this chapter in the Teaching in Focus section.
- Prepare for licensure exams as you deepen your understanding of chapter concepts in the Developing Professional Competence section.

- Gauge and further develop your understanding of chapter concepts by taking the quizzes and examining the enrichment materials in the Chapter 6 Study Plan.
- Visit Topic 9, "Managing the Classroom," to watch ABC videos, explore Assignments and Activities, and practice essential teaching skills with the Building Teaching Skills and Dispositions unit.

References

Boynton, M., & Boynton, C. (2005). *The educator's guide to preventing and solving discipline problems.* Alexandria, VA: Association for Supervision and Curriculum Development.

Darling-Hammond, L. (1997). *The right to learn.* San Francisco: Jossey-Bass.

DeVries, R., & Zan, B. (2003). When children make rules. *Educational Leadership, 61*(1), 64–67.

Dewey, J. (1944). *Democracy and education.* New York: Free Press.

Dunklee, D. R., & Shoop, R. J. (2002). *The principal's quick reference guide to school law: Reducing liability, litigation, and other potential legal tangles.* Thousand Oaks, CA: Corwin Press.

Erwin, J. C. (2003). Giving students what they need. *Educational Leadership, 61*(1), 19–23.

Farrell, C. (2010). *Corporal punishment in the United States.* Retrieved August 7, 2010, from http://corpun.com/counuss.htm

Glasser, W. (1998). *Choice theory.* New York: Harper Collins.

Kohn, A. (2005). Unconditional teaching. *Educational Leadership, 63*(1), 20–24.

Kounin, J. S. (1970). *Discipline and group management in classrooms.* New York: Holt, Rinehart and Winston.

Lemlech, J. K. (2004). *Teaching in elementary and secondary classrooms.* Upper Saddle River, NJ: Merrill/Prentice Hall.

Loeper, J. L. (1973). *Going to School in 1776.* New York: Macmillan.

Lumpkin, A. (2007). Caring teachers: The key to student learning. *Kappa Delta Pi Record, 43*(4), 158–160.

Manning, L., & Bucher, K.T. (2003). *Classroom management: Models, applications, and cases* (2nd ed.). Boston: Allyn & Bacon.

Marzano, R. J. (2003a). *Classroom management that works: Research-based strategies for every teacher.* Alexandria, VA: Association for Supervision and Curriculum Development.

Marzano, R. J. (2003b). *What works in schools: Translating research into action.* Alexandria, VA: Association for Supervision and Curriculum Development.

McCloud, S. (2005). From chaos to consistency. *Educational Leadership, 62*(5), 46–49.

Noddings, N. (1992). *The challenge to care in schools: An alternative approach to education.* New York: Teachers College Press.

Stevenson, C. (2002). *Teaching ten to fourteen year olds* (3rd ed.). New York: Longman.

Prensky, M. (2010). Shaping tech for the Classroom: 21st-century schools need 21st-century technology. Retrieved April 9, 2010, from http://www.edutopia.org/adopt-and-adapt

Ray, B. (2010). Guest Blog: Making the Case for Social Media. Retrieved April 9, 2010, from http://www.edutopia.org/social-media-case-education-edchat-steve-johnson

Weinstein, C. S., Romano, M., & Mignano, A. (2011). *Elementary classroom management: Lessons from research and practice* (5th ed.). New York: McGraw-Hill.

Glossary

A

Academic freedom A form of expression that allows teachers to use their judgment in making decisions about what to discuss, what to assign as readings, what teaching strategies to use, etc.

Academic rigor The content of what we teach is meaningful, and our expectations of the learning of that content are demanding.

Academies Early secondary schools designed to teach content intended to prepare students to participate in business and trade.

Accountability Holding a person or program responsible for an outcome.

Achievement gap Disparity among students, with some excelling while others languish with respect to learning and academic success.

Action research Research conducted by teachers in their classrooms around a concept or question that captures their interest; results of research may be added to the teaching knowledge base.

Active engagement Involving students in meaningful experiences that promote learning; providing an environment for creativity and collaboration, all with increased learning as the goal.

Adequate Yearly Progress School report that consists of a number of elements determined by each individual state with guidance from No Child Left Behind requirements. AYP data are kept by race, socioeconomic status, and gender. Typical components of the AYP report include graduation rate, attendance, math scores, reading/language arts achievement data, and other indicators of student progress.

Advocate for students Support and defend students, always putting their needs first.

Aesthetics The determination of what is beautiful and artistic.

Alternative assessment Generally any assessment other than traditional paper-and-pencil and/or forced-choice assessment.

Alternative school School designed for students who are not successful in a traditional school setting.

American Federation of Teachers (AFT) America's second largest professional association for teachers.

Analytic rubric Specifies separate parts of an assessment task, product, or performance and the characteristics of various levels of success for each.

A Nation at Risk: The Imperative for Educational Reform Report commissioned by President Reagan in 1983 that referred to U.S. public education as a "rising tide of mediocrity." In response, various proposals for reform and improvement surfaced.

Assessment Gathering evidence of student learning.

Assimilation Process of bringing persons of all races and ethnicities into the mainstream by having them behave in ways that align with the dominant culture.

Assistive technology Devices and services that benefit students with disabilities by helping them communicate, increasing their mobility, and aiding in multiple ways that enhance their capacity to learn.

Associative play Children begin to share toys and communicate verbally.

At-large election Voters may vote for any candidate regardless of the area in the district the candidate represents.

At-risk students Those who are in serious danger of not completing school and/or who may be heading toward nonproductive or counterproductive lifestyles.

Attention deficit hyperactivity disorder (ADHD) A learning disability in which students demonstrate three defining characteristics—inattention, hyperactivity, and impulsivity—in persistent patterns that are more severe than in others of the same age.

Authentic assessment Students show what they know and can do in a real-life setting or situation.

Axiology Branch of philosophy that addresses values, both in ethics and aesthetics. Ethics is the determination of what's right and what's wrong. Aesthetics is the determination of what is beautiful and artistic.

B

Backward design An approach to planning for teaching and learning that starts with deciding on the desired learning results (curriculum), then identifies how to collect the evidence necessary to know if the results have been achieved (assessment), and then proceeds to choosing how to help students acquire the desired knowledge and skills (instruction).

Benchmarks Statements of what students should know and be able to do at specific developmental stages.

Bilingual education The delivery of instruction in two languages.

Bilingual Education Act of 1968 Provided funds to assist non-English-speaking students (mostly Hispanic) who were dropping out of high school at a rate of about 70%.

Black Codes Prior to the Civil War, predominantly in the South, Black Codes were enacted to prohibit the education of slaves.

Block grants Grants that provide funding with few restrictions for its use, allowing states and school districts the freedom to use the money in ways that meet their specific needs.

Block schedule A schedule allowing for longer class periods; a block schedule may be composed of a wide variety of schedule options.

Bloom's taxonomy A classification system of thinking and processing skills that range from simple to complex; used to classify various levels of learning objectives and experiences.

Blueprint for Reform Part of the 2010 proposal to reauthorize the Elementary and Secondary Education Act.

Bond referendum Allows school districts to borrow money stipulated for specific projects. The school board asks voters in the district to approve the borrowing of the money (the bond) that will be repaid over a period of time.

Breach of contract Contracts are binding on both parties. If a person signs one and then backs out or takes a different job, or if the district backs out, the person or the district may be sued for damages.

Brown v. Board of Education In 1954 Chief Justice Earl Warren declared that segregating children based solely on race was wrong and illegal. Some schools integrated peacefully; others did not.

Buckley Amendment Also known as the Family Educational Rights and Privacy Act (FERPA) of 1974. Allows parents and guardians access to their students' academic records and requires written parental permission for the records to be shared with anyone else. When students turn age 18, they have control over who sees their records.

Bullying Relationally aggressive behavior; a type of emotional or physical violence where individuals use relationships to harm others.

C

Case knowledge When experienced teachers face a new student, a new learning problem, or new materials, they have a memory bank of other similar situations on which to draw.

Case law Based on the doctrine of *stare decisis*, a Latin phrase meaning "let the decision stand;" once a decision is made in a court of law, that decision sets a precedent for future cases of a similar nature until challenged or overturned.

Categorical grants Money that is allocated or funds that are earmarked for specific purposes.

Charter school A public school that is freed in specific ways from typical regulations required of other public schools.

Child abuse Any act that results in death, serious harm, or exploitation of children.

Child neglect A form of abuse resulting from the failure to act in the best interest of children.

Civil Rights Act of 1964 Stipulates that if schools discriminate based on race, color, or national origin, they are not eligible for federal funding.

Classroom assessment Encompasses every deliberate method of gathering information about the quantity and quality of learning.

Classroom climate The everyday environment of teachers and students working together.

Classroom community A classroom where students and teacher tend to be like-minded and have common beliefs, understandings, and aims.

Classroom management The establishment and enforcement of rules and disciplinary actions; teacher strategies to ensure an orderly classroom environment.

Clinical internship Also known as student teaching or clinical practice; involves extended fieldwork in which teacher candidates teach lessons and, for a designated period of time, take over all classroom duties.

Coleman Report Report written in 1966 that concluded that family and community factors such as poverty and parental levels of education prevented some children from learning, that no matter what schools did, some children would not be successful in school.

Collective bargaining Act of negotiating with employers and/or states to gain additional benefits for members of the bargaining group; a right practiced in most states by teacher associations and unions. States often allow unions to negotiate with school boards concerning elements of teacher contracts and working conditions.

Collegial Relationships with other teachers that promote growth through sharing of professional expertise.

Common Core State Standards Initiative Efforts to develop and promote common national standards by the National Governors Association (NGA) and the Council of Chief State School Officers (CCSSO).

Common schools Community-supported elementary schools for all children established in response to many economic, social, and political factors.

Community The neighborhood, town, city, and/or county in which a person lives.

Comprehensive high school High schools that attempt to meet the educational needs of all adolescents on a single campus.

Compulsory education law Requires children to attend school until a specified age.

Consequences Implies more natural ramifications for wrongdoing than the word *punishment*, which can be arbitrary.

Constructive correcting Assigning consequences in ways that serve as student learning experiences.

Constructivism A way of approaching instruction that builds on progressivism as students are challenged to construct, or discover, knowledge about their environments. Process is valued in progressivism, often more than product. The theory is that students who learn through the processes of construction, discovery, and problem solving will be better able to adapt to a changing world.

Content Knowledge and skills that are taught.

Content standards Specific knowledge students should have and skills they should be able to do.

Contract An agreement between parties that includes the rights and responsibilities of each. When teachers begin jobs in schools they sign initial contracts.

Cooperating teacher A classroom teacher who serves as the host and mentor during clinical practice.

Cooperative learning Loosely defined, any instance of students working together in small groups.

Cooperative play Children actively coordinate ways to keep interaction going.

Copyright laws Federal laws that protect the rights of a creator or author to own intellectual property and to prevent others from copying or distributing it without permission. Intellectual property includes written material, original audio and visual work, and computer programs. Copyright laws also provide guidelines for authorized use of someone else's intellectual property.

Core Knowledge An organization that proposes there is a body of lasting knowledge that should determine the curriculum in PreK–8 schools.

Core subjects Generally considered language arts, math, science, and social studies.

Corporal punishment Physical punishment practiced in some school settings.

Council of Chief State School Officers An organization composed of school superintendents and other school leaders.

Council for Exceptional Children (CEC) National organization that represents the needs of students with exceptionalities and fosters appropriate education for them.

Criterion-referenced test Student scores indicate levels of mastery of a subject and do not depend on how other students perform.

Critical thinking Higher-order thinking involving observing, comparing and contrasting, interpreting, analyzing, seeing issues from a variety of perspectives, weighing variables, and then making decisions and solving problems.

Cultural identity Results from the interactions of many factors, including language, religion, gender, income level, age, values, beliefs, race, and ethnicity.

Culturally responsive teaching What teachers do to make multicultural education a reality.

Cultural pluralism Involves the recognition that our nation is populated by a rich variety of people of varying races and ethnicities, and thus cultures, all with potential to contribute positively to our common goal of a productive, free society.

Culture A composite of social values, cognitive codes, behavioral standards, worldviews, and beliefs that characterize a group of people.

Curriculum The educational term for what students experience in schools.

Cyberbullying Using technology to bully.

Cybercitizenship Responsibly using technology in ways that do not harm others.

D

Dame schools In colonial days, dames were respected women who, usually without formal schooling, had learned to read and write and who turned their homes into schools where parents paid to have their children educated.

Deductive reasoning A process that begins with a general statement from which more specific statements are assumed to be true.

Democratic classroom A classroom setting that promotes choice, community, authentic learning, and a relevant, creative curriculum; students participate in the establishment of behavioral expectations.

Departmentalization School organizational pattern in which teachers teach their own subjects and meet occasionally with other teachers who teach the same subject.

Depression Mental illness characterized by a deep sense of sadness and a loss of interest or pleasure in activities.

Developmental appropriateness Teaching and learning that matches students' physical, cognitive, social, emotional, and character development.

Diagnostic assessment Assesses student knowledge and skill levels before beginning a unit of study; commonly referred to as pretesting.

Dialects Deviations from standard language rules used by identifiable groups of people.

Differentiation of instruction Varying instruction based on the needs of students.

Direct instruction A general lesson model that includes a distinct opening, presentation of information, practice, and teacher feedback and review.

Dispositions Attitudes and beliefs that guide and determine behavior.

Distance learning Involves the acquisition of knowledge and skills through instruction delivered using technology.

District school board Governing body composed of elected citizens responsible for setting policies that affect the operation of schools.

District superintendent Functions as the school district's chief executive officer; hired by the board and serves at its pleasure.

Dropouts Students who do not complete high school.

Due process The steps a district must take to pursue the charges when a tenured teacher is threatened with dismissal; important principle that requires guidelines to be followed to ensure that individuals are protected from arbitrary or capricious treatment by those in authority.

E

Early childhood education The care and education of the youngest students in the United States, typically considered birth through age 8.

Ebonics Black English, one of the best known and most controversial dialects in the United States.

Educational technology Any technology that assists teachers in teaching and students in learning.

Education for All Handicapped Children Act (Public Law 94-142) Federal law passed in 1975 that guaranteed a free and appropriate education to all children with disabilities in the least restrictive environment; renamed Individual with Disabilities Education Act in 1990.

Education Maintenance Organization (EMO) An organization contracted to take over the management of a public school for profit.

Education summit Organized meeting to advocate for school improvement.

Effective schools Schools that meet the learning needs of the students who attend them.

Effective Schools Movement Originated in the 1970s to develop research pertaining to the assertion that all children can learn; purpose was to find schools deemed effective for all children and identify common characteristics.

Elementary Level of school that usually includes grades K through 5.

Elementary and Secondary Education Act Enacted during the presidency of Lyndon B. Johnson to provide extra funding, called Title I funding, for schools with high numbers of children from low-income homes.

Emotional intelligence quotient (EQ) A set of skills that accompany the expression, evaluation, and regulation of emotions. A high-level EQ indicates a person's ability to understand others' as well as his or her own feelings, respond appropriately to them, and, in general, get along.

Encore courses Also known as related arts or exploratory courses; all courses other than what are considered the core courses of math, English language arts, social studies, and science.

English as a second language (ESL) Students receive individualized assistance; unlike bilingual education, ESL services are delivered only in English; little or no emphasis is placed on preserving native language or culture; and ESL teachers do not need to speak another language.

English-language learners (ELL) Non-English speakers and students with limited English proficiency.

Entitlements Grants given to certain segments of the population that have specific needs; the federal government deems these individuals entitled to extra assistance.

Epistemology Branch of philosophy that addresses the dilemma of determining truth and ways of acquiring knowledge.

Era of standards A time when content standards determined curricular learning goals; generally considered 1990 through the present.

Essentialism A philosophy of education based on the belief there is a core curriculum that everyone in the United States should learn. This core can shift in response to societal changes but should always be basic, organized, and rigorous.

Ethics Standards of conduct based on moral judgments; the determination of what's right and what's wrong.

Ethnicity An individual's country of origin and ancestry.

Eurocentric Contributions and traditions centered on European values.

Evaluation Judgments about, and the assigning of values to, the *results* of assessments.

Excise tax Tax on luxury items such as boats and travel trailers.

Exemplars *Samples* of work that fit various criteria for scoring so students actually see what a product looks like that earns a particular number.

Existentialism Primary emphasis is on the individual. As a philosophy of education, existentialism contends that teachers teach the whole person, not just math, reading, science, or any other particular subject. Each student searches for personal meaning and personal understanding. If learning about a subject area increases a student's sense of self, then it's worthwhile.

Expectations A word with positive connotations that may be used in place of *rules,* a word with negative connotations.

Expenditure per pupil The average amount of money spent from federal, state, and local sources on an individual student.

Explicit curriculum What teachers are expected to teach, what students are expected to learn, and what society expects of schools; also referred to as the formal curriculum.

Exploratory courses Also known as related arts or encore courses, all courses other than math, English language arts, social studies, and science; may include art, music, physical education, industrial arts, languages, drama, computer education, and others.

Expulsion Semipermanent or permanent dismissal from school for a semester or for an indefinite period.

Extracurriculum Includes the organized experiences students have that are beyond the formal curriculum.

Extrinsic incentives Incentives that are imposed or originate outside the individual.

F

Fair use Specific limitations on the use of copyrighted materials.

Family Educational Rights and Privacy Act (FERPA) of 1974 Commonly called the Buckley Amendment, allows parents and guardians access to their students' academic records and requires written parental permission for the records to be shared with anyone else. When students turn age 18, they have control over who sees their records.

Feeder system Configuration of schools in a district; typically in one feeder system of schools, early childhood/elementary schools feed into middle schools that feed into a particular high school.

5-E lesson plan A way for teachers to guide students through a cycle of inquiry learning; most commonly used for science exploration.

Field experience Observing and/or participating in actual classrooms; also referred to as practicum experiences.

Formal curriculum Encompasses what is intentionally taught, what is stated as the goals of student learning.

Formative assessment A series of assessments in a variety of formats that help monitor student progress.

For-profit schools Schools operated by private companies for profit.

Full-service school A public school that provides a comprehensive program of education and includes student and community services such as after-school and family education programs.

Functional behavioral assessment (FBA) A management plan through a team of educators using a process that looks for events and actions that may lead to misbehavior and devises strategies to help students abide by classroom expectations.

G

Gender The sense of being male or female, as opposed to sex, which refers to anatomical differences.

Gender bias The favoring of one gender over the other in specific circumstances.

Gender equity The fair and balanced treatment of males and females.

Gender stereotyping Occurs when perceived gender differences are assumed for all people.

Gifted and talented Exceptional learners who demonstrate high levels of intelligence, creativity, and achievement.

Global awareness Involves understanding environmental, societal, cultural, political, and economical concepts and issues that impact our world.

Graduation rate Percentage of students who graduate from high school with a regular diploma in the standard number of years.

Grade Judgment of assessment quality (evaluation) with a number attached to it.

Grant Funds provided by a source to pay for equipment or services requested by teachers and others.

Great Books The writings of those considered to be the great thinkers throughout the history of Western civilization, such as Homer, Shakespeare, Melville, Einstein, and many others.

Grievance A formal complaint filed by an individual teacher or group of teachers against a district.

Guided practice Opportunities for students to work independently on applying knowledge in a non-threatening setting that includes teacher feedback.

H

Head Start The largest provider of government-funded preschool education, employing one of every five U.S. preschool teachers.

Hidden curriculum Curriculum that is not explicit or openly expressed; similar to the informal curriculum but with negative connotations.

Hierarchy of needs Maslow's (1908–1970) theory that all human beings experience the same needs.

Highly qualified Those who meet government guidelines for teacher quality in public schools.

High school completion rate As defined by the U.S. Department of Education, the "percentage of students, measured from the beginning of high school, who graduate from a high school with a regular diploma in the standard number of years"; also known as graduation rate.

High schools Schools that most often encompass grades 9 to 12.

High/Scope An approach to early childhood education built on consistency and few transitions during the day.

High-stakes tests Standardized tests that have far-reaching consequences.

Holistic rubric A grading instrument that uses one scale for an entire project.

Homeschooled Refers to students who receive most of their academic instruction in their homes.

Homework Independent practice outside the classroom.

I

Idealism A philosophy based on the belief that ideas are the only reliable form of reality. Idealists believe the physical world changes continually and that ideas are what should be taught.

Implicit curriculum Curriculum that is implied and subtle; the informal curriculum.

Incentives A word that may be used in place of the overused and value-laden word *rewards*.

Inclusion Students attend their home school with their age- and grade-appropriate peers, participate in extracurricular activities, and receive special education and support services to the maximum extent possible in the general education classroom.

Individualized educational program (IEP) A plan developed for a student by educators, the family, and others as appropriate, involving details of how to reach specific goals. A student's IEP must be revisited annually and student progress evaluated.

Individuals with Disabilities Education Act (IDEA) Also referred to as PL94-142 (and the revised version of the Education for All Handicapped Children Act of 1975), this act made special education services a right, not a privilege, because it required schools to place students in least-restrictive environments within public schools.

Individuals with Disabilities Education Improvement Act Reauthorization of IDEA in 2004 that compiled all U.S. laws that affect children with disabilities into one statute.

Inductive reasoning Given specific statements, a general conclusion may be logically assumed.

Informal curriculum What students learn that isn't written in a lesson plan or necessarily intentionally transmitted to students.

Information literacy Involves recognition of when information is needed, knowing how to access information, and judging information credibility.

In loco parentis Serving in place of parents.

Inquiry learning When students pursue answers to questions posed by others or developed on their own, they are involved in inquiry learning. Observation, questioning, hypothesizing, and predicting are all part of inquiry-based learning.

Instruction Encompasses the strategies used to convey the curriculum with the desired end result of student learning.

Instructional software Software designed specifically for student use to learn about concepts and/or practice skills related to a subject area.

Instructional time Time available for teaching and learning.

Instrumental aggression Aggression based on attempting to meet a specific goal, such as grabbing a particular toy or establishing dominance in an activity; most common among boys.

Integrated curriculum Involves making connections among subject areas through the use of a unifying topic or theme.

Intelligence The capacity for knowing and learning.

Intelligence quotient (IQ) The results of a test that affixes a number to intelligence.

Intelligent design Includes a belief that certain features of the universe and of living things are best explained by an intelligent being (God), not by the process of natural selection espoused by evolution.

Interdisciplinary Term often used to describe curricular links or connections among subjects.

Interdisciplinary team The preferred organizational structure for middle-level education, involving a team of two to five teachers working with a distinct group of students for an entire year.

Intermediate grades Typically grades 4 and 5 in an elementary setting.

Internet Computer network that allows people around the world to search for information, share resources, and communicate.

Interstate New Teacher Assessment and Support Consortium (INTASC) Organization that sets standards for what new teachers should know and be able to do.

Intrinsic incentives Incentives that come from within and result from students' natural drives.

J

Jigsaw Strategy involving students becoming experts on particular topics and then teaching those topics to the other students.

Junior high Schools developed in 1909 to be a bridge between elementary and high school; typically grades 7 to 9.

K

Kalamazoo Case Established that the legislature could tax for support of both common and secondary schools, propelling public high schools into school systems in every state.

Kindergarten German for "children's garden," the school year that precedes first grade.

L

Language Primary means of communication; transmits knowledge and passes on culture.

Language minority students Students whose native language is other than English, regardless of their current level of English proficiency.

Latin grammar school First established in 1635 in Boston for boys whose families could afford to send them on for more education beyond the dame school; considered the forerunner of modern high schools and specifically prepared boys to attend Harvard University, established in 1636.

Learning A complex and dynamic process involving thinking, perception, experience, and memory.

Learning disabled (LD) A general category of students with disorders involving problems understanding or using language that results in significant differences between learning potential and achievement.

Learning modalities Auditory (hearing), visual (seeing), tactile (touch), and kinesthetic (movement); all four are used in the process of learning, but individuals tend to favor one or two over the others.

Learning styles Ways in which individuals learn most effectively and efficiently.

Least restrictive environment (LRE) The setting within which students with disabilities can function at capacity; generally the setting with students who do not have disabilities that also meets the educational needs of the students with disabilities.

Lesson plan Devising experiences for students as part of the formal curriculum.

Liable To be responsible for; liability is what teaching is all about—accepting responsibility for students while they are under our supervision.

Limited English proficiency (LEP) Students with LEP may speak and understand some English, but not enough to be successful in classes taught in English without additional assistance.

Literacy Involves ability to analyze and apply knowledge and skills necessary to solve problems within a discipline.

Logic Reasoning that attempts to avoid vagueness and contradictions. To use logic simply means to think clearly to understand a situation, solve a problem, or draw a conclusion. There are two basic kinds of reasoning, or logic, commonly addressed in school. One is **deductive reasoning**, a process that begins with a general statement from which more specific statements are assumed to be true. Another kind of logic, **inductive reasoning**, works the other way: Given some specific statements, a general conclusion may be assumed.

Long-range plans Lesson plans that may encompass a nine-week timeframe, a semester, or a year.

Looping School practice that keeps a teacher with a particular group of students for more than 1 year.

M

Magnet school A public school with a specific emphasis or theme and curriculum and instructional programs tailored with unique opportunities that attract certain students.

Manipulatives Hands-on objects that enhance and illustrate concepts and skills.

Massachusetts Act of 1642 First compulsory education law in the New World; required all white children to attend school.

Mentor An experienced teacher who uses experience and wisdom to answer questions and help guide new teachers.

Meta-analysis A research technique involving the analysis of multiple studies.

Metaphysics Branch of philosophy that addresses the search for reality and purpose. The word *metaphysics* means "beyond the material or the physical." Those who study metaphysics look for answers that go beyond scientific experiments.

Methods courses Courses that emphasize particular strategies for specific subjects and will probably incorporate opportunities to actually apply what you are learning.

Micromanagement Managing to a level of detail that is inappropriate for a particular position. For instance, when school board members go beyond policy making into what is considered day-to-day operations, they may be seen as micromanaging.

Middle school Schools for young adolescents with a distinct philosophy that embraces both academic rigor and developmental appropriateness; may include any combination of grades 5 to 9.

Mini-lecture Shortened, focused version of the lecture.

Montessori An approach to early childhood education with mixed-age grouping and self-pacing.

Morrill Act In 1862 the government granted states 30,000 acres of land for every senator and representative in Congress in 1860. The income the state generated from this land was to be used to support at least one college.

Multiage classroom Classroom where children in two, three, or more grade levels learn together.

Multicultural curriculum Curriculum that purposefully includes contributions and viewpoints from the perspectives of different cultures, ethnicities, races, genders, and socioeconomic levels.

Multicultural education An instructional approach that celebrates diversity and promotes equal educational opportunities.

Multimedia Using more than one medium to communicate information.

Multiple intelligences theory (MI) A theory developed by Howard Gardner that intelligence is multidimensional, that individual brains work in ways that give each of us our own personal intelligences; includes nine intelligences.

N

National Assessment of Educational Progress (NAEP) Only standardized test systematically administered to a sampling of students across the United States. The NAEP is administered to fourth, eighth, and twelfth graders in math, reading, writing, science, history, economics, geography, civics, foreign language, and a variety of the arts; often called the nation's report card.

National Board of Professional Teaching Standards (NBPTS) Board that sets standards, establishes policies, and issues certificates designating teachers with skills to perform effectively.

National Council for the Accreditation of Teacher Education (NCATE) Agency that scrutinizes university teacher education programs. About two thirds of states require university teacher education programs to be accredited (authorized to prepare teachers) through NCATE.

National Defense Education Act of 1958 Called for strengthening of science, math, and foreign language programs; teachers were given training in the use of new methods and materials in hopes of bringing American student learning up to, and beyond, the levels of learning in other countries.

National Education Association (NEA) The largest professional education association in the United States, with a total of over 5 million members including teachers, administrators, professors, counselors, and other educators.

National Governors Association Organization of governors enabling them to share expertise and tackle dilemmas collectively.

National Middle School Association (NMSA) Organization that provides standards for the preparation of teachers for grades 5 to 9, and advocates for the needs and education of young adolescents.

Nature Refers to the genetically inherited influences on who we are.

Neighborhood school Students in a geographic area attend school close to their home.

New England Primer First published in 1690 for children in upper elementary and secondary levels. Published for over 150 years with few substantial changes over its lifetime, the *New England Primer* included a spelling guide based on the alphabet denoted in brief rhymes and pictures, the Lord's Prayer, the Apostles' Creed, the Ten Commandments, a list of the books of the Bible, the Puritan catechism, and numbers 1 to 100.

No Child Left Behind Act of 2001 (NCLB) Federal law (2001–2010) that holds schools accountable for student learning, regardless of student diversity. States are required to test all students in grades 3 to 8 annually to determine progress.

Normal schools Publicly funded secondary schools specifically designed to prepare teachers for the classroom.

Norm referenced Tests used to compare students; administered to a group of students selected because they represent a cross section of U.S. students (norm group).

Norms Expectations that are foundational, including physical norms for preserving the health and safety of students, moral norms pertaining to respect for others, and societal norms for politeness and individual responsibility.

Northwest Land Ordinance of 1787 Divided federally owned land in the wilderness into townships and required that schools be built.

Null curriculum What is not taught in school.

Nurture Refers to the influence of the environment, including everything that happens except for what can be accounted for genetically.

O

Obesity Extreme overweight as indicated by body mass index (BMI), a measure of how much a person weighs relative to height.

Objective Concise statement about what students are expected to learn and be able to do as a result of the lesson.

Old Deluder Satan Act Because education was considered the best way to fight the devil, the act (also known as the Massachusetts Act of 1647) established that every town of 50 or more households must provide a school.

Open enrollment A plan that allows students to choose from among virtually all the schools in a school district.

Overlapping A teacher's ability to multitask, to take care of several things at once.

P

Pacing guide A document that dictates the timing of content coverage; helps ensure that all grade-level standards are part of the curriculum.

Parallel play Children agreeably sharing the same space but are not communicating.

Paraprofessional A teacher aide or assistant teacher; typically not a certified teacher.

Parochial schools Schools affiliated with religious organizations.

Partnership for 21st Century Skills Leading advocacy organization focused on infusing 21st-century skills into education.

Pedagogy The combining of curriculum and instruction to foster learning.

Perennialism A philosophy of education based on a core curriculum with themes and questions that endure, that are everlasting; as life changes and times change, the real substance and truths of life remain the same.

Performance assessment May be a project, a demonstration, a creation, or anything that requires the application of knowledge and skills.

Performance-based pay Involves paying teachers more when they produce whatever results are designated as desirable.

Performance standards Designated levels of the knowledge or skills that are considered acceptable at a particular grade level.

Philosophy *Philo* means "love," and *sophos* means "wisdom." Philosophy, then, means "love of wisdom." This love of wisdom, or philosophy, becomes a means of answering fundamental questions.

Philosophy of education The *love of wisdom* regarding teaching that expresses itself in attitudes and actions every day in the classroom.

Portfolio Assessment tool for which either students or teachers assemble a cohesive package of representative evidence of student learning.

Portfolio for teacher preparation A cohesive package of representative products; may either document growth or display best work, depending on purpose.

Postmodernism Grew out of a sense that those in power control those who don't have power. This control, postmodernists believe, is manifested through major institutions like schools.

PowerPoint Presentation program used by teachers to deliver instruction and by students to demonstrate skills and display project products.

Practicum experiences Involve observing and/or participating in actual classrooms; also referred to as field experiences.

Pragmatism A philosophy that says that student-centered perspectives integrated with firsthand experiences are most effective.

Praise Complimenting others for real or perceived positive actions or attributes.

Praxis Series Battery of tests published by the Educational Testing Service (ETS) that may be used to determine the qualifications of individuals to be licensed or certified to teach in a variety of disciplines and grade levels.

Preschool A semistructured environment for 3- and 4-year-olds housed in a school setting; care is enhanced by exposure to basic educational concepts.

Pretesting Assessing student knowledge and skill levels before beginning a unit of study; also called diagnostic assessment.

Primary grades Typically grades K to 3.

Principal Oversees every aspect of school life and answers to the district for all that occurs at the school. The principal's role involves administrative tasks such as facility maintenance, attendance, discipline, parent/community relationships and communication, transportation, and all manner of paperwork. Principals are also instructional leaders with knowledge of, and experience with, the teaching and learning process.

Private schools The two elements that make schools public—public funding and public accountability—are both absent in private schools.

Privilege gap Gap between the haves and the have-nots.

Problem-based learning (PBL) Focusing student attention and effort on a real-life problem that has more than one solution path or product.

Problem solving Process involved in finding a solution to a problem.

Processing Sending a student out of the classroom with the purpose of reflection and planning for better choices.

Process standards Processes that support content learning by explaining how the content might be best learned and how to use the content once it is acquired.

Profession An occupation that meets certain criteria, including (1) extensive training to enter, (2) inclusion of a code of ethics, and (3) service as the primary product.

Professional development Efforts to help teachers improve their knowledge and skills.

Professionalism A way of being involving attitudes and actions that convey respect, uphold high standards, and demonstrate commitment to those served.

Progressive education In 1896 John Dewey established a method of involving students in their own learning through cooperative groups, which grew into a major movement with far-reaching implications; interests guide what is learned about traditional subjects.

Progressivism A student-centered philosophy of education that focuses on curriculum of interest to students. Progressivists view education as more than preparation for the future; it is life itself. The progressive philosophy of education endorses experiential learning full of opportunities for student discovery and opportunities to solve problems.

Property taxes Values of property are determined, and a small percentage of the assessed amount (usually less than 1%) is collected annually and used for local services.

Proximity The accessibility of teacher to students.

Public domain A work is in the public domain if it is more than 75 years old or is published by a federal agency; work in the public domain is not protected by copyright.

Public Law 94-142 (PL94-142) Common way of referring to the Individuals with Disabilities Education Act (IDEA), an act that made special education services a right, rather than a privilege.

Public schools Public schools are funded through some form of taxation and are accountable to the community through elected or governmental officials who have policy and oversight responsibilities.

R

Race Term used to classify people according to their physical characteristics that are nature given. Race classifies people at birth.

Race to the Top A federal initiative challenging states to make bold efforts to improve teaching and learning; over $4 billion in federal money awarded to states on a competitive basis.

Racism A form of prejudice that may be perpetuated by individuals or governments stemming from a belief that one race is superior to another.

Reading across the curriculum Infusing the curriculum with reading, regardless of content area.

Realism Based on the belief that some facts are absolutes no matter who recognizes them. Realists contend that the only way to know these absolutes is to study the material world.

Reduction in force Occurs in schools when there are fewer students, budget cuts, or the cancellation of a program. Reduction in force (rif) may also apply to tenured teachers. The general rule of "riffing" is that the last hired are the first to go if it becomes necessary.

Reflection Thinking about what is done, how it's done, and the consequences of actions or inactions, all with the goal of being a better teacher.

Reflective practitioner A teacher who thinks critically about teaching and the consequences of actions or inactions, all with the goal of being more effective with students.

Reform To change, to make different, or to improve.

Reggio Emilia An approach to early childhood education for ages 3 months to 6 years based on relationships among children, families, and teachers.

Related arts courses Also known as exploratory courses or encore courses; all courses other than math, English language arts, social studies, and science; may include art, music, physical education, industrial arts, languages, drama, computer education, and so on.

Relational aggression Subtle actions that may hurt emotionally rather than physically; may include name-calling, gossiping, or saying mean things just to be hurtful; most common among girls.

Reliability The degree to which an assessment yields a pattern of results that is repeatable and consistent over time.

Resilience The ability to bounce back and meet life's challenges.

Resource teacher A special education teacher who helps students develop strategies for school success.

Ripple effect An effect that occurs when one action directly affects another.

Role play Getting students up and moving as they dramatize a scenario to make a point or prompt students to think in divergent ways.

Romanticism A philosophy of education that contends the needs of the individual are more important than the needs of society; also known as naturalism.

Routine An expected action that occurs in a given circumstance to accomplish a task efficiently.

Rubric Assessment tool that makes explicit what is being assessed, lists characteristics of degrees of quality, and provides a rating scale to differentiate among these degrees.

Rural Indicates an area with fewer than 2,500 people and a minimum of retail stores and services.

S

Scaffolding The support given to children to help them move through progressive levels of learning.

School choice Method of letting parents decide which schools their students attend.

School connectedness Student bonding and engagement in the school experience.

School culture The prevailing atmosphere of a school that provides the context of learning experiences; as places where people work together and learn together, schools function according to their cultures.

School district An organizational structure of local schools defined by geographic boundaries.

School-to-Work Federal government program initiated to bring real-world, work-related skills and understanding to students through courses and experiences that introduce them to career possibilities.

School venues The variety of ways Americans "do school" in the more than 120,000 schools in the United States. The most prominent venues are public schools and private schools.

Self-contained classroom An organizational structure involving one teacher and a group of students for whom the teacher is accountable much of the school day.

Self-efficacy An "I can" belief in oneself that leads to a sense of competence; the concept of self-efficacy is solidly grounded in the accomplishment of a continuum of increasingly difficult challenges.

Settlement houses Established by early American reformers to confront the problem of urban poverty; community service centers that provided educational opportunities, skills training, and cultural events.

Sexual harassment Behavior with sexual implications that is neither wanted nor welcome; may include obvious looks with lewd intent, taunts with sexual innuendo, touching, kissing, groping, and any behavior that has sexual connotations.

Sexual orientation The sex to which a person is romantically or socially attracted is considered a person's sexual orientation.

Single gender All male or all female.

Single-member elections Only those who live in a specific area can vote for the representatives in their area.

Sin tax Tax on items some consider vices, such as alcohol and cigarettes.

Site-based management Public school management structure in which governance is in the hands of those closest to it, generally teachers, administrators, and parents.

Social cognition Process of relating to others and thinking about them and oneself.

Socialization Occurs through a variety of influences including home, family, church, print and electronic media, peers, and school.

Social reconstructionism A philosophy of education that looks to education to change society, rather than just teach about it. Social reconstructionism as an education philosophy calls on schools to educate students in ways that will help society move beyond all forms of discrimination to the benefit of everyone worldwide.

Socioeconomic status (SES) Status based on economic level and other sources of power.

Software Computer programs that are written to perform specific applications; application software and instructional software are two basic types used in schools.

Special education services Services provided by schools to help students with disabilities function and learn in ways optimal to each.

Special education students Students with disabilities that require services enabling them to function and learn in ways optimal to each individual.

Special interest group Group of people with a common mission who work to have an impact.

Stages of cognitive development Jean Piaget (1896–1980) recognized distinct differences in children's and adolescents' responses to questions that directly correlated to their chronological ages and categorized these differences into stages.

Stages of moral reasoning Noted developmental psychologist Lawrence Kohlberg contends that people pass through distinct stages as they develop morally.

Standard English A composite of the language spoken by educated middle-class people in the United States.

Standardized test Test given to multiple groups of students, designed for specific grade levels, and typically repeated annually. These tests are administered and scored under controlled conditions, and their exact content is unknown to everyone except the test makers before they are administered.

Standards Expectations for what individuals should know and be able to do.

Standards-based reform movement Efforts to improve teaching and learning through content standards; another way of expressing the era of standards.

Standards-based test Test written using the content of a specific set of standards.

State board of education Volunteers who are either elected or appointed by the governor; state legislatures give state boards oversight authority; boards act in regulatory and advisory capacities.

State department of education Operates under the guidance of the governor, legislature, and state board of education; also known as state office of education or perhaps department of public instruction.

State superintendent The one person given responsibility for managing the state department of education; also known as chief state education officer or commissioner of education.

Structured English immersion Approach includes significant amounts of the school day dedicated to the explicit teaching of the English language, with other content supporting instruction but not as the primary focus.

Structured observation Early field experiences involving looking for specific things and responding to prompts that purposefully call attention to certain aspects of the classroom.

Student self-monitoring Students assume control of their own behavior as they develop a sense of ownership for that behavior.

Students with exceptionalities Learners with abilities or disabilities that set them apart from other learners.

Student teaching Also known as clinical internship or clinical practice; involves extended fieldwork in which teacher candidates teach lessons and, for a designated period of time, take over all classroom duties.

Substance abuse A pattern of alcohol or drug use that can lead to detrimental and habitual consumption, impaired functioning at school and work, and legal difficulties.

Suburban Indicates neighborhoods and small- to medium-size towns that are located on the fringe of cities or are their own distinct locations.

Summative assessment A formal assessment involving judgments about the success of a process or product; most often occurs at the end of a unit of study.

Superintendent A school district's chief executive officer; hired by the district school board; advises the board and carries out board policies.

Suspension Time out of school that may range from 1 day to less than a semester, but is usually for 10 days or less.

T

Tableau Freeze-frame role-playing with students choosing a book passage, striking a pose that depicts the passage, and holding the pose while a narrator reads the passage.

Tax cap An upper limit to taxation.

Teacher leader A teacher with additional responsibilities such as chairperson of a grade level of teachers or perhaps a subject-area specialist who works with other teachers to help them improve their knowledge and/or skills; more generally, teachers who prove to be leaders in their schools, as well as in their districts and states, simply by being dynamic, well-informed classroom teachers.

Teacher study groups Building professional, collegial communities within schools. Small groups of teachers select books and journal articles to read, talk about what they have read, and discuss how it might be applied to their teaching.

Teacher think-aloud An instructional strategy in which teachers think out loud about how to approach a problem, make sense of new information, use self-restraint in volatile situations, consider options, discard what doesn't work, and begin to refine what makes sense.

Teach for America Most widely known of all alternative licensing programs; TFA recruits individuals who are college seniors or recent graduates who agree to teach in high-needs rural or urban schools for at least 2 years.

Tenure Continuing contract status; a teacher with tenure is entitled to a contract each year unless the district has reason to not renew it or the teacher decides to go elsewhere. In most states tenure doesn't guarantee a particular position in a particular school, but it does guarantee employment in the district.

Glossary

Thinking skills Skills that aid in processing information.

Think-pair-share Teachers expose students to information, give a prompt, ask a question, or provide an experience and then challenge them to think about it in a particular way and perhaps record their thoughts on paper (T). Students then choose a partner (P) and share their thoughts with another student (S).

Time-on-task Productive learning time.

Title I funding Federal compensatory funds provided through the Elementary and Secondary Education Act given to public schools where more than 50% of the students qualify for free or reduced-price meals; used to supplement regular school funding in schools with high numbers of students from low-income settings.

Title IX of the Education Amendments Act of 1972 Prohibits government money from being used for anything that discriminates on the basis of gender.

Token economy A system of giving symbolic rewards for appropriate behavior and withholding or taking away rewards for inappropriate behavior.

Town schools Early American schools established for whole communities; while some schools still limited curriculum to reading, writing, and the classics, specialized schools in the form of academies became popular.

Traditional public schools Schools that have no admission criteria, other than perhaps residency in a particular attendance zone.

Transition When students change activities or locations, they are in transition; generally a time when most classroom disruptions happen.

Transparent Decisions are made with full disclosure of information and reasoning.

Trends in International Mathematics and Science Study (TIMSS) International tests that compare students worldwide; administered every 4 years since 1995.

Truancy Nonattendance during compulsory education, not including excused absences generally granted for health reasons.

Tyler Rationale Ralph Tyler developed four questions that should be asked throughout the stages of curriculum development.

U

Unconditional teaching Accepting students for who they are, not for what they do.

Unfunded mandate A legally enforceable law without monetary support provided.

Unit of study Organizes curriculum, instruction, and assessment around a major theme or distinct body of content; provides planned cohesion.

Unobtrusive intervention Consequences that do not disrupt instruction.

Urban Indicates cities with large downtowns and dense populations.

V

Validity The degree to which an assessment measures what it is supposed to measure.

Virtual schools Schools that deliver instruction only through distance learning.

Vocational Education Act of 1963 Quadrupled the amount of money allocated for vocational education.

Voucher Government-issued piece of paper that represents part of a state's financial contribution for the education of a student; parents choose a school and present the voucher, and the government allocates funding to the school accordingly.

W

Watchdog group Community members who join forces to keep an eye on school district accountability by examining policies and practices.

Wayside teaching Teaching that occurs inside and outside the classroom through attitudes, values, habits, interests, and classroom climate.

Whole child Attending to student developmental stages and needs, along with teaching them grade-level and subject-area content.

Withitness Refers to a teacher's awareness of what's going on in the whole classroom, enabling the teacher to step in when needed to keep the environment positive; originated with Jacob Kounin.

Writing across the curriculum Infusing the curriculum with writing, regardless of content area.

Y

Young adolescents Students between ages 10 and 15.

Z

Zero tolerance School-imposed nonnegotiable consequences for certain infractions. For instance, the consequence for fighting may be automatic suspension for 3 days.

Zone of proximal development The level at which a child can almost, but not completely, grasp a concept or perform a task successfully; theory proposed by Lev Vygotsky.

Index